# ROBERT THE BRUCE

# Robert the Bruce
## KING OF SCOTS

*Ronald McNair Scott*

BARNES
&NOBLE
BOOKS
NEW YORK

This edition published by Barnes & Noble, Inc.,
by arrangement with Peter Bedrick Books.

1993 Barnes & Noble Books

ISBN 1-56619-270-6

Printed and bound in the United States of America

M 9 8 7 6 5 4 3

# CONTENTS

# ILLUSTRATIONS

# PREFACE

The life of Robert Bruce coincides with the wars of Scottish independence when a small kingdom struggled for its existence against an overbearing neighbour. In this struggle Bruce played an increasingly prominent part and eventually became the deliverer of his country. His name therefore appears constantly in the state papers of the time and the thirteenth- and fourteenth-century chronicles. The fascination for the historian is that, in addition to these sources, there is another so full of vivid descriptions of the events and characters of the period that a bare recital of facts can be transmitted into a biography of great human interest.

In 1375, less that fifty years after Bruce's death, John Barbour, Archdeacon of Aberdeen, produced his epic life of Robert Bruce, *The Brus*. In his opening canto he declares his intention to tell nothing but the truth, 'to put in wryt a suthfast story'. Wherever it has been possible to check his account against contemporary documents scholars have confirmed his reliability. Occasionally the order of events is transposed but the accuracy of his detail has been accepted by every subsequent historian.

Barbour was born some seven years before Bruce died. Over the years preceding the completion of his work, when he was gaining position in the Church and at the Scottish court, he had the opportunity to meet many of those who had taken part with Bruce in the extraordinary adventures which seem to belong to the realm of fiction rather than of fact. No doubt, when old men tell their tales, they sometimes heighten and embellish the dramatic incidents of their past, but the essential truth is there. The liveliness of Barbour's descriptions bears the stamp of eyewitness accounts. The reader is justified in a willing suspension of disbelief.

The encouragement and criticism I have received, in the writing of this book, from my family, friends and correspondents have been invaluable: in particular I would like to thank, first, General Sir Philip Christison Bt, G.B.E., C.B., D.S.O., M.C., D.L., who put at my disposal the research notes he accumulated over the decade before he wrote his account of the Battle of Bannockburn for the Scottish National Trust; second, Major General The Earl of Cathcart, D.S.O., M.C., who made available to me the manuscript history of his family, written by his grandfather. His ancestor, Sir Alan Cathcart, was among the young men who joined Bruce in his bid for the throne and is the only person whom John Barbour mentions by name as one of his informants. Lastly, no writer on the period can fail to mention his debt to Professor G. W. S. Barrow's monumental work on *Robert Bruce and the Community of the Realm*.

The Scottish Highlands

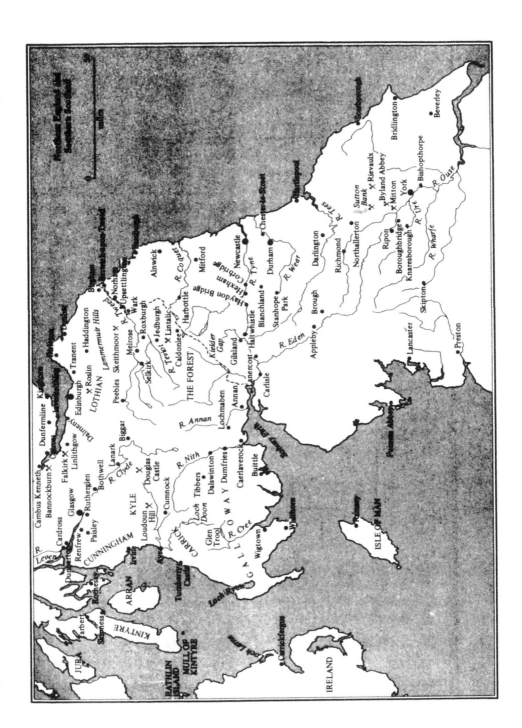

Northern England and
Southern Scotland

Beverley

Bridlington
Bishopthorpe

R. Ouse
Sutton
Bank
Rievaulx
Byland Abbey
Mitton
York
R. Ure

Ripon
Boroughbridge
Knaresborough
R. Wharfe

Northallerton
Skipton

Richmond
Darlington

R. Tees

Durham
R. Wear
Brough
Appleby
Preston

Newcastle
R. Tyne
Stanhope
Park
Blanchland
Lancaster

Alnwick
Mitford
Hexham
Corbridge
Haltwhistle
Haydon Bridge
R. Eden

R. Coquet
North
Harbottle
Gilsland
Lanercost
Carlisle
Annan

Upsettlington
Wark
Roxburgh
Jedburgh
Lintalee
Caldonlee
Kielder
Gap
Lochmaben

Melrose
R. Teviot
THE FOREST
R. Annan

Haddington
Roslin
Skeithmoor
Selkirk

Tranent
Lammermuir Hills
Peebles

Edinburgh
LOTHIAN
Biggar

Dalmeny
Linlithgow
Lanark
Bothwell
R. Clyde
Douglas
Castle
R. Nith
Dalswinton
Dumfries
Caerlaverock
Buittle

Dunfermline
Falkirk
Glasgow
Rutherglen
Cumnock
Tibbers
Furness Abbey

Cambus Kenneth
Bannockburn
Cardross
Renfrew
Paisley
KYLE
Loudoun
Hill
Loch
Doon
CARRICK
Glen
Trool
R. Cree
Wigtown
Whithorn
ISLE OF MAN
Peel

R.
Leven
CUNNINGHAM
Irvine
Ayr
Turnberry
Castle
Loch Ryan
GALLOWAY

Dunoon
Rothesay
ARRAN
Skipness
Tarbert
KINTYRE
JURA
MULL OF
KINTYRE
RATHLIN
ISLAND

Loch Lomond

Carrickfergus
Loch Larne
IRELAND

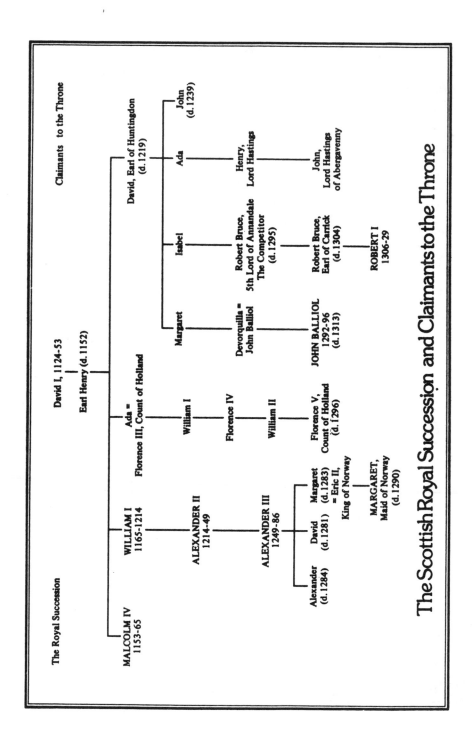

The Scottish Royal Succession and Claimants to the Throne

# The House of Bruce

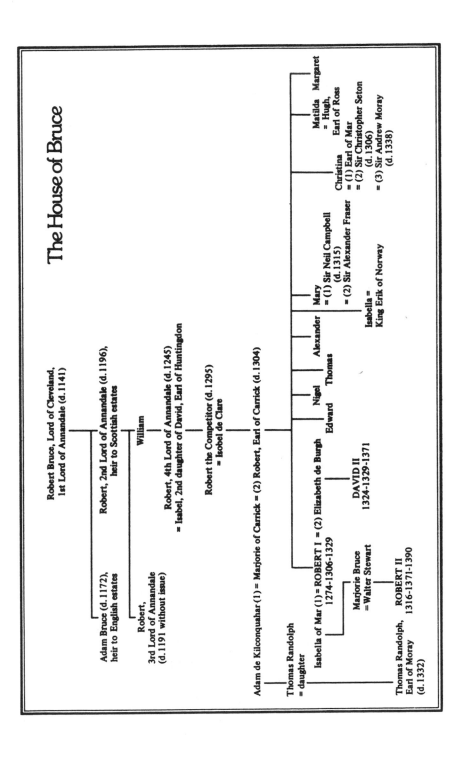

Robert Bruce, Lord of Cleveland,
1st Lord of Annandale (d.1141)

Robert, 2nd Lord of Annandale (d.1196),
heir to Scottish estates

Adam Bruce (d.1172),
heir to English estates

William

Robert,
3rd Lord of Annandale
(d.1191 without issue)

Robert, 4th Lord of Annandale (d.1245)
= Isabel, 2nd daughter of David, Earl of Huntingdon

Robert the Competitor (d.1295)
= Isobel de Clare

Adam de Kilconquahar (1) = Marjorie of Carrick = (2) Robert, Earl of Carrick (d.1304)

Thomas Randolph
= daughter

Isabella of Mar (1) = ROBERT I = (2) Elizabeth de Burgh
1274-1306-1329

Edward    Nigel    Thomas    Alexander    Mary
                                          = (1) Sir Neil Campbell
                                             (d.1315)
                                          = (2) Sir Alexander Fraser

Matilda    Margaret
= Hugh,
Earl of Ross

Christina
= (1) Earl of Mar
= (2) Sir Christopher Seton
      (d.1306)
= (3) Sir Andrew Moray
      (d.1338)

Isabella =
King Erik of Norway

Marjorie Bruce
= Walter Stewart

DAVID II
1324-1329-1371

ROBERT II
1316-1371-1390

Thomas Randolph,
Earl of Moray
(d.1332)

# CHRONOLOGY

| | |
|---|---|
| 1274 | Birth of Robert Bruce on 11 July. |
| 1286 | Death of Alexander III. Election of guardians. The Turnberry Bond. |
| 1289 | Treaty of Salisbury. |
| 1290 | Treaty of Birgham. Death of Maid of Norway. Edward I invited to arbitrate. |
| 1291 | Edward I accepted as superior lord of Scotland. |
| 1292 | Balliol crowned and renders homage. Edward I repudiates Treaty of Birgham. |
| 1293 | King John (Balliol) summoned before English Parliament and convicted of contumacy. |
| 1294 | War between Edward I and Philip IV of France. Welsh revolt. |
| 1295 | King John replaced by Council of Twelve. Treaty between France and Scotland. Bruce's grandfather dies. |
| 1296 | Outbreak of war between England and Scotland. Sack of Berwick. King John abdicates. The Ragman Roll. Freeholders pay homage to Edward I. |
| 1297 | Insurrection. Andrew Moray, William Wallace. Capitulation of Irvine. Battle of Stirling Bridge. Andrew Moray dies of wounds. |
| 1298 | Wallace knighted and appointed guardian. Edward I invades Scotland. Battle of Falkirk. Bruce and Comyn appointed guardians. |

1299    Lamberton third guardian. Scots take Stirling Castle.

1300    Bruce resigns guardianship. Replaced by de Umfraville. English invasion. Truce.

1301    Soulis appointed sole guardian. English invasion.

1302    Truce. Bruce submits to Edward I. Marries Elizabeth de Burgh.

1303    Battle of Roslin. Peace treaty between France and England, excluding Scots.

1304    Bruce's father dies. Comyn surrenders. Bond between Bruce and Lamberton. Stirling captured by Edward I.

1305    Wallace captured and executed. New ordinance for government of Scotland.

1306    Death of Comyn. Douglas joins Bruce. Bruce crowned at Scone: defeated at battles of Methven and Dalry: escapes to Dunaverty and then Rathlin. His brother Nigel captured at Kildrummy Castle and executed. His wife, sisters and daughter captured at Tain.

1307    Bruce lands at Turnberry. Guerrilla war in southwest Scotland. His brothers Alexander and Thomas captured in Galloway and executed. Bruce defeats English at Glen Trool and Loudon Hill. Rising in Moray. Edward I dies. Bruce moves north, falls ill.

1308    Battle of Inverurie. 'Herschip' of Buchan. Battle of Brander. Earl of Ross submits to Bruce.

1309    St Andrew's parliament. Scotland north of the Tay under Bruce's control.

1310    Edward II invades Scotland.

1311    Bruce raids northern England.

1312    Bruce again raids northern England. Treaty of Inverness between Scotland and Norway.

1313    Bruce captures Perth. Reconquers southwest Scotland and Isle of Man.

1314    Douglas captures Roxburgh. Randolph captures Edinburgh. Battle of Bannockburn.

1315    Act of Succession. Marriage of Princess Marjorie. Edward Bruce invades Ireland.

1316    Edward Bruce crowned King of Ireland. Death of Princess Marjorie.

1316–17  Bruce in Ireland.

1318    Berwick taken by Scots. Edward Bruce slain in Ireland. Succession to Scottish throne settled on Princess Marjorie's son Robert Stewart.

1319    Edward II besieges Berwick. Douglas and Randolph invade England. 'The Chapter of Myton'. Two-year truce.

1320    The Declaration of Arbroath. Soulis's conspiracy.

1322    Edward II's last invasion of Scotland. Bruce raids England. Defeats Edward II at Old Byland, Yorkshire.

1323    Harclay attempts peace treaty. Executed by Edward II. Official negotiations lead to thirteen-year truce.

1324    Pope recognizes Bruce as King of Scotland. Queen Elizabeth gives birth to male heir.

1326    Treaty of Corbeil between France and Scotland. Succession to Scottish throne settled on David Bruce, remainder to Robert Stewart.

1327    Deposition of Edward II. Truce broken. Edward III advances on Scotland. Outwitted by Douglas and Randolph at Stanhope Park, Durham. Bruce invades Northumberland.

1328    Treaty of Edinburgh. Marriage of David Bruce to Edward III's sister Joan.

1329    Death of Bruce, 7 June.

1330    Death of Douglas.

1332    Death of Randolph.

# PART ONE
# 1285–1306

Our nation lived in freedom and quietness until Edward, King of England, under colour of friendship and alliance, attacked us, all unsuspecting, when we had neither King nor Head and our people were unacquainted with wars and invasions.

*Scottish Declaration of Arbroath, 1320*

.

# I

On 14 October 1285 Alexander III, King of Scotland, married as his second wife Yolande of Dreux, descended from Count Robert I of Dreux, a son of Louis VI of France.[1] It was a marriage welcomed by his subjects. His first wife Margaret, daughter of Henry III of England, had died in 1275 having borne for her husband a daughter and two sons, Margaret, Alexander and David. But within the space of three years all were dead: the younger son in 1281 unmarried, the elder in 1284 without issue and in 1283 the daughter, who was married to Erik II, King of Norway, died in childbirth leaving as heir to the Scottish and Norwegian thrones a sickly infant Margaret, the Maid of Norway.[2] The succession stood in jeopardy.

Alexander III was of a sanguine temperament and during his ten years as a widower, as the *Lanercost Chronicle* sourly reports, 'he used never to forbear on account of season or storm, nor for perils of flood or rocky cliffs but would visit none too creditably matrons and nuns, virgins and widows by day or by night as the fancy seized him, sometimes in disguise, often accompanied by a single follower.'[3]

His marriage to the young Frenchwoman, it might be expected, would concentrate his attentions and give promise of a male heir to the throne.

For over two hundred years, since Birnam Wood came to Dunsinane and the forces of Malcolm III had defeated and slain Macbeth, the House of Canmore had been the rulers of Scotland. During the reigns of eight succeeding kings of that blood, by conquest or by treaty, the realm had been enlarged so that when Alexander wed Yolande she became the queen of a kingdom which differed little in extent from the Scotland of the present day.

But the population was much smaller. The inhabitants numbered fewer than 500,000. The majority were Celts, mainly north of the Forth and Clyde and in the southwest. There were Norsemen in Caithness, Sutherland and the Western Isles, Anglo-Saxons in Lothian; and along the east coast in ports that sound like a drum roll – Inverness, Elgin, Aberdeen, Perth, Montrose, Dundee, Edinburgh, Berwick – were colonies of foreign merchants: Germans from the Hanseatic towns, Scandinavians from the kingdom of Norway, Frenchmen from Gascony and, more numerous than the rest, Flemings from the Low Countries. Aberdeen was virtually a Flemish enclave and in Berwick they had their own headquarters, 'the Red Hall', held directly from the Crown on condition that they would always defend it against the King of England.[4]

The country too was infinitely wilder. Vast forests of the native Scottish pine abounded, dark and impenetrable, in which wolves and the wild boar still roamed and wide wastes of moor and bog, mountain and water covered much of the land. Apart from the king's highway, the *via regis*, few roads were capable of carrying wheeled traffic except in a dry summer. Transport was mostly by pack horse along tracks which might become impassable in winter. Bridges were few and far between. Within little more than a decade the great forests and deep ravines, the mist-hung hillsides and rugged tracks were to become the salvation and refuge of desperate men.

But in the year of Alexander III's wedding Scotland was still at peace: a prosperous and settled kingdom. For nearly a hundred years her English neighbours, torn by internal feuds and continental wars, had little leisure to turn a predatory eye northwards and Norway, having launched a formidable armada against the west coast in 1263, had seen her ships tossed and scattered by a violent storm and the stragglers who landed in Ayrshire easily defeated at the battle of Largs. In 1266 by the Treaty of Perth the Norwegians ceded the Isle of Man and the Western Isles, except the Orkneys and Shetlands, to Scotland in return for a monetary tribute and a growing collaboration between the two countries was cemented by the marriage of Alexander's daughter to the Norwegian King.[5]

Thus for the thirty-six years that he had reigned Alexander III and his people had enjoyed a period of tranquillity unparalleled by any other western kingdom at that time. In this fostering climate of peace, agriculture and trade made steady progress. Under the lead of the Scottish Church, which had been strengthened and enlarged by many royal grants of land, improvements had been made in the art of tillage and the management of livestock. New clearings and new grazings had been brought into production by the joint efforts of landlord, thane and peasant. An expanding export trade in wool, hides, timber and fish with England, the Low Countries, the Hanseatic towns and Scandinavia had brought an increased flow of riches to the merchants and landowners which percolated throughout the whole society. The eastern ports hummed with activity. Berwick, at one extremity, was described by a contemporary English writer as 'a city so populous and of such trade that it might justly be called another Alexandria, whose riches were the sea and the water its walls.'[6] At the other extremity Inverness was a shipyard for mighty vessels.[7]

But affluence without security is a cause more for anxiety than for comfort. It is because the turbulent elements among the Scottish people had, by the reign of Alexander III, been brought under control by the network of a feudal organization that trade flourished, the traveller could ride unharmed, the peasant could reap his crops and the craftsmen and purveyors clustered in the royal burghs could pursue their avocations without one hand upon their swords.

The feudal system was based on the concept that all land belonged to the king and that he leased large provinces to his leading noblemen as tenants-in-chief in return for their oath of fealty and their pledge to bring to his aid, in time of war, a stipulated number of armed knights. In like manner, in a descending gradation of sub-tenure, these vassals of the Crown divided the land which the king had granted to them into smaller estates which they leased to knights and gentlemen in return for their service in war and attendance in peace. They, in turn, leased their land to lesser men who cultivated it with or without husbandmen and serfs and would present themselves to their masters at the call to arms, with shield and spear.

It had a profound economic base. War, in the Middle Ages, was the central factor of political life and the dominating element in war was the mailed warrior mounted on his horse. The ruler who aspired to enlarge or protect his possessions required a force of armed cavalry: a force which by its combination of shock and mobility was as irresistible against men fighting on foot as tanks against savages.

To mount and arm such a warrior required a long purse. Horses bred for carrying and staying power, suits of chain link mail beaten out by the armourer for individual fitting, helmets, shields, lances, swords, battle axes and maces, squires for arming, grooms for the horses: all these were costly. To manage the horses, to wield the weapons required continuous training. The knight was a fighting specialist. He had no time to earn his living so he was allotted land for his service from which he could draw rents in money or in kind to defray his expenses. He was both the mailed fist of the king and the shield of his subjects.[8]

The system originated among the Franks. It was perfected in England under William the Conqueror and his sons and was introduced into the Celtic kingdom of Scotland by David I on his assuming the throne in 1124.

David had been brought up in the English court where his sister was married to Henry I of England. He had been greatly favoured by his royal brother-in-law. In Scotland, with English support, he had established himself in Lothian and Strathclyde as a virtually independent ruler within the kingdom of his brother, King Alexander I.

In England, by marriage and kingly sanction, he had acquired the huge 'Honour of Huntingdon' with broad lands spreading across the counties of Huntingdon and Northamptonshire. There, among his tenants-in-chief, were a clutch of Anglo-Normans deriving from the same region on the borders of Normandy and Brittany, the Morevilles, the Soulises, the FitzAlans, the Bruces. When David I took over the governance of an unruly kingdom, it was to these he looked to set up military fiefs in sensitive areas each with its castle and Norman lord.

Other Anglo-Normans followed in their train: Comyns and Balliols, Sinclairs and Frasers, Mowbrays and Hays, and were granted charters for land in Scotland. Contemporaneously. the great Celtic landowners, who had hitherto held their land by tribal custom, had their possessions and privileges confirmed by charters from the Crown. On the whole this proceeded smoothly. There was no dispossession of existing landowners. The lands granted were from estates which had been forfeited to the Crown or where native families had died out or from the royal demesnes.

Gradually, the kingdom became dotted with castles, some great stone edifices built on upthrusts of rock such as Edinburgh or Stirling, some on precipitous sea cliffs such as Turnberry or Dunaverty. But the majority were simple mottes, huge earthen mounds surrounded by wooden stockades and deep ditches with a central tower skirted by wooden living quarters, each forming a sentinel for the security of the area and a focus for the local community.

Such central government as existed was provided by the king and the officers of his household: the constable, the king's chief military officer, flanked by the marischal in special charge of the cavalry element; the chamberlain who provided for the costs of administration from the royal rents, feudal dues and other imposts; the chancellor, the keeper of the royal seal and Crown records who besides presiding over the king's chapel was virtually a secretary of state for all departments. He was invariably a cleric and was assisted by numerous chaplains and clerks to undertake the necessary written documents for the ordering of the kingdom. The fourth great officer was the steward responsible for the management of the royal household. David I had granted this office to Walter FitzAlan in 1136. William I, David's grandson, made it hereditary in the family. Thereafter, the FitzAlans were known as Stewarts, the ancestors of the royal house of that name.

Outside the household were the chief administrative and judicial officers of the Crown: the justiciar of Scotland north of the Forth and Clyde, the justiciar of Lothian and the justiciar of Galloway. Below them were the sheriffs, some thirty in all, who acted as royal agents in the local districts into which the kingdom was divided. They were the sinews of the administration, presiding over courts for free men to use, collecting and accounting for royal revenues, supervising the royal castles in their sheriffdoms. All these were appointed by the king and were usually drawn from the earls and barons who were already prominent landowners in their areas.

By the closing years of Alexander III's reign intermarriage between the Anglo-Norman and Celtic magnates was far advanced. Already a third of the ancient Celtic earldoms were held by men of Anglo-Norman descent, and although many of the leading men held estates in both English and Scottish kingdoms, the cordial relations between Alexander III and his brother-in-law Edward I posed no threat of divided loyalties. The administration had never been more stable, the country more prosperous, the throne more secure.

Not for another five hundred years were such conditions again to obtain and it is no surprise that succeeding generations were to look back on Alexander III's reign as a golden age hauntingly evoked in the words of the first of Scotland's poets Andrew Wyntoun:

Quhen Alysandre our King was dede
That Scotland led in lure and le★
Awaye was sons of ale and brede
Of wyne and wax, of gamyn and glé†
Our gold was changed into lede
Cryst born into virgynté
Succour Scotland and remede
That stad‡ is in perplexité.[9]

Into that age Robert Bruce was born with a mind and temper, courage and magnetism to meet and match the horrors which the future was soon to let loose upon his country.

★tranquillity  †abundance  ‡placed

# 2

Robert Bruce was born on 11 July 1274 at Turnberry Castle, of which the remains can still be seen perched on the cliffs which plunge steeply into the waters of the Firth of Clyde.[1] He was the eldest child of a fruitful and happy marriage which had begun in romantic circumstances.

His father, the sixth Robert of that name, at the age of twenty-four had enrolled in a crusade to the Holy Land under the banner of Prince Edward, soon to become King Edward I of England. Among his knightly companions was Adam de Kilconquahar, great-grandson of Duncan, Earl of Fife. Adam was killed in the Palestine defence of Acre leaving as widow his young bride, already with child, Marjorie, Countess of Carrick in her own right.

Powerful as may have been the forces which called Adam de Kilconquahar to arms, there must have remained in the mind of the countess a residue of resentment that he had so soon exchanged his marriage bed for the wars and when the sixth Robert, after his safe return in 1272, called on her with news of her husband's death it is understandable that in her most vulnerable period of widowhood she should have welcomed the supporting presence of the young crusader in her house.

Legend has it that her attendants were instructed by one means or another to delay his departure, with the happy result that she shortly became his wife and over the years bore him a large family of five sons and five daughters.[2]

It was a marriage that, from the worldly point of view, had everything to commend it. The Countess Marjorie was the last of her line. Her father Neil, Earl of Carrick, was the only direct descendant of Fergus Lord of Galloway, a Celtic prince who, in the reign of King David I, exercised an almost independent power over the southwest

9

of Scotland. In 1256 when Marjorie was still a baby, her father died leaving her sole possessor of the great Celtic kingdom of Carrick. Her new husband who, on his marriage, became by right of his wife Earl of Carrick, was already the heir to the vast estates of his father, Robert the Competitor, whose principal Scottish possession of Annandale marched with Carrick.

The Bruces were members of that Anglo-Norman élite through whom the kings of England and Scotland maintained their sovereign rule. Reputedly descended from Lodver, the Norse Earl of Orkney in the tenth century, the Bruces first made their impact on the British Isles when Adam de Brus, whose grandfather had migrated to Normandy, accompanied William the Conqueror to England. He was given the task of reducing Anglo-Saxon resistance in Yorkshire and as a reward for his services was granted numerous manors in and around that county. His eldest son, the first Robert, became one of the great magnates of northern England, Lord of Cleveland and a royal justice for Henry I. In 1124 his possessions were notably increased. In that year King David I, who was his feudal overlord in England, succeeded to the Scottish throne and one of his first acts was to grant to his most important tenant-in-chief the lordship of Annandale and 200,000 acres. Straddling the western route, the lordship of Annandale was a key to one of the gateways of Scotland. From that date the Bruces became the virtual Wardens of the Western Marches.

The first Robert combined the shrewdness of a Norman and a Yorkshireman. Having advised King David I in vain against a Scottish invasion of England in 1138, he resolved the problem of his dual loyalty by divesting himself, in the nick of time, of his Scottish possessions in favour of his younger son, the second Robert, and fought stoutly on behalf of his English sovereign at the Battle of the Standard. The second Robert for his part, although only fourteen, donned his armour and ranged himself in the ranks of the Scottish king. Tradition has it that father and son met on the eve of the battle and in a moving scene each tried to persuade the other to refrain from risking his life on the following day but without avail. Fortunately neither suffered injury in the fray.

The second Robert lived to a ripe old age. He had two sons, the third Robert of that name and William, who both predeceased him so that on his death in 1196 his inheritance passed to William's eldest son, the fourth Robert. There is a certain monotony in the Bruces' choice of Christian names.

In 1209 the fourth Robert married Isobel, younger daughter of David, Earl of Huntingdon, the youngest of King David I's three grandsons of whom the two elder, Malcolm IV and William I, had succeeded him in turn on the Scottish throne. This marriage was to have a profound effect on the future of the Bruces.

Isobel held large estates in her own right both in England and Scotland, and when the fourth Robert died in 1245 and Isobel in 1252, the fifth Robert (the Competitor) received lands in both countries of such extent as to make him one of the most influential men in either Scotland or England.[3]

In 1238 a dazzling prospect opened before him. Queen Joan, the wife of Alexander II, died childless and there was no apparent heir. To safeguard the succession the King called his magnates together and in their presence and with their consent designated the fifth Robert as his heir presumptive.[4] But the period of anticipation was brief. In May 1239 Alexander married again and sired on this second wife, Marie de Courcy, a son who was born in September 1241: the future Alexander III. Nevertheless, the fact that the kingdom of Scotland had once been within his grasp was deeply engraved on Robert's mind and when, nearly fifty years later, the opportunity seemed once more to arise, the old man roused himself from his retirement to make a masterful bid for the throne.

Meanwhile in May 1240 Robert the Competitor had married Isobel de Clare, daughter of the Earl of Gloucester and niece of the Earl Marshall of England. Linked as he thus became to the innermost circles of the English ruling families, he devoted many of his abilities to the service of Henry III of England,* fighting for him against Simon de Montfort on the disastrous field of Lewes, acting as a trusted intermediary between the English and Scottish thrones, and carrying out his duties as Sheriff of Cumberland and Governor of Carlisle.[5]

The *Lanercost Chronicle* writes:

> He was of handsome appearance, a gifted speaker, remarkable for his influence and, what is most important, most devoted to God and the Clergy. It was his custom to entertain and feast more liberally than all other courtiers and was most hospitable to all his guests nor used the pilgrim to remain outside his gates for his door was open to the wayfarer.[6]

His devotion to God and his indomitable character were made

---

*cf note I

equally evident when in 1270 he resigned all his offices and at the age of sixty, accompanied by his son the sixth Robert, embarked on the long voyage to the Middle East to face the rigours of a crusader's life in the Holy Land. When he returned in 1272 his old friend and master Henry III had died and a new vigorous monarch, Edward I, was on the English throne. It was time for him to settle quietly on the family estates and enjoy the pleasures of his second marriage to a neighbouring widow, Christiana of Ireby, which took place in May 1273, and to anticipate with confidence the benediction of the formidable Saint Malachy.

The curse of Saint Malachy had exercised his mind ever since he came to manhood. More than a hundred years earlier in 1148 Saint Malachy, Archbishop of Armagh, on his way to Rome from Ireland had spent the night at the house of the second Robert in the town of Annan. Hearing that a thief had been captured shortly before and was awaiting sentence, he asked, as a boon from his host, that the man's life should be spared. His request was granted and he blessed the household. But as he set out on his journey the next morning he saw the thief hanging from the gallows. Outraged by the duplicity of his host, he revoked his blessing and laid a perpetual curse on the family of the Bruces.[7]

When Robert the Competitor became heir presumptive to Alexander II, it was clear to him that steps must be taken to remove what appeared to many of the superstitious a grievous disability. He journeyed to the saint's tomb and on his knees beside it prayed that the curse might be lifted. He repeated these visits on many occasions. Finally in 1272, on his way back from the Holy Land, he confirmed by a charter, still preserved at Clairvaux, a perpetual rent 'to God and the Blessed Mary and to the house and monks of Clairvaux in order to maintain lights before the blessed Malachy and for the good of his own soul and the souls of his predecessors and successors.'[8] He could well feel that a benediction was now his due.

Lochmaben Castle, at the head of the Annandale Valley, in which he dwelt with his new wife, was a powerful stone-built fortress, sited on a promontory jutting into the waters of the loch, the embracing arms of which were joined by a canal surrounding it on all sides by water. It was some sixty miles from his son the Earl of Carrick's castle at Turnberry, a long day's ride but close enough to assume that according to the ordinary pattern of family relationship there would have been constant visits between the two households and that he would have attended the christening of his first grandson, Robert Bruce.

Of Robert Bruce there is no written record from the time of his birth certificate in July 1274 until July 1286, when in the Paisley *registrum* his signature is appended as witness to a deed of Alexander Macdonald of Islay in company with his father the Earl of Carrick, the Bishop of Argyll, the vicar of Arran and the clerk of Kintyre as well as other personages.[9] During these twelve years he would have spent much of his time with his foster brothers and sisters, children of the woman to whom, as was then customary, he would have been handed over at birth to be suckled.

Again from 1286 to 1292 there is no record, but as the child is father of the man, so from the known history of the man can be deduced the upbringing of the child.

The Robert Bruce who, when he was a hunted man, beguiled his haggard followers on the hillside by reading to them a French romance, must have had book learning in his youth. He would have spoken the Norman-French of his peers and in the Celtic household of his parents absorbed from their retainers the Gaelic language which was dominant from Galloway in the southwest up through the western Highlands to the mountains of Inverness. In his grandfather's house too he would have heard spoken and learnt the northern English, which was to become the broad Scots of later generations and was then the common speech from the borders to Strathclyde, and from Lothian to the trading ports on the eastern seaboard. He would have become trilingual at an early age: an accomplishment most necessary for one who was to draw supporters for his struggle from all three spheres.

And since in his prime Robert Bruce was ranked with the Holy Roman Emperor Henry and Sir Giles D'Argentan as one of the three most accomplished knights in Christendom,[10] it is certain that as soon as he was able he was trained in the handling of arms and the management of horses. The society in which he lived was a military one and martial prowess was sought with an obsessive passion. When knights could not exercise their skill on the field of battle, they took part in tournaments which were immensely popular all over Europe.

These combined the stimulus of risk and the possibility of profit. The defeated knight forfeited his horse and arms or had to pay ransom to reclaim them. So rich were these prizes that often knights made up teams to share the gains or dilute the losses, or wealthy backers would club together to equip a promising but indigent competitor and participate in his spoils. The reputations of consistent champions were internationally known and those in the top rank, such as Robert Bruce became, carried with them an aura of success which had a psychological effect in the clash of war.[11] In the love-hate syndrome which can be detected in Edward I's relationship to Robert Bruce, the chivalric fame of the latter may well have played its part. But their meeting was still in the future. Meanwhile the towering figure of Edward I, seven feet from mailed feet to crested helmet, was to cast a long shadow on Scotland.[12]

# 3

The year 1286 was ushered into Scotland by storms so thunderous and recurrent that many a wiseacre shook his head and doleful men predicted the imminence of calamity. A strengthening rumour rippled through the countryside that 18 March was to be the Day of Judgement. On that very day Alexander III called together at Edinburgh Castle the lords of his council in conference and after the meeting entertained them at dinner. The feast was long, the *Lanercost Chronicle* relates, the cups were filled, the King was in tearing spirits, chaffing his companions about the prophecies of doom, passing to one of his barons a dish of lampreys, bidding him to eat and make merry for he should know that this was judgement day, to which the baron replied, 'If this be judgement day we shall arise with full bellies.'

As the red wine of Gascony mounted in his veins, the vision of Yolande, the young bride he had left in the royal manor of Kinghorn, twenty miles away, became more and more alluring. In spite of the tempestuous weather outside and the remonstrances of his nobles, he called for his horse and followed by three squires made haste along the road to the ferry at Dalmeny. When he reached the village the ferrymaster urged on him the hazards of the crossing and begged him to return to Edinburgh.

'Are you afraid to die with me?' asked the King.

'By no means,' replied the ferrymaster, 'I could not die better than in the company of your father's son,' and forthwith rowed them across the two miles of turbulent water to the burgh of Inverkeithing.

Landing in profound darkness they were met by Alexander, the royal purveyor, who, recognizing the King's voice, called out, 'My Lord, what are you doing here in such storm and darkness? How often have I not tried to persuade you that these midnight rambles will do you no good? Stay with us and we will provide you with all that you want until the morning light.'

But the King, still impelled by the dual urge of royal duty and private pleasure, asked only for two countrymen to guide him and set off with his escort along the coast road to Kinghorn. In the howling wind and darkness the little party soon lost all contact with each other and next morning the King was found dead on the seashore below the cliffs, his neck broken.[1]

A great grief fell upon the kingdom and apprehension for the future. The heir apparent was a small girl in a foreign land, and although at Scone in 1284, in the presence of Alexander III, the magnates of the realm had promised, failing his direct issue, to recognize his grand-daughter Margaret, the Maid of Norway, as 'their liege lady and sovereign Queen', many who had so promised under the eye of their King when the possibility seemed remote, now that the King was dead began to have reservations. No woman had ever before become the ruler of Scotland. Some harked back to the old Celtic tanist tradition under which when a king died, the nearest male relative took over the reins of power: others began to edge closer to one or other of the two powerful families, the Comyns and the Bruces, who numbered among their members males of the royal blood. Like two stiff-legged dogs circling with hackles raised the two families eyed each other ready to launch into action if any move was made by their rival. The whiff of civil war was in the air.

But Alexander III had left behind him a firm infrastructure of government. The chancellery, the civil service of the time, was largely manned by clerics. The Church had her fingers on the pulse of administration and the Church was the one single coherent institution which covered the whole country. Next to the Crown she was the largest landowner in the kingdom. Her many tenants – lairds, thanes and smallholders – were men of the native race, rooted deep in the soil, a solid substratum of Scottish men beneath the shifting oligarchy of Normans whose lands and loyalties were split between Scotland and England. With undeviating purpose, but often by devious means, she was determined to preserve the independence of Scotland and the Scottish Church.

As soon as the royal funeral had taken place on 29 March 1286, Bishops Wishart of Glasgow and Fraser of St Andrews dispatched two Dominican friars to Edward I, brother-in-law of the late King and hitherto a good friend to their country, to inform him of the event.[2] A month later, when Queen Yolande's claim to be pregnant proved illusory, they summoned to Scone the bishops, abbots and priors, the earls and barons and good men of the country to pledge their fealty to the young Queen over the water, Margaret of Norway, the last survivor of the House of Canmore, and to swear, on pain of excommunication by the bishops, to protect and uphold the peace of her land.[3] To this end a regency was appointed to represent the community of the realm, *communitas regni Scotie*, the whole body of the free subjects of the Crown.

The regency consisted of six guardians of whom two were earls, those of Buchan and Fife, two were churchmen, the Bishops of St Andrews and Glasgow, two were barons, James Stewart and John Comyn.[4] Of these the first-named three were responsible for Scotland north of the Forth and the other three for the south. Deliberately, neither Robert the Competitor nor John Balliol of Galloway, both of whom had pretensions to the throne, was elected but of the guardians the Earl of Buchan, the Bishop of St Andrews and John Comyn were there to safeguard the interests of John Balliol, whose sister was married to John Comyn. The others were supporters of Robert Bruce.

It was in all a carefully thought-out constitutional compromise and, as a neighbourly gesture and diplomatic courtesy, three envoys, the Bishop of Brechin, the Abbot of Jedburgh and Sir Geoffrey de Mowbray, were commissioned by the Scone parliament to seek out Edward I in Gascony and acquaint him with the arrangement. In the meantime a seal was struck for the guardians without which no ordinance in the future would be accounted valid.

Edward I received the envoys early in September 1286 at the town of Saintes. He was then actively engaged in arriving at an agreement with the King of France over various disputed territories in Normandy, Limousin and other areas, defining the boundaries of Gascony and reforming its government: enterprises which were to occupy his attention until his return to England in August 1289. He dismissed the envoys courteously with expressions of goodwill to the guardians and the promise, at their request, to shelve a border dispute which was causing friction between the two countries.[5] But he kept his own counsel about the future he had already envisaged for Scotland.

Edward I was one of the most able and ably advised of all the monarchs of England. The foundations of English legislature and parliament were laid in his reign: the pretensions of the Church were reduced and contained; the system of feudal levies was adapted and transformed to provide a fighting force of immense flexibility and power.

He was a man of commanding presence, tall, handsome and spare. On the field of battle he was fearless: in his private life chaste. He was sober in his mode of living, dressed simply and was constant in his religious devotions.

But the overriding element in his character was his unquestioning belief that whatever he desired was right and in the interests of all concerned. A contemporary wrote:

> He is valiant as a lion, quick to attack the strongest and fearing the onslaught of none. But if a lion in pride and fierceness, he is a panther in fickleness and inconstancy, changing his word and promise, cloaking himself by pleasant speech. When he is cornered he promises whatever you wish but as soon as he has escaped he forgets his promise. The treachery or falsehood by which he is advanced he calls prudence and the path by which he attains his ends, however crooked, he calls straight and whatever he likes he says is lawful.[6]

When the news had come of his brother-in-law's death, he pondered deeply on the consequences. Hitherto, if he was involved in continental warfare, he had known that he had a friendly ruler at his back. Now no such certainty obtained. The French already had links with Scotland through Alexander's widow Yolande de Dreux, and could strengthen them to their advantage. Above all, the Maid of Norway, with the Scottish kingdom as her dowry, would soon excite the interest of royal suitors from the courts of Europe. It was essential that he had as much control of Scotland as he had of Wales.

His first move was to make sure that there should be no consort for the young Queen of Scotland other than his youngest and only surviving son, Edward of Carnarvon, who had been born in 1284. For that end he had already prepared the way. On 29 March 1286, within a few days of Alexander's death, he had put the Maid of Norway's father, King Erik, in his debt by making him a personal loan of two thousand pounds sterling[7] and had resolved the problem of his own son's marriage being within the forbidden degrees of the Church by obtaining from the Pope, in May of that year, a bull dispensing with the impediments of affinity and legitimizing any issue that might result.[8]

The groundwork had been laid but young Edward was barely two years old and the time was not yet ripe for the next move forward.

The return of the Scottish envoys to their country, bringing with them the approbation of Edward I, was a welcome support to the guardians in a critical situation. During the envoys' absence trouble had flared in the southwest of Scotland. Robert the Competitor and his son the Earl of Carrick, gathering their retainers together, had seized the two royal castles of Dumfries and Wigton and the Balliol stronghold of Buittle,[9] and on 20 September 1286 had entered into a sworn agreement with James Stewart, one of the guardians, Angus Macdonald, Lord of the Isles, the Earls of March and Menteith and other noblemen to band themselves together.[10]

Robert the Competitor had been stirred from his retirement by two strong motives: first, to secure his base by hemming in the Galloway domain of his rival John Balliol and so keeping open the Nithsdale route between Annandale and Carrick; second, by seizing the castles and signing the Turnberry bond to indicate to King Edward, his old companion in arms and fellow crusader, that at a nod from his royal head the Bruces had the potential to take over the government of Scotland.

But no sooner was it known that the guardians had received the backing of Edward I than the raised fists were folded in peace. Robert the Competitor was too shrewd a magnate to pursue his purpose without the support or tacit approval of the English monarch.

A calm descended upon the country and for four years the guardians, backed by a permanent council of magnates, were able to carry out their administration without further incident. In 1289 their number was reduced to four. The Earl of Buchan died from old age and the Earl of Fife, described by the *Lanercost Chronicle* as 'cruel and greedy beyond average',[11] was murdered by his kinsmen. It was fortunate that among the survivors were the two bishops. For these were the professionals: trained in law and diplomacy and determined to uphold the national identity of Scotland. Their skills were shortly to be needed in the negotiations with Edward I.

As soon as Edward I returned to England in the late summer of 1289 he moved cautiously towards his objective. Exercising his moral authority as brother-in-law of the dead King and great-uncle of the young Queen, he invited the King of Norway and the Scottish regency to send commissioners to confer on her future. The King of Norway sent ambassadors. Edward himself appointed the Earl of Pembroke, the

Bishop of Winchester, the Earl of Surrey and Antony Bek, the militant Bishop of Durham, to act on his behalf, and the Scottish regency empowered three of the guardians, John Comyn of Badenoch and the two bishops, together with Robert the Competitor, to treat 'with due care, in all possible contingencies, for the honour and liberty of the Scottish realm.'[12]

The plenipotentiaries met at Salisbury in October and by 6 November had reached an amicable agreement: that the Queen should be sent to Scotland or England by 1 November 1290 but without prejudice to the question of her marriage; that if it was in England she landed she should be delivered to Scotland provided it was in a safe and peaceful condition, and that the Scots should refrain from engaging her in any marriage contract without the consent of her father and great-uncle.[13]

Encouraged by the smooth passage of these negotiations, Edward I, within a few weeks of the Treaty of Salisbury being signed, brought at last into the open the project on which he had been quietly working over the past three years. He produced a bull from Pope Nicholas IV granting dispensation for the marriage of Margaret, now six years of age, to his five-year-old son.[14]

This proposal for the union of the Crowns was received in Scotland with wary approval. For a hundred years there had been peace between the two countries and, with that peace, prosperity. The marriage of Margaret and young Edward would give assurance of that peace continuing: the authority of the Queen would be enhanced by her relationship to a powerful monarch and the pretensions of ambitious vassals would be abated. On 17 March 1290, therefore, letters were sent to the Kings of England and Norway in the names of the four guardians, ten bishops, ten earls, twenty-three abbots, eleven priors and forty-eight barons, speaking for the whole community of Scotland, agreeing to the marriage in principle.[15]

But the churchmen of the chancellery were not unaware that the see of York nursed claims for supremacy over the Scottish bishoprics and the Scottish magnates who had done homage for their English lands to Edward I in person knew well the imperious temper of that monarch and his consolidating ambitions. Even King Erik of Norway had his reservations and when a Yarmouth ship, specially equipped by Edward I with sweetmeats, fruit and gingerbread for the comfort of Maid Margaret, arrived in May 1290 at Bergen to carry her back to England, he dismissed it empty-handed.[16]

So the Scottish commissioners conducted their negotiations with all the caution of a reluctant virgin in the presence of an ardent suitor, and when the Treaty of Birgham was signed on 18 July 1290 in the village of that name, there had been written in specific conditions for the protection of Scotland's independence as strong as any parchment could create.

The laws, liberties and customs of Scotland were to be observed at all times. The great offices of state were to be held only by Scotsmen. No writ of common law or letter of special favour could be issued except by the 'King's Chapel', the royal chancellery. No taxation of the Scots should be levied except for the needs of the Scottish kingdom. No vassal of the Scottish Crown was to do homage for his Scottish lands outside the kingdom. No Church matters were to be subject to interference outside the kingdom. No Scottish subject was to be answerable at law outside the kingdom. No parliament dealing with Scottish affairs was to be held outside the kingdom.

The whole emphasis was on the separateness of the Scottish kingdom from that of England. There was to be a union of the Crowns indeed, but the two countries were to remain as distinct sovereignties ruled respectively by their native queen and king.[17]

Agreement to these terms was endorsed by Edward I at Northampton on 28 August 1290 and many historians have applauded his statesmanship in showing such consideration to the demands of the weaker party. On the surface this would appear to be so. But it is noticeable that after the resounding affirmation that the Scottish kingdom should be 'separate, apart and free in itself without subject to the English Kingdom', there is slipped in a clause 'saving the rights of the King of England . . . which may justly belong to him':[18] a clause identical to that he inserted in the Forest Charter Laws forced upon him by his barons and on the strength of which he claimed legal justification when he reneged on his undertakings. Even while the commissioners were still discussing the Treaty of Birgham Edward I sent Walter Huntercomb with an armed force on 4 June 1290 to seize the governorship of the Isle of Man. An integral part of the Scottish realm, of strategic importance, was thus transferred into an English protectorate.[19] In August he attempted still further pressure by asking the Scottish regency to allow Antony Bek, his chief negotiator at the Treaty of Birgham, to be viceroy in Scotland for Queen Margaret and her husband designate and to accept his ruling in all matters appertaining to the 'governance and peaceful state of the realm' – yet another pointer to the fact that however accommodating his reaction to the Treaty of Birgham, his settled purpose remained the subservience of the Scottish kingdom to the national interest of England.

Nevertheless, for the moment the Scottish rulers conditioned themselves to see only his Janus face of peace and throughout September, that best of months in Scotland, a mood of optimism spread through the country at the prospect of the royal marriage. A voyage by sea of the Maid of Norway to the Orkneys was put in hand and to that outlying possession of the Norwegian Crown a deputation from the kingdoms of Scotland and England made their way while other magnates began to gather at Perth to await her progress south and her inauguration at Scone.

But all was for nothing. The little Queen Margaret fell ill on the voyage from Norway to Orkney and soon after landing there, on 26 September 1290, she died in the arms of the Bishop of Bergen. The succession to the throne was now wide open.[20]

# 4

No sooner did the news of the Queen's death reach Scotland early in October than Robert the Competitor, although in his eightieth year, gathered a strong force of armed men together and hastened to Perth where the Scottish Council was in session, with the intent to overawe them against any action inimicable to his interests. The Earls of Mar and Atholl were rumoured to be mustering their forces in his support and few can doubt that in his train was a young squire of sixteen years, already trained in weaponry and well aware of his family's claims, his grandson Robert Bruce.

Down in the south, John Balliol, Lord of Galloway since his mother's death earlier in the year, with the connivance and encouragement of his neighbour and friend Antony Bek, Prince Bishop of Durham and right hand man of Edward I, declared himself 'heir to Scotland'. A swarm of other claimants dusted their pedigrees and burnished their arms. But none was preponderant enough to gain the Crown by force and all eyes turned towards the English King whose apparent consideration for the independence of Scotland had so recently been shown and whose reputation for impartiality had been recognized by the Crowns of Europe when he was appointed arbiter between the conflicting claims of Peter of Aragon and Charles of Anjou to the kingdom of Sicily.

Bishop Fraser urged him by letter to move to the border in force to prevent bloodshed and pressed the claims of John Balliol.[1] In riposte the seven Earls of Angus, Atholl, Lennox, Mar, Menteith, Ross and Strathearn rallied to the side of Bruce and claimed that they alone had the ancient right of instituting a king and had invited Edward of England to arbitrate.[2]

No wolf invited by a flock of sheep to nominate their leading ram could have felt more satisfaction at this juncture than Edward I. In response to their appeals he set in train his movement northward. But at Hardby in Lincolnshire his beloved consort Eleanor fell ill and in November 1290 died of fever.[3] All matters of state were immediately put aside. Although his marriage to this half-sister of the King of Spain at the age of fifteen had been one of dynastic convenience arranged by his father, he had for thirty-five years devoted himself to her with a fidelity and attachment notable in any class and rare indeed among monarchs. 'I loved her dearly during her lifetime,' wrote Edward, 'I shall not cease to love her now that she is dead.'

Her body was borne in stately progress to its last resting place in Westminster Abbey, and at every nightfall stopping place a cross was erected in her memory, the last at Charing Cross.[4] Her death wrought an evil change in Edward's nature. The savage streak, inherited from his Angevin ancestors, 'the Devil's breed', which had expressed itself in his youth by acts of wanton cruelty, had been tamed and softened by her gentleness. From now on, without her restraining influence, it was to break out in barbarous reprisals against those who thwarted his purpose.

Raw from his bereavement, he delayed no longer to reveal his ambitions. Confidentially informing his barons in council that he intended to subjugate Scotland as he had Wales,[5] he moved north to Antony Bek, the Bishop of Durham's castle at Norham on Tweed and from there invited the representatives of Scotland and the various competitors to meet him on 30 May 1291,[6] with the assurance that their appearance on English soil would not be taken as a precedent.[7] At the same time, he gave orders to his armed forces to join him on 3 June.

The Scotsmen, assuming that his action was that of an unbiased arbitrator, duly arrived in his presence. He received them with ostentatious ceremony surrounded by the high officers of his court, and began the proceedings by informing them through his chief justice that he had come to resolve the dispute among the claimants to the Scottish throne not as friend and umpire but as lord paramount and feudal superior of the Scottish realm. 'Can you,' his address concluded, 'produce any evidence to show that I am not the rightful Suzerain?'[8]

Taken aback, the Scots asked for time to consider their reply and were granted twenty-four hours and then, after their expostulation, three weeks, by which time King Edward knew that he would have his army at his side.[9]

If the Scots had chosen to invoke the legalistic formulas by which the King liked to cloak his designs, they would have pointed out that if he genuinely believed he was lord paramount he could already, on the Maid of Norway's accession to the throne, have claimed the right according to feudal law of administering her heritage while she was still a minor, and the right as her guardian of marrying her to whom he chose. Instead, by signing the Treaty of Birgham, he had accepted that Scotland was an independent kingdom and had guaranteed that it should so continue.

They could have reminded him that though by the Treaty of Falaise between Henry II of England and King William I 'the Lion' of Scotland, King William had agreed in 1174 to accept the over-lordship of England in order to be released from captivity, this treaty had been abrogated by Richard I, Coeur de Lion, in 1189, and that when Alexander III, on Edward I's accession to the English throne in 1278, did homage to him for his English lands, he stated categorically, 'I become your man for the lands which I hold of you in the Kingdom of England for which I owe you homage, saving my Kingdom. To homage for my Kingdom of Scotland no-one has any right but God alone, nor do I hold it of any but of God.'

But guided almost certainly by Bishop Wishart of Glasgow, that continuing champion of Scottish freedom, they went straight to the vital point: that they could not answer for a future king of Scotland. In a memorable letter, 'in the name of the community of Scotland', delivered to King Edward at the end of May, they wrote, after a courteous preamble referring to his claim to suzerainty:

> Sire, to this the good men who have sent us here say that they know full well that you would not make so great a demand if you did not believe that you had good right to it: yet of any such right or demand made or used by yourself or your ancestors they know nothing. They answer, with such authority as they possess, that they have no power to reply in the absence of a ruler over them to whom such a demand should be addressed and who could reply to it. For even if they did reply it would not increase your right nor take away from the right of their liege lord. But the good men of the Kingdom are willing that whoever shall be King shall perform to you whatever right and law require, for he and no-one else will have the power to do this. Meanwhile they can only refer to the oath they took after the death of the late King, saving your faith and theirs and to the treaty confirmed in your presence at Northampton.[10]

Brushing aside this petition as containing nothing to the purpose (*nihil tamen efficax*),[11] Edward demanded that as his title was disputed by none his overlordship should be recognized by all.

The Scots were in a helpless situation. Edward lay on their borders with a formidable army at his command. Their country had been so long at peace that it was ungeared for war. The natural military leaders were bitterly divided by the empty throne. They had no alternative but acceptance or annihilation. Nine conferences were held between 2 and 13 June, but the upshot was that all the claimants to the Crown swore to the King in person and then publicly repeated their oaths before the assembled lords that they accepted King Edward I as their feudal superior with lawful right to decide their case;[12] and shortly afterwards the guardians of Scotland and the magnates of the realm agreed to hand over to him the custody of their country and its castles in exchange for his solemn promise that within two months of his award he would restore them to him 'who shall gain the right, by judgement, of royalty', and that on the death of a Scots king he would demand nothing but homage and the rights incidental to it.[13]

With Scotland in the hollow of his hand, Edward acted with calculated promptitude: on 13 June 1291 on the green at Upsettlington, a little village on the Scottish side of the Tweed opposite Norham Castle, he received the fealty of the guardians and the magnates there present. The four guardians resigned into his hands the office which they had received from 'the community of Scotland' and were reappointed 'by the most serene prince, by God's grace illustrious King of England, superior Lord of Scotland', with the addition of a fifth guardian, an English baron, Brian FitzAlan of Bedale. A new chancellor was installed with an Englishman as his colleague. The constables of the Scottish castles resigned their charges and were reappointed as his sworn liege men.

Then, setting out from Upsettlington, he made a ceremonial progress by way of Haddington, Edinburgh and Linlithgow to Stirling. At Stirling he issued a proclamation that by 27 July, on pain of severe penalties, all men of substance throughout the kingdom should swear fealty to him in person or to representatives appointed by him for that purpose. He returned by Dumfermline, St Andrews and Perth with abbots and priors, barons and knights, freemen and burghers coming to kneel before him, and arrived in Berwick in time to open on 3 August the preliminary hearings of the great court case for the throne of

Scotland. All this with such speed and panache that any resistance by unwilling Scots had no time to consolidate.

The great court case was to become a showpiece trial by which not only Scotland and England but all Europe were to be made aware with what detailed care and respect for legal opinion the matter was conducted. It was indeed a splendid façade.

The court was composed of 104 auditors: twenty-four from Edward's council, forty nominated by Robert the Competitor, and forty nominated by John Balliol. By the very nature of these appointments it was clear that attention would be concentrated on the pleas of the two principal rivals and that the claims of the other candidates were regarded as unsubstantial. Nevertheless, on 3 August all the competitors appeared before the King and lodged their petitions, each tracing his descent in detail from the royal ancestor through whom he made his claim. These petitions were sewn up in a leather bag, sealed with the seals of the Bishops of Glasgow and St Andrews and the Earls of Buchan and Mar, and then deposited in Berwick castle.[14] Thereupon King Edward, who had urgent business in England, adjourned the hearing until 2 June 1292. On that date the court reassembled and was adjourned once more until 14 October. Meanwhile copies of the pedigrees had been sent to France to be considered by some of the greatest law scholars in Europe.

The auditors began by debating the pleas of Bruce and Balliol before entering on the claims at large. Both were descended from David, Earl of Huntingdon, brother of King William I the Lion, whose stock had ended with the Maid of Norway. David had left no sons behind him. His heirs were three daughters whose living representatives were: a grandson of the eldest daughter, John Balliol, a son of the second daughter, Robert the Competitor, and a grandson of the third daughter, John Hastings, Lord of Abergavenny.

John Balliol claimed the throne as representative of the senior branch, Robert the Competitor as being the nearer descendant with the further arguments that he had been nominated as heir by Alexander II when that king was childless and that he had the support of the seven earls who, by ancient right and tradition, had the power to elect a king.

The scales of justice could be weighted either way by adequate precedents. The Frenchman Bonet, the supreme authority at that time of canon law, gave as his opinion that the succession ought to go to the claimant who was born first even though he was descended from the younger line,[15] and the Master General of the Franciscans came to the same conclusion not on this ground but as nearer in degree, citing from the Bible the unexpected precedent of the daughters of Zelophehad.[16]

On the other hand, the principle of primogeniture, although not yet established, was gradually gaining acceptance. King Edward at first inclined to Bruce and said so in private. But Antony Bek, the shrewd Bishop of Durham, as Fordun reports, posed him his question: 'If Robert of Bruce were King of Scotland, where would Edward King of England be? For this Robert is of the noblest stock of all England and together with him the kingdom of Scotland is very strong in itself and in times gone by a great deal of mischief has been wrought to the Kings of England by those of Scotland.' At this the King, patting him on the head – as it were – answered in the French tongue, *'Par le sank Dieu vous avez bun chanté'*, which is to say, 'By Christ's blood thou hast sung well. Things shall go otherwise than I arranged at first.'[17]

The Scottish auditors, being unable to agree by what laws and customs the right of succession should be determined, referred the matter to those auditors appointed by the King. Each of these auditors in turn was interrogated by none less than the King himself. Aware by now of his wishes and that as recently as April 1290 he had defined the rules of succession for the kingdom of England by seniority, they gave him the agreeable answer that judgement should be given by the laws and customs of England, and that as between the nearer descendant of the younger daughter and the more remote descendant of the elder daughter, the progeny of the elder daughter must be exhausted before that of the younger had any claim.

On 6 November Bruce was informed that on the pleadings presented he had failed to make out his case. On 7 November, by a document now in the British Museum, sealed by Bruce and Gilbert de Clare, Earl of Gloucester, he delegated his claim to the throne to his son, the Earl of Carrick, and his heirs. Two days later the Earl of Carrick, whose wife had died earlier in the year, resigned his earldom to his own son and heir, the eighteen-year-old Robert Bruce, the future king.[18] Whatever the outcome of the court case, the Bruces were determined that their claim should remain on record.

They made two further attempts to prevent the elevation of John Balliol. On 14 June 1292 Bruce the Competitor had entered into an agreement with the Count of Holland that if either should win the Crown he would hand over to the other as his fief a third part of the kingdom. The Count of Holland now came forward with the unlikely story that David, Earl of Huntingdon, on behalf of himself and his heirs, had resigned the rights to the Scottish throne in exchange for a grant of land at Garioch in northeast Scotland and that in consequence his stock was disbarred, whereas the Count was in direct descent from Ada, the sister of King William the Lion, and entitled to the throne.[19] However, whether bribed by Balliol, as his fellow Dutchmen believed, or not, after a short debate he withdrew his plea. Finally, the Bruces threw their weight behind the claim of John Hastings that Scotland was held of the king as any other fief under common law and was therefore divisible between the three descendants of Earl David and that in consequence they were entitled to a third share of the income and land.[20]

But the court had come to its decision. On 17 November 1292, in the great hall at Berwick, the King's judgement was read to the crowded assembly by his chief justice, Roger le Brabazon. Of the thirteen competitors seven had withdrawn their claims and three had been dismissed for want of prosecution. In regard to the remaining three, the King pronounced that the kingdom of Scotland was indivisible, which cut out John Hastings, that the senior branch of Earl David's stock had precedence over the junior, which cut out the heirs of Robert the Competitor, and that John Balliol was heir at law to the vacant throne.[21]

It was at this stage that, according to Fordun:

> The Earl of Gloucester, holding Robert the Bruce by the hand, in the sight of all, spoke thus to the King: 'Recollect O King what kind of judgement thou hast given today and know that thou must be judged at the last', and straightaway at the Earl's bidding the aforesaid Robert Bruce withdrew, nor did he ever tender homage or fealty to John of Balliol.[22]

The great court case was over; but on the mind of the young Robert Bruce, now Earl of Carrick, who had listened to the many family conclaves during the years which had followed the death of Alexander III, was deeply imprinted the conviction that an injustice had been done and that his grandfather was the rightful king of Scots.

Formalities now followed each other pell-mell. On 19 November the constables of those Scottish castles previously placed in Edward's hands were ordered to surrender them to John Balliol, and the guardians of Scotland to hand over the realm. The great seal they had used was broken in four and the fragments sent to the English treasury and a fresh seal was cut for the new king.[23]

On 20 November John Balliol swore fealty for his kingdom as held of his superior lord.[24] On 30 November he was crowned at Scone by John St John as deputy for the infant Earl of Fife,[25] whose family held the hereditary right of crowning the monarch and on 26 December, in his capacity as invested king, he once more rendered homage to his lord superior: as complete a vassal king as the documents of English jurists could make him.[26]

John Balliol was King of Scotland but this unfortunate man, pilloried to posterity as Toom Tabard, the Empty Jacket, derived few benefits from his royal status.

There was little of Scots about him. He was a native of Picardy with vast possessions in France. He was married to the daughter of John de Warenne, Earl of Surrey, one of King Edward's leading military commanders, and had substantial landed interests in England. His only direct link with Scotland was his recent inheritance of the wild and unruly domain of Galloway and the fact that his sister was married to a former guardian, John Comyn of Badenoch, head of the 'Red' Comyns, the senior branch of a baronial family which vied with the Bruces as the most powerful influence in Scotland. A savage little vignette appears in the contemporary *Rishanger Chronicle:*

> John [Balliol] hurried to Scotland glittering in his crown. But the Scots consenting or not received him with extreme annoyance. They dismissed his attendants, familiar to him and of his own race, and deputed strangers to act as his administrators . . . But he, simple and stupid, almost mute and speechless . . . did not open his mouth . . . Thus he dwelt among them for a whole year, as a lamb among wolves.[27]

Within a week of his enthronement this meek lamb experienced both the perfidy and pressure of his superior lord. A burgess of Berwick who had lost his triple law suit in the court of the Scottish guardians appealed to the King of England against their decision. There is suspicion of prearrangement about this action, for contrary to the usual law's delays, Edward had called in the record of the proceedings to his own court within the next fortnight and reversed one of the judgements.

Immediately Fraser, Bishop of St Andrews, John Comyn, Earl of Buchan, Patrick Graham and other supporters of Balliol lodged a petition in the name of King John that Edward should keep to the promise he had made in Northampton in August 1290 and reiterated at Norham in June 1291 that he would preserve the laws and customs of Scotland and should abide by the solemn agreement he had signed in the Treaty of Birgham that no Scottish lawsuit should be dealt with outside the kingdom.

To this Edward roundly replied that any promises, concessions or ratifications made during the interregnum, when the throne of Scotland was vacant, were 'for the time being' only and that henceforward nothing ever placed on parchment should keep him from hearing appeals from Scotland and that he would cite King John himself to appear before him if he so thought fit.[28] So much for the integrity of a monarch who, on his gravestone, had engraved by a piece of prodigious irony *pactum servo* – I keep my word. He followed up his outburst by extracting from the Scottish King on 2 January 1293 two instruments, one in Latin, one in French, by which the Treaty of Birgham was declared 'null and void' and Edward was released from 'every article, concession or promise' therein contained.[29]

Nothing could more clearly demonstrate to the Scots what Edward understood by homage and the rights that appertained and they writhed in impotence.

But worse humiliation was to follow. King Edward had a set of standing orders drawn up by his lawyers for the hearing of Scottish appeals of a character unheard of in the history of appellate justice. By these rules the King of Scotland in person was required to attend in England the hearings of every appeal against him and if the English court adjudged a miscarriage of justice, he was to be held personally liable for damages, both to the appellant and to his lord superior.

The climax of this measured harassment was reached in October 1293 when King John was summoned to appear in person before the English parliament to hear an appeal against him by John Macduff, younger son of Malcolm, Earl of Fife. On presenting himself as requested, he was treated with deliberate discourtesy and made to stand at the bar like a private malefactor. Stiffened before the ordeal by his councillors, he showed at first a commendable firmness. He refused to answer to the charge on the grounds that he was King of Scotland and dared not nor was able to act in any matter affecting his kingdom without the advice of the good men of his realm, nor could he ask for any adjournment for that would imply that he recognized the jurisdiction of those before whom he was cited.[30]

The court thereupon declared that he was guilty of extreme contempt in that it was directed against the sovereign who had conferred upon him the dignity of the Crown, and that for this contumacy he should not only pay damages to the appellant but should also hand over to the King of England the three principal castles in his realm together with their attendant towns until he had purged his contempt. At this King John's nerve failed him. Browbeaten by Edward and insulted by Parliament, he stood firm no longer. Before the court's resolution could be passed into a decree, he submitted a humble petition to his lord superior, craving that time should be given him to consult his subjects and promising to report the result to the first Parliament after Easter. King Edward thereupon adjourned the next hearing to 14 June 1294. But as in the inexorable progress of a Greek tragedy, pride is followed by retribution, so now it happened to Edward.

Philip the Fair of France had observed the arbitrary manner in which Edward had treated the Scots as a prerogative of his overlordship. With ironic malice he decided to follow his example. Edward, in his capacity of Duke of Aquitaine, owed him fealty. Claiming that English seamen had attacked French ships without provocation, he cited Edward to appear in person before the parliament in Paris and there submit to the judgement of his lord superior. When Edward failed to attend, King Philip came down into the parliament, pronounced him contumacious and on 19 May 1294 seized his lands in Gascony as forfeit. On 24 June Edward retaliated by renouncing his homage as duke and despatched a formal declaration of war.

The opportunity had now come for those smarting under his subjection to regain their independence. In September 1294, on the very eve of the Edward's departure from Portsmouth with his assembled forces for Gascony, the Welsh rose in revolt and compelled him to turn away from the expedition on which he had based his hopes of recovering his duchy.

By May 1295 he had crushed the Welsh rebellion but in the meantime the Scots, having lost all confidence in King John, had elected four bishops, four earls and four barons to manage the government of the country in his name,[31] and had sent commissioners to negotiate an alliance with France. On 23 October 1295 an offensive and defensive league was concluded between the two countries and this was ratified by the Scottish parliament in February 1296.[32]

But before this Edward had got wind of the affair. He made an immediate decision that the conquest of Scotland had priority over that of Gascony and with his accustomed energy had summoned his feudal host to meet him at Newcastle on 1 March 1296 and a fleet of ships to be assembled in East Anglia and to sail along the east coast to join him on the same date.[33] The Scottish Council in the name of King John issued a national call to arms for all free men to rendezvous at Caddonlee, four miles north of Selkirk.[34]

During all the time since the rebuttal of their claims, the Bruces had played no part in the affairs of Scotland. Robert the Competitor retired from public life and remained quietly on his estates until his death on 1 April 1295; but not before he had signified his contempt for the new king by rigging, in the previous year, the election of his own nominee to the bishopric of Galloway in the face of royal objection.[35] His son, determined not to compromise his claim to the throne by doing homage to Balliol, departed in 1292 on a long visit to King Erik of Norway, accompanied by his eldest daughter Isobel.[36] Within a year she was married to her host and her father remained at their court until he returned, on his own father's death, to succeed to the lordship of Annandale and the English estates. In October 1295 he was appointed Governor of Carlisle by King Edward.[37]

In his absence his son and heir, Robert Bruce, the future king, to whom he had handed over the earldom of Carrick in November 1291, had become the virtual head of the lively and united family which remained in Scotland, consisting of his four brothers, Edward, Thomas, Alexander and Nigel, and his four sisters Mary, Christina, Matilda and Margaret. During this time, he would have been in close contact with his grandfather, Robert the Competitor, and, on his behalf, visited the family possessions in the Midlands and Essex and paid his respects at the English court. There it must be assumed he found favour with King Edward for loans from the Royal Exchequer were put at his disposal. It is probable that it was from London in September 1293 that he despatched his magnificent wedding gift to his sister Isobel of blue, scarlet and fur-trimmed gowns, bed linen, coverlets of gold and green, silver plate and dishes for the table.[38]

Soon after his father's return in 1295 Robert married Isabella, daughter of the tenth Earl of Mar, whose great lands lay along the northeastern coast of Inverness; but it was a short-lived marriage, for after giving birth to a daughter, Marjorie, in 1296, Isabella died.[39]

When the call to arms was issued by King John, the conduct of the Bruces was clear and consistent. They had never recognized his coronation. They had never given up the hope of their succession to the Scottish throne. They had never paid homage to him. They abode by the vows of fealty they had made to King Edward in 1292 and reiterated in 1296 and he, in turn, to fasten their loyalty and excite their hopes, had promised that if the revolt was crushed and Balliol deposed, the elder Bruce, now Governor of Carlisle, should succeed to the Scottish throne.[40] So they ignored the summons as did the Earls of Angus and Dunbar and many other magnates who followed their lead. In consequence all were instantly deprived of their Scottish possessions. That those of the Bruces were handed out by Balliol to his kinsman, John Comyn, Earl of Buchan, only intensified an already bitter feud.[41]

The Scottish and English forces were gathering their strength when a love affair sparked off the conflict. Robert de Ros, an Englishman, Lord of Wark on Tweed, had fallen in love with a Scottish girl. As an earnest of his wish to marry her, he joined forces with her countrymen and promised to deliver to them his castle. His brother, hearing of his purpose, sent an urgent request to King Edward for his help. An advance guard of the English was promptly dispatched, but Robert de Ros with men from Roxburgh fell upon them as they lay camped for the night and cut them to pieces. The first blood had been shed. 'By God's blessing,' exclaimed Edward when he heard the news, 'as the Scots have begun, so shall I make an end.'[42]

His army made a rapid advance to relieve Wark and on 17 March 1296 King Edward made his quarters there and remained until after the celebration of Easter on 25 March.

Elevated by this greatest of Christian festivals, both sides immediately proceeded to acts of unnecessary barbarity. On 26 March, leaving their country's eastern approaches unguarded, the Scots, under the Earl of Buchan, poured over the border at its western end, put to sword and flame the scattered villages on the English side and swept to the walls of Carlisle in an attempt to take it by storm. But the gates were fast bolted by the Lord of Annandale and the ramparts manned by the citizens under the command of his son, the Earl of Carrick.[43]

The Scots, having no siege engines, retraced their steps and a few weeks later turned east over the Cheviots and ravaged far and wide into Northumberland, burning churches, nunneries and villages and crowning their aimless exploits by the incineration of two hundred little scholars in a school at Corbridge.[44] From a military point of view these raids were useless and did nothing to distract King Edward from his advance up the main eastern route to Scotland.

As it was, he was able to transport his army unopposed over the Tweed, twenty miles upstream from Berwick, and invade the town. An initial assault was made from the sea but the four leading ships went aground and the defenders, sallying forth, set them on fire and slew their crews. Elated by their success, they manned their precarious defences of earthen mound and palisade and jeered at the English and their King. But their confidence was ill founded. Under King Edward's lead, his armoured knights crashed through the rotting timbers and drove their adversaries in disorder into the narrow streets and closes of the town. The foot soldiers followed and dreadful slaughter ensued. On the orders of the King that none should be spared, men, women and children were hewn down in their thousands and their corpses gave out a stench so overpowering that when all was over, deep pits had to be dug to bury their remains. For two days the massacre continued until Edward, riding among his men, observed a woman in the very act of childbirth being put to the sword, and at last called off the carnage.

Among the dead all honour must be given to the thirty Flemish merchants, who, in strict compliance to their ancient treaty with the Scottish Crown, resisted fiercely in their depot, 'the Red Hall', until it was engulfed by flames and all were burned.

The citadel alone remained intact; but the governor, Sir William Douglas, agreed to surrender himself as hostage so that the garrison might depart unharmed.[45]

The sack of Berwick, the pearl of Scotland's commerce, was a crippling blow to her revenues and trade. Never again was the town to recover its ancient eminence. Edward at once had marked it down as the headquarters of his Scottish administration. With feverish energy he collected a vast work force from the neighbouring counties to surround it with massive fortifications – Edward himself set an example by personally shifting earth in a wheelbarrow[46] – and brought up from the south English clerks and English merchants to replace the inhabitants who now lay cluttered in a common grave.[47]

By a macabre coincidence, while the smoke still rose thinly from the smouldering ruins a letter was brought by the Abbot of Arbroath to King Edward in which King John renounced his fealty.[48] So late and so ineffective. 'O foolish knave! What folly he commits!' exclaimed the English King. 'If he will not come to us, we will go to him.'[49]

Learning that the Countess of Dunbar had handed over its castle to a Scottish force while her husband was with the English and that the Earl of Buchan was gathering a powerful host on the heights surrounding the town of Dunbar, he ordered his army, under the Earl of Surrey, to march northwards.

The disciplined columns of the English came up with their opponents on 27 April and began to deploy in the deep valley beneath the slopes of the Lammermuirs, on which the Scots were massed, in order to cross the intervening burn. Stalwart though the Scottish knights had shown themselves in many a tiltyard, they had no experience of the tactics of serious warfare. As the English began to disappear into the dead ground below, they assumed they were seeking to escape. Breaking their ranks, they charged down the hillside in a tumultuous rabble only to meet an ordered battle line which overwhelmed them at the first onslaught. Thousands of Scottish foot soldiers were slain and the knights surrounded and made prisoner. Among those taken on the field of battle and from the castle of Dunbar were the greater part of the principal nobility who had supported Balliol, and no organized resistance remained.[50]

The rest of Edward's campaign was a military promenade. Roxburgh, Dumbarton and Jedburgh castles surrendered in quick succession and Edinburgh castle after eight days. Stirling castle was found abandoned with only a porter to hand over the keys. In unresisting Perth, Edward celebrated the feast of John the Baptist and there received letters of abject submission from King John. On 10 July this unhappy monarch appeared before his overlord at Montrose and yielded to him his person and his kingdom, bewailing the errors into which he had fallen 'through evil counsel and our own simplicity', and in the presence of all assembled to witness his humiliation had the blazon of the royal arms embroidered on his tabard ripped off and cast upon the floor. Toom Tabard, King Nobody, was king no more.[51]

Leaving the Earl of Lancaster to transport his captive to the Tower of London,★ Edward made leisurely progress northward through Aberdeen and Banff as far as Elgin to demonstrate his might and receive the homage of prominent Scots in the districts through which he passed. Returning by Perth, he commanded that the hallowed Stone of Destiny, upon which from generation to generation the kings of Scotland had been enthroned, should be taken from the abbey church at Scone and delivered to Westminster Abbey. The plunder of this sacred relic and the royal regalia which he had already removed from Edinburgh castle were arrogant signals to all in Scotland that henceforth their country was not a kingdom but a dependent part of England.[52]

On 28 August he held a parliament at Berwick to which every landholder in Scotland was summoned to appear with signed and sealed instruments of fealty – The Ragman Roll [53] – not to a new king of Scotland – 'Have we nothing else to do but win kingdoms for you?' he replied scornfully to the Lord of Annandale's reminder of the promise of a throne – but to Edward, king of England. He had at last achieved the object to which he had been moving, step by step, by cunning and by force – the incorporation into one kingdom of England, Wales and Scotland.[54]

He remained for three weeks in Berwick ordering the administration of his new province. Scotsmen were no longer to be governed by Scotsmen but by Englishmen with no lineal or landed ambitions in that area. The Earl of Surrey was made viceroy, Sir Hugh Cressinham, treasurer, Sir Walter of Amersham, chancellor, and Sir William Ormesby, chief justice.[55] The castles throughout Scotland were garrisoned by English troops, the Church benefices filled with English priests, the day to day business controlled by English bureaucrats from their headquarters in Berwick. Scotland, bereft of its natural leaders who were either immured in English prisons or drawn by the pull of their English possessions to Edward's camp, appeared prostrate at his feet.

★ cf note II

# 5

In the autumn of 1296 Edward returned to England to deal with the problems of the French war, disdainfully remarking as he crossed the border that it was 'a good job to be shot of shit' (*bon besoigne fait qy de merde se deliver*).[1]

His satisfaction was premature. The fall of Berwick, the collapse at Dunbar, the abject figure of John Balliol, the unopposed progress through the burghs of his new conquest had given him and his lieutenants a false impression of the people they now proposed to govern. The Earl of Surrey was so unconcerned about his duties as Viceroy of Scotland that he retired to his Yorkshire estates leaving the direction of affairs to Hugh de Cressingham. This portly ecclesiastic, sensual and money-loving, concentrated his energies on extracting from the subject Scots, by taxes and sequestration, funds which his master so urgently required for the war against France. He was ably abetted by William Ormesby, the Chief Justice, who with a dog-like fidelity hunted out all who had not signed instruments of fealty, proclaimed them outlaws and seized their properties and goods.[2]

But Scotland had been stunned and not subdued. A growing band of outraged and dispossessed men took refuge in the forests and mountains of their native land. The pent-up resentment of a proud and spirited race, smouldering like a peat fire below the surface, burst into flame and by May 1297 the whole of Scotland, outside Lothian, was in revolt led by two outstanding men: Andrew Moray and William Wallace.

Andrew Moray had been captured at Dunbar together with his father, Sir Andrew Moray, and his uncle. Escaping from his prison in Chester,[3] he made his way to the hereditary lands of his family in the Mounth, the great mountainous mass which divides the Spey river from the Tay. There he raised the standard of rebellion at his father's castle at Avoch and to him rallied not only the warlike men of Moray, but also the burghers of Inverness under Alexander Pilche. Together they so harried and ambuscaded the English that anguished cries for help were sent to King Edward.[4]

Down in the Selkirk forest William Wallace, son of a knightly family from the parish of Paisley, was living an outlaw life since neither he nor his eldest brother, Sir Malcolm, had bowed their heads at Berwick. A giant of a man with a mane of brown hair and piercing eyes, Wallace had become a magnet for the discontented. He had recently married a young woman who lived in Lanark. Visiting her by stealth, as a marked man, he clashed with an English patrol. Fighting his way clear, he retreated to her house and as his pursuers hammered on the front door he escaped by the back to the rocky Cartland Crags. Enraged by the failure to capture him, Sir William Heselrig, Sheriff of Lanark, ordered the house to be burned and all within it, wife and servants, to be put to the sword. From that day Wallace vowed an undying vengeance against the English.

Gathering together a band of desperate men, he fell by night on the sheriff and his armed guard, hewed the sheriff into small pieces with his own sword and burned the buildings and those within them.[5]

For the first time one of the high officials of the hated conquerors had been slain and a ripple of jubilation spread through the oppressed.

Men flocked to Wallace's banner and with a growing force he turned eastward to where the chief justice was holdings his courts at Scone. On the way there he was joined by that stormy petrel, Sir William Douglas, late commander of the castle at Berwick, with a body of mounted men. Leaving the foot soldiers to follow, Wallace and Sir William, with all the horsemen of the party, galloped ahead in the hope of surprising the chief justice at his sessions. But in the nick of time he was warned of their approach and fled in the clothes he stood up in, relinquishing to his attackers a rich haul of booty.[6]

The gesture of Sir William was typical of the man. Cruasader, warrior, egoist, he had gone his own way throughout his life with very little regard for anyone else. He had flouted the guardians of the interregnum and insulted the authority of King Edward by abducting and forcibly marrying Eleanor de Ferrers, an English widow, while she was staying with relatives in Scotland.[7]

Nevertheless, in that heraldic age, the adherence of this great nobleman immediately conferred on Wallace's band of outlaws the cachet of respectability. Sir William Douglas's kinship to the family of Moray and the fact that his first wife was the sister of James Stewart, Wallace's feudal lord, linked the two areas of insurrection. Behind his move it is reasonable to discern the fine hand of Robert Wishart, Bishop of Glasgow.

Nobody was more opposed to the domination of England than the Scottish Church, and this opposition had been intensified since the parliament of Berwick by King Edward's repeated presentations of English priests to Scottish benefices. Nobody had a better network of communication to direct and coordinate subversive activities.

Both these aspects were personified in the frail body of the bishop. He had pledged his fealty to King Edward at Berwick, but for him the Church came first and he regarded his recurrent pledges as no more than pawns in the struggle, given under duress, discarded without compunction whenever the defence of his country required it. For he remembered only too well the blatant manner in which the English King had repudiated his most solemn promises. As news of the spreading revolt reached him on the ecclesiastical grapevine, he turned his attention to his fellow guardian in the days of the interregnum, James Stewart.

This cautious man with his vast possessions in Bute, Kyle Stewart and Renfrew, Teviotdale, Lauderdale and Lothian, his hereditary position as royal steward, his freedom from any distracting landholdings in England, his overlordship of William Wallace, had for weeks been hovering on the edge of a decision. The example of his neighbour and relative, Sir William Douglas, the return of Wallace to the west where he chased the cocksure Antony Bek, Bishop of Durham, from the episcopal palace in Glasgow and trapped and burned an English garrison in Ayr, together with the urgings of Bishop Wishart, proved decisive. Early in June 1297, at the same time as Macduff of Fife, a son of an Earl of Fife, and his two sons raised their standard of revolt in the east, he summoned his knights to take the field against the English and join him at the town of Irvine in the west.[8]


When news of Sir William Douglas's defection reached King Edward, he was deeply involved in English problems. Knowing of old the contrariness of this opinionated knight, he did not take the matter seriously enough to alert the English forces but sent orders to the Governor of Carlisle, the elder Bruce, to instruct his son to muster the men of Annandale and with them proceed to the Douglas lands and seize the Douglas castle.

So Robert Bruce, the young Earl of Carrick, rode from Carlisle to Annan and Lochmaben to summon his father's vassals, and when he had gathered a sufficient force together drew up to the Douglas stronghold. During his journey there he had much on which to ponder. His father had always been a follower of King Edward, more at home with the civilities of the English court and the blander climate of his English estates than with the rougher life of the north. But Robert Bruce was Scottish born and Scottish bred. With his brothers and sisters he had roamed the Carrick lands of his Celtic mother or ridden beside his tough old grandfather through the hills and valleys of Annandale. He had played his part indeed on the English side and in return had been granted a postponement of his debt repayments to the English exchequer:[9] but that was when he was ranged against the Comyns for whom John Balliol had confiscated the Bruce estates in Scotland. Now the Comyns and John Balliol were captives and the leaders who had taken the field against the English in Ayrshire were the very men who had supported his grandfather's claim to the Scottish throne.

That claim Bruce had never forgotten. Brought up in the knowledge that in his veins ran the royal blood of the House of Canmore, convinced of the injustice of the court decision which had denied his family their regal inheritance, his abiding ambition was to retrieve the crown his grandfather had struggled for and lost. That purpose dominated his actions. Hitherto it had been served by Edward I's promise to Bruce's father that the Scottish throne would be his when Balliol was deposed. But Edward had reneged. The Scottish throne had been incorporated in that of England. The single devil of Balliol had been swept away only to be replaced by the sevenfold devil of the Plantaganet king. By assuming the sovereignty of Scotland, Edward I had become the chief obstacle to Bruce's objective and the catalyst to fuse the two elements in Bruce's nature, his love of his native land and his determination to rule it.

So, as he rode up the long valley of Annandale, this young man of twenty-two, already admired by men for his skill at arms and by women for his courtesy, took the crucial decision of his life.

When he reached the castle, which was held by Sir William's wife, he called his followers around him. 'No man,' he said, 'holds his flesh and blood in hatred and I am no exception. I must join my own people

41

and the nation in which I was born. Choose then whether you go with me or return to your homes.'[10]

Many of the knights who accompanied him were vassals of his father, who was still pledged to King Edward, and decided that they must abide by their overlord's allegiance and so departed. But with those who were left and with the men of Douglas and Lady Douglas, who had been advised of his decision, he moved northeastward through his domain of Carrick, gathering recruits as he went, and joined the steward and the bishop at Irvine.

Meanwhile the humiliated Antony Bek had alerted King Edward to the strength of the insurrection. On 4 June the King empowered Henry Percy and Robert Clifford, the two foremost barons in the border shires, to raise levies from Lancaster, Westmorland and Cumberland 'to arrest, imprison and try all disturbers of the peace in Scotland', and instructed all sheriffs and castle governors to give them every aid.[11]

With commendable speed the two commanders collected a powerful body of armed knights and, moving fast along the Annandale and Nithsdale route, reached towards the end of June the English-held castle of Ayr, a few miles south of Irvine where the Scottish forces were encamped.

No battle ensued. Almost as soon as Percy and Clifford had dismounted, envoys arrived under a flag of truce to ask if they had authority to treat with the Scottish leaders.

Dissension had broken out in the Irvine camp between those who supported Balliol and those who supported Bruce. Andrew Moray and William Wallace were fighting in the name of John Balliol whom they still regarded as king, and may well have been sceptical of young Bruce's sudden conversion to the Scottish cause. Bishop Wishart, James Stewart, his brother John and Alexander Lindsay considered that, by his abdication, John Balliol had renounced his rights and that Robert Bruce's father was the natural successor to the Scottish Crown and the true focus for the upsurge for independence. Sir William Douglas agreed with nobody.

Moray and Wallace preferred to fight on their own terms and in their own centres of resistance and departed forthwith. Without their support the forces of Stewart and Bruce were in no position to make headway against the English invasion. Their men were mainly foot soldiers: those of the English were armed knights. The contest would be glaringly unequal and a defeat damaging to the growing confidence of the Scottish people.

News had reached Scotland of a clash between King Edward, his Church and his barons. The Archbishop of Canterbury had instructed his clergy to pay no taxes on pain of excommunication, and the two great magnates in England, Roger Bigod, Earl of Norfolk, the Earl Marshall, and Humphrey Bohun, Earl of Hereford, the Constable, had refused to serve overseas, retiring to their fiefs and calling up their vassals. Many other of the barons had followed their example. There was the possibility of civil war in England. The forces of Percy and Clifford were the only English armed troops in the field. It was a time to keep them engaged in negotiations so that Moray and Wallace could pursue their activities undisturbed by attack. Such must have been the reasoning which led the subtle bishop and canny steward to ask for parley.

Percy and Clifford, in their turn, were aware of the uncertain situation in England and had no desire unnecessarily to hazard forces, reluctantly conscripted, which they might desire at home. So talks began.

After days of discussion the English made certain promises, and on 9 July 1297 the Scottish leaders agreed to surrender to King Edward's pleasure and produce hostages as pledges of good faith.[12] Bruce, in particular, was required to hand over his infant daughter, Marjorie, but it is clear that he was unwilling to do this; the bishop, the steward and Sir Alexander Lindsay took it upon themselves to act as sureties on his behalf.[13]

In the upshot, Sir William Douglas failed to produce his hostages on the appointed day and was imprisoned in Berwick castle, where, wrote Henry Percy, he was 'very savage and very abusive'.[14] A year later he died, leaving behind a son of three years, James Douglas, who was to become the most famous and devoted of all the followers of Robert Bruce, the future king.

Sir Alexander Lindsay made his own peace. The bishop was held prisoner. Robert Bruce and James Stewart neither surrendered nor produced hostages, and remained at large deprived of their lands. Bruce's father was relieved of his post as Governor of Carlisle and retired to his English estates, where he remained until his death in 1304.

★　　★　　★

After the capitulation of the nobles at Irvine, the leadership of resistance remained entirely in the hands of Moray and Wallace and their efforts were attended with such success that on 10 July Hugh de Cressingham wrote to the deputy treasurer in London that 'not one of the Sheriffs, bailiffs or the officials of the Lord King . . . can at this time raise a penny of the revenues of their bailiwicks on account of the multitude of different perils which daily and continually threaten them',[15] and a fortnight later, in still more urgent tones, to the King:

> By far the greater part of your counties in the Scottish Kingdom are still not provided with keepers because they have been killed, besieged or imprisoned or have abandoned their bailiwicks and dare not go back. And in some shires the Scots have appointed and established bailiffs and officials. Thus no shire is properly kept save for Berwickshire and Roxburghshire and they only recently.[16]

With many of his barons hostile, King Edward was desperately trying to raise an army to cross to Flanders in support of the Count of that country, with whom he had formed an alliance against France.[17] When he received Cressingham's request he had no English to spare for Scotland. He therefore released a number of the Scottish nobles, among them the Earl of Buchan and Alexander Comyn, whom he had captured at Dunbar on condition that they returned to their fiefs to quell the disturbances and then followed him overseas with their feudal levies.[18]

But when the noblemen arrived in Scotland they found the disturbances very much more serious than they had expected. They sent various messages to King Edward expressing their loyalty and hopes of success, but in practice they remained inactive, waiting to see how matters would evolve and taking no steps to prevent their retainers drifting away to join the insurgents. Hugh de Cressingham had no doubt that they were playing a double game and warned the King to give no credence to their protestations. As an English chronicler shrewdly remarks, 'even when the Lords were present with the King in body, at heart they were on the opposite side.'[19]

By early August Moray had broken out of the Mounth and seized all the English-held castles in the north, including Inverness, Elgin and Banff.[20] Sir Henry Lathom, Sheriff of Aberdeenshire, had joined in the revolt and handed over the castle at Aberdeen.[21] Wallace, having built up his forces in the forest of Selkirk, moved northeast after the capitulation of Irvine, cleared Perthshire and Fife and, after making contact with Moray on the Tay, settled down to besiege the castle of Dundee. The whole area north of the Firth of Forth, with few exceptions, was in Scottish hands.

At last the Earl of Surrey, whom King Edward had appointed his viceroy in Scotland, bestirred himself. He was now an elderly man whose long military experience had taught him that foot soldiers in their hundreds could be scattered like chaff by a handful of armed knights. He had little doubt that with the Scottish lords, the core of their chivalry, sitting on the sidelines or in prison or in the retinue of his master, he would brush aside the common folk of Moray and Wallace like a fly from his face.

Marshalling at Berwick a formidable host of heavy cavalry and footmen, he marched towards Stirling where the crossing of the Forth was the key to the north.

On hearing news of his approach, Moray and Wallace joined forces and moved south to defend this vital position. One cannot admire enough the courage and determination of these two young men who were going to pit their inferior forces, woefully lacking in mounted men, against the armed might of a rich and powerful kingdom. The posture they took up bore all the marks of brilliant generalship. Overlooking a loop of the Forth river which was crossed by a single bridge was an abrupt rock, the Abbey Crag, from which a neck of ground led back to the nearby Ochil Hills, giving a safe retreat in the event of failure. Below the northern exit of the bridge and the causeway that prolonged it, was an area of boggy ground almost entirely encircled by the Forth. On this crag the Scottish commanders deployed their men.

The English forces spent the nights of 9 and 10 September on the south side of the river. They were supremely self-confident. Hugh de Cressingham had already advised Percy and Clifford that there was no need for their additional support.

James Stewart and the Earl of Lennox, who had been hovering on the outskirts with a troop of cavalry, uncertain whether to join Moray and Wallace, rated equally low the chances of the Scottish forces. To avoid a butchery of their countrymen they approached the Earl of Surrey with the suggestion that they should inaugurate a parley. The earl agreed, but Stewart and Lennox returned from the Scottish leaders with a blank refusal. Two Dominican friars were then dispatched to Moray and Wallace with offers of generous treatment if they would yield. 'Tell your commander,' was their reply, 'that we are not here to make peace but to do battle to defend ourselves and liberate our kingdom. Let them come and we shall prove this in their very beards.'[22]

Sir Richard Lundin, a Scottish knight, who had gone over to the English from Irvine in disgust at the dissension in the Scottish camp, asked the Earl of Surrey to send him up river with a detachment to a ford where he could cross with sixty men abreast and take the Scotsmen in the rear, but his suggestion was ignored and the earl retired to bed.[23]

At dawn on 11 September a party of English infantry were sent over the narrow bridge but were recalled because the earl had overslept. Hugh de Cressingham, fuming with impatience, urged that no more time should be wasted and the earl gave him the order to cross. Riding arrogantly two by two, the cavalry were led by him over the bridge. From early in the morning until eleven o'clock the column moved forward until Moray and Wallace decided that the time had come to split the English army. The main force of the Scots fell upon the leading ranks on the causeway while a picked body of men seized the bridgehead and began to cut away its timbers. Jostled from the causeway, the heavy horses of the armed knights plunged and wallowed in the deep mire on either side, unable to manoeuvre or charge, tumbling their riders to the ground. Behind them their comrades on the south side were powerless to help them for the bridge was destroyed.[24]

A bloody massacre took place. Hugh de Cressingham met his fate at the hands of the Scottish spearmen. His body was flayed and his skin in small pieces was sent throughout the country as tokens of liberation from the accursed regime of which he was the symbol.[25] Only Sir Marmaduke Tweng managed to hew his way through his opponents and take refuge in the castle of Stirling.[26]

The Earl of Surrey had not crossed the bridge. Aghast at the slaughter beyond it, he lost his nerve and galloped in such haste to the border that his horse had nothing to eat between Stirling and Berwick and foundered on arrival.

The rank and file and the baggage trains of the English were less fortunate than their commander. As they retreated down the road to Falkirk, James Stewart and the Earl of Lennox, who were lurking in the woods on either side until the issue had been decided, poured out with their men to kill the fleeing groups and seize the laden wagons of booty.[27]

The repercussions of the English defeat were immense. For the first time an army of professional knights had been overcome by the common folk. The dissenting barons in England were so shocked that they patched up an agreement with the regency who were ruling in the absence of the King abroad, and all talk of civil war was suspended.

In northeast Scotland, the Earl of Strathearn, the Earl of Buchan and the Comyns and other noblemen in that area, who had been making face-saving gestures to suppress the patriots, threw off their allegiance to the English Crown. In the southwest, Robert Bruce, who had gone to ground after the capitulation of Irvine, emerged to rouse the men of Carrick and Galloway to such effect that Sir Robert Clifford made two punitive expeditions, before and after Christmas 1297, from Carlisle to Annandale to try to check his activities.[28] Outside the strongest castles all English resistance ceased. Moray and Wallace were masters of the realm.

But Moray had been severely wounded at Stirling Bridge. He survived long enough to send a letter in his name and that of Wallace on 11 October 1297, to the mayors of the communes of Lübeck and Hamburg, that 'the Kingdom of Scotland had, by God's grace, re-covered by battle from the power of the English and that, in conse-quence, the ports of Scotland were once more open to their merchants',[29] but soon afterwards he succumbed to his wounds.[30]

A famous folk hero, William Wallace, was now to take upon his shoulders the sole government of the realm. Behind him was the Church, manning the chancellery, the civil service of that time, which had been displaced by King Edward but now returned to its adminis-trative duties. 'The common folk of the land followed him as their leader and ruler',[31] but the most striking tribute to his personality and pre-eminence was the drawing together of the feuding magnates under his leadership in a common front against the English.

In March 1298 in the forest of Selkirk, which Wallace had made the base of his armed forces, the earls, barons and knights, the bishops, abbots and friars who were then in Scotland met to resolve the future of the realm. In the presence of them all, William Wallace was dubbed knight by Robert Bruce, Earl of Carrick,* and by the general voice of those assembled proclaimed guardian of the kingdom.[32] From that

* cf note III

47

date edicts were issued in the name of 'William Wallace, Knight, Guardian of the Kingdom of Scotland and Commander of its armies in the name of the famous prince, Lord John, by God's grace, illustrious King of Scotland, by consent of the Community of that realm.'

Between the battle of Stirling and the Forest Parliament, Wallace had led his army south. There was famine in the lowlands. To gain corn and cattle he ravaged the northern counties of England from late October 1297 into the New Year until snowstorms and severe frost forced him back to Scotland laden with immense spoil. 'During that time,' writes the English chronicler Guisborough, 'the praise of God ceased in all the monasteries and churches of the whole province from Newcastle-upon-Tyne to Carlisle: for all the monks, canons regular and other priests, the servants of the Lord had fled, with one may say, the whole of the common folk from the face of the Scots.'[33]

During the absence of Wallace on this campaign, Bishop Fraser of St Andrews, who had remained in France since the parliament at Berwick in 1296, disenchanted by and hostile to King Edward, passed away. Acting on Wallace's instructions, the St Andrews chapter elected in his place the Chancellor of Glasgow Cathedral, William Lamberton, friend and compatriot of Bishop Wishart. He was to become one of the key figures in opposition to English rule.[34]

Meanwhile King Edward had been having little success in Flanders to which he had sailed on 22 August 1297. Matters had come to a stalemate and on 9 October a short Armistice was signed between France and England which was then prolonged to 6 January 1299. King Edward had now the opportunity to turn his attention to Scottish affairs.

He landed in England on 14 March 1298 and by 25 May had transferred the headquarters of government to York, where it remained for the next six years. Scotland was to become the obsession of his remaining life and even beyond the grave, for it is said he gave instructions that on his tomb should be inscribed the vengeful words, 'The hammer of the Scots'.

Such a hammer he now began to fashion. Writs were sent to his tenants in chief to join him with their vassals, horses and arms. Other armed knights were recruited at his own expense. A corps of Gascon lords, knights and crossbowmen were summoned from the duchy. Orders were given for the paid conscription of numerous Welshmen, archers and footmen.[35] A fleet of ships was commissioned to ensure supplies. Reconciliation was arranged with the recalcitrant Earls of

Hereford and Norfolk, respectively Constable and Earl Marshal of the Kingdom, and their powerful forces were put at his disposal.

A wave of patriotic fervour supported his preparations. From ecclesiastical pens issued a stream of propaganda. Wallace was depicted as an ogre of unspeakable depravity who skinned his prisoners alive, burned babies and forced the nuns of the Holy Church to dance naked before him.[36] So when King Edward mustered his troops at Roxburgh on 25 June some 2500 heavy cavalry and 12,000 foot had answered his summons.

This vast army with its attendant baggage train set off along the Lauderdale route to Edinburgh. The clank of armed knights, the tramp of footmen, the creak of wagon wheels sounded in a silent land from which man and beast had vanished. There was neither fodder nor food nor information to be found. The inhabitants had fled to the forests driving their cattle and sheep before them, leaving behind a scorched and wasted land. By 15 July the English army had reached Kirkliston beyond Edinburgh. Here King Edward learnt that Dirleton and two other castles in East Lothian were held by the Scots and sent Antony Bek to capture them while he remained encamped.[37]

The whereabouts of Wallace and his men was still unknown. The food ships due at Leith had been delayed by contrary winds and the army was faced with starvation. The few ships that had struggled through happened to carry only barrels of wine.[38] When this was issued to raise the spirits of the troops, the effect on the empty stomachs of the Welshmen, who always got the worst of the meagre rations, was disastrous. They got very drunk, brawled with the English soldiers, killed some and were killed in turn and then grew mutinous and threatened to decamp to the enemy.[39]

The whole expedition was in danger of collapse. Indeed, King Edward had already decided to return to Edinburgh when the tide of fortune, due no doubt to the intervention of Saint John of Beverley to whose shrine the King had made a pilgrimage on his way north, turned miraculously in his favour. Antony Bek returned with the news that Dirleton had surrendered and that the other two castles had been abandoned by their defenders; the food ships had made harbour at Leith and a message was received from the Earl of Dunbar that the Scots were only thirteen miles away in Callendar Wood beside Falkirk.

A wave of elation swept through the army. All discord ceased. The quarry had been viewed. The hunt was on. Immediately breaking camp, King Edward led his troops along the road to Falkirk and bivouacked just east of Linlithgow, each man sleeping on the ground with his horse beside him, the King among his men, the horses 'tasting nothing but cold iron, champing their bits'.[41]

In the dead of night a cry of alarm aroused the sleeping warriors. The King had been trampled upon by his charger and was injured. But the King, despite two broken ribs, had himself hoisted into his high-back saddle and set his knights in motion through Linlithgow in the early light of morning. They had not gone far when the rising sun glinted on lances lining the top of a nearby hill, but as they pressed towards them the spearmen melted away. It was not until they reached the bank of the West-Quarter burn, where a halt was called for the King and Antony Bek, Bishop of Durham, to hear Mass, that they saw in full daylight Wallace deploying his troops on the slope of Slamman Moor.[42]

Wallace's main anxiety was the overwhelming superiority of the English cavalry, and he made his dispositions with this in mind. Immediately to his front was a boggy marsh, to his right scattered woodland and rocks and on his left the deepening valley of the burn. On the hard ground behind the marsh he drew up his men in four schiltrons (shield rings): packed circles of spearmen drawn up with their long spears slanting outward with butt on earth and the front rank kneeling. Round each schiltron wooden stakes were driven into the ground and roped together. Between the schiltrons he lined the Ettrick archers, equipped with their short bows, under the command of John Stewart, brother of James Stewart. On the crest of the hill behind he placed his slender force of cavalry, contributed by several earls: too few to be effective in attack but of decisive value in pursuit of a demoralized foe.[43]

Wallace's logical action would have been to retreat before the English army, wasting the land as he went, and let hunger defeat the enemy, but there is reason to believe that he was overruled by his impatient troops and hence his famous valediction, 'I have brought you to the ring: hop if you can'.[44]

On the English side King Edward divided his cavalry in four brigades of some six hundred knights each: the first under the Earls of Hereford, Norfolk and Lincoln, the second under Antony Bek, Bishop of Durham, the third under his own command and the fourth in reserve under the Earls of Arundel, Gloucester, Oxford and Pembroke. He proposed, before joining battle, that there should be a pause during which men and horses, none of whom had eaten for twenty-four hours, should be fed. But his commanders were chafing for action and he yielded to their importunity.[45]

The first brigade charged immediately to their front but, checked by the bog, swung leftwards in a half circle. The second brigade swung likewise in a half circle to the right and the two horns converged behind the schiltrons and scattered the Scottish cavalry who fled into the woods behind. Then turning inwards they overwhelmed the Scottish archers whose arrows were not powerful enough to penetrate their armour and slew their commander, John Stewart.

The schiltrons were left exposed. Again and again they were charged by the mounted knights but their ranks remained unbroken. It was then that King Edward ordered up the Welsh longbowmen and the crossbowmen and slingmen of Gascony. A deadly hail of arrows, bolts and stones was poured into the schiltrons until the gaps in their ranks became too wide to be filled and the mail-clad knights broke into the weakened rings. Once the human fortress was breached hundreds upon hundreds of the Scottish foot were slain. Macduff and his two sons who had faithfully supported Wallace since they took arms against the English in 1297 were left dead upon the field. Wallace escaped into the surrounding woods with a handful of followers.[46]

The battle of Falkirk was notable for two innovations that were profoundly to affect military tactics until the introduction of gunpowder. Wallace's hedgehog of spears shattered for ever the accepted principle that the foot man was always at the mercy of the mounted knight. This was again triumphantly disproved at Courtrai four years later when the pikemen of Flanders, with no longbow against them, broke the chivalry of France. King Edward's brilliant riposte by switching from hand to hand fighting to the long-range missile marked the beginning of modern war and, when properly exploited, gave to England its great victories at Crécy and Agincourt in succeeding reigns.

King Edward had won a battle and destroyed the authority of William Wallace, but otherwise his expedition was profitless. Like Napoleon in Russia some five hundred years later, he had come unprepared for a situation in which people of the invaded land, to their own material loss, destroyed everything which could be of service to him. He was desperately short of supplies and unable to carry his pursuit further north.

After resting a fortnight in deserted Stirling while his ribs knit together, meanwhile sending a raiding party to set fire to Perth and St Andrews,[47] which had been abandoned by the Scots as they retired beyond the Tay, he turned back towards his base at Carlisle with the intention of rounding up Robert Bruce and his men on the way. But Bruce, who had been making sporadic raids in the southwest from his headquarters in Ayr, was warned of his approach and slipped away into the wilds of Carrick, after burning the town and destroying its castle.[48] When King Edward arrived he found an empty shell.

He proposed immediate pursuit. But his army was already short of commons, his tenants-in-chief who had done unpaid service demanded leave to depart, and he was left with no choice but to fall back on Carlisle, which he reached on 8 September, after seizing Lochmaben Castle,[49] the ancestral home of the Bruces, which lay across his route.

From Carlisle, as his followers dispersed for the winter, he sent out fresh summonses to reassemble an army at that town on 6 June 1299 to renew the struggle.

# 6

After Falkirk the guardianship of the country returned into the hands of the magnates. William Wallace had no fief and no vassals behind him. His leadership had depended upon his aura of success and when that was dissipated he had no platform of recovery. For the next seven years he remained in obscurity, harrying the English whenever he could with bands of lawless men, or acting as messenger to the King of France or His Holiness the Pope for his friend William Lamberton, Bishop of St Andrews.[1]

But something of his unselfish dedication to the cause of Scotland brushed off, for a short time, on the feuding barons. The new guardians were Robert Bruce, leader of the resistance in the southwest, and John Comyn 'the Red' of Badenoch, kinsman of the Earl of Buchan and representative of the pre-eminent family beyond the Tay.[2] It was a surprising and uneasy alliance and argues generosity of mind and patriotism on the part of Robert Bruce, for the guardians were still acting in the name of the abdicated King, John Balliol, and thus effectively blocking his family's claim to the throne.

Under the guardians' rule the normal machinery of government continued to operate throughout the major part of Scotland, for in spite of the Scottish defeat at Falkirk the English had not sufficient troops to occupy the country, and from 1298 to 1303 the only area under their full control was East Lothian, where their garrisoned castles were thicker on the ground than in other parts.

It was against Roxburgh, the most westerly of these, that the Scots made their first full scale raid in July 1299. The assembled forces of the two guardians and those of the Earls of Buchan, Menteith and Atholl and of James Stewart, Sir Robert Keith, Sir Ingram de Umfraville and other barons[3] were accompanied by the Bishop of St Andrews, who had newly returned from France after evading the ships which King Edward had detailed to intercept him.[4] The Scottish attack was abortive. The castle was too strongly held to be taken without heavy casualties and these they were unwilling to risk in view of the preparations that King Edward was putting in train to renew the conflict. They returned to Peebles in the forest of Selkirk to consider their next move.

Frustrated and quarrelsome after the failure of their expedition, they were soon at odds, as can be noted from the report of a spy planted among them by the Constable of Roxburgh Castle which is now preserved in the Public Record Office in London:

> At the council, Sir David Graham demanded the land and goods of Sir William Wallace because he was leaving the Kingdom without the leave or approval of the Guardians. And Sir Malcolm, Sir William's brother, answered that neither his lands nor his goods should be given away, for they were protected by the peace in which Wallace had left the Kingdom. At this the two knights gave the lie to each other and drew their daggers. And since Sir David Graham was of Sir John Comyn's following, it was reported to the Earl of Buchan and John Comyn that a fight had broken out without their knowing it: and John Comyn leapt at the Earl of Carrick and seized him by the throat and the Earl of Buchan turned on the Bishop of St Andrews, declaring that treason and *lèse majesté* were being plotted. Eventually the Stewart and others came between them and quietened them. At that moment a letter was brought from beyond the Firth of Forth, telling how Sir Alexander Comyn and Lachlan Macruarie were burning and devastating the district they were in, attacking the people of the Scottish nation. So it was ordained then that the Bishop of St Andrews should have all the castles in his hands as principal captain and the Earl of Carrick and John Comyn be with him as joint-guardians of the Kingdom. And that same Wednesday, after the letter had been read, they all left Peebles.[5]

For the time being the old feud between Bruce and Comyn was patched up by the influence of the bishop whose whole thought was for the liberty of the kingdom and the independence of the Church. His bishopric was north of the Tay in Comyn land: his career had hitherto been in the southwest, the preserve of the Bruces, so no better link between the two could have been chosen. The Comyns returned to their homeland to deal with their erring relative and Bruce to Annandale in an attempt, which proved unsuccessful, to regain his hereditary castle at Lochmaben. Lamberton, Umfraville and Keith remained in Selkirk forest to watch the southern approaches, and other forces were placed under the command of Sir John Soulis to besiege the English garrison in Stirling Castle which had been left behind by King Edward after his victory at Falkirk.

In November news was brought to the Scots that King Edward was raising an army to rescue the beleaguered defenders[6] and the scattered guardians came together at the Tor Wood near Stirling to protect Sir John and his men against the threatened invasion. But their support was not needed. The levy ordered by King Edward to foregather at Berwick to raise the siege of Stirling was ignored. The military tenants of Antony Bek, Bishop of Durham, his right hand man, refused to serve beyond their shire and other desertions were so serious that Edward could not proceed so the castle fell to the Scots.[7]

Heartened by this display of weakness, the guardians wrote to King Edward that, through the mediation of King Philip of France, they would agree to a truce,[8] but the King peremptorily refused and on 30 December 1299 issued further writs for a full and formally constituted feudal levy to meet him at Carlisle on 24 June 1300.

Before then the temporary advantage enjoyed by the Scots was dissipated by renewed dissension among the guardians. The Comyn faction argued that the main effort against the English should be directed in support of the men of Galloway, but this was unacceptable to Bruce and his friends. The men of Galloway were a law unto themselves and the sustaining thread through their history was a traditional hatred of the men of Carrick dating from the quarrels between Gilbert and Uhtred, the sons of Fergus, a century before. Ever since the abdication of their titular lord, John Balliol, they had spent as much time raiding their neighbours in Carrick and Annandale as harrying the English. To support them was in no way to preserve the amity of the guardians.

John Comyn, who had already evinced his hot temper at the meeting in Selkirk Forest, responded to these arguments by declaring vehemently that he would no longer serve with the Bishop of St Andrews. The Earl of Atholl and James Stewart, both supporters of Bruce, intervened on behalf of the bishop, but in the end it was Bruce who resigned and his place was taken by Sir Ingram de Umfraville, a kinsman of Balliol's and ally of the Comyns.[9] Bruce's resignation may have been partly in the interests of harmony but more surely because he felt that if the Comyns were going to meddle in Galloway his presence was needed in Carrick to preserve his family interests in the southwest, and it is there that for the next two years he confined his activities. The remaining magnates, apart from the Earl of Buchan who in fact went to Galloway to try to enlist the support of the leading men against the English, held a parliament at Rutherglen on 10 May to prepare for a summer campaign.

Events overtook them. King Edward's further writs for a feudal levy had been obeyed. On midsummer's day 1300 he held a court at Carlisle accompanied by his young Queen, Marguerite, sister of the King of France, whom he had married the previous year, [10] and there reviewed the assembled troops. So great was their number, according to a contemporary ballad, that the hills and valleys resounded to the neighings of horses and the ground was carpeted with tents, wagons and all the impedimenta of war. The chivalry of England, in its splendour, was marshalled in four great squadrons and an auxiliary force placed under the command of Antony Bek, Bishop of Durham, 'ever at hand when there was fighting'. So with an army comparable to that which he had commanded at Falkirk, King Edward crossed the Solway Firth into Scotland while a fleet of fifty-eight ships guarded his flank and kept watch on the coast of Galloway. The conquest of the southwest seemed imminent.

But the outcome was a dismal anticlimax. After capturing the castle of Caerlaverock and its handful of defenders, this menacing force achieved nothing. [11] King Edward marched them along the coastal plain as far as Wigton, hampered by appalling weather, and then retraced his steps. [12] At Kircudbright on his outward progress, shadowed by the Scottish guardians in the rugged hills to the north, the King was waited on by the Earl of Buchan and John Comyn with Scottish proposals of peace: the restoration of John Balliol to the throne and the return to the Scottish magnates of their forfeited English estates. He regarded these terms as impertinent and dismissed them with contempt. [13]

Stung into rashness by Edward's response, Buchan, Comyn and Umfraville descended from the sheltering hills and attempted to oppose his crossing of the river Cree but, after the first charge of his armoured knights, fled in disorder into the boggy moors to their rear where heavy cavalry could not pursue them, leaving Sir Robert Keith, Marischal of Scotland, prisoner in his hands. [14]

By the end of August King Edward was back in Sweetheart Abbey, hard by Caerlaverock, angry and frustrated. If his parade of power was meant to draw adherents to his cause, it had failed entirely. His barons refused to continue their feudal service beyond the prescribed two months, his foot soldiers, drawn mainly from the northern shires, were deserting in their hundreds.[15]

It was at this unpropitious moment that the Archbishop of Canterbury reached him after a long and arduous journey and, at the King's request, read aloud before the assembled court a papal bull, indited more than a year ago, which he had brought with him.[16] In this Pope Boniface VIII, after detailing in lucid phrases the devious means by which King Edward had imposed upon the trusting Scots, ordered him to desist from inflicting injuries on that unhappy people and withdraw from a country which 'as thou knowest my son' is and was a fief of the Holy See.[17] The archbishop followed this recitation by an address imploring the King 'for the love of Mount Zion and Jerusalem' to yield to the Pope's decree.

'By God's blood,' the King exploded, 'I will not keep my peace for Mount Zion nor silence for Jerusalem but while there is breath in my nostrils, I will defend my right, which all the world knows, with all my power.'[18]

The shaken archbishop was ushered from his presence and later informed that the King would consult his barons and then reply to the Pope.

The papal broadside was the culmination of Scottish diplomacy at the Vatican. Pope Boniface VIII, elected supreme pontiff in 1294 after a series of ineffective predecessors, was a determined and ambitious prelate. He believed that all the princes on earth owed sovereignty to the Vicar of Christ and that the Church of Rome, as it were the United Nations, should be the acknowledged arbiter of international disputes. His conversion to the cause of Scottish independence had been inspired, as early as the summer of 1298, by the arguments of William Lamberton who had been in Rome awaiting his consecration as Bishop of St Andrews, which took place on 1 June of that year. It had been confirmed by the passionate pleadings of David Moray, uncle of Andrew Moray, the young hero of Stirling bridge. David Moray had been appointed Bishop of Moray by Robert Bruce and John Comyn when they were joint guardians, and had followed his compatriot Lamberton to the Holy See for the laying-on of hands.

The public opposition of the Pope compounded the problems facing King Edward. His barons stubbornly refused military service until he reformed the Forest Charters, and the French King constantly postponed the translation of the truce between them into a formal peace treaty. In these circumstances King Edward recognized the need for a breathing space for manoeuvre. On 30 October 1300, at the instance of King Philip of France, he agreed a truce between England and Scotland to last until 21 May 1301 and, as a mollifying gesture to the Pope, released from prison Robert Wishart, the Bishop of Glasgow.[19]

But no sooner had he settled his differences with his barons and rallied them behind him in his rejection of the papal bull than he set in train measures for yet another invasion of Scotland, his sixth campaign, to take place in the summer of 1301. His intention was once again to deal with the Scottish stronghold in the southwest.[20]

Robert Bruce, since his relinquishment of the guardianship, had been building up his forces in Carrick and had made himself master of Turnberry Castle. It is probable that during that period he had visited the Bruce possessions in Northern Ireland and the northeast Highlands of Scotland as reservoirs of reinforcements. He kept his distance from the Comyns and his only link with them would appear to have been through William Lamberton, Bishop of St Andrews, who was desperately trying to prevent a complete breach between the two families.

It was with this aim, one must assume, that early in 1301 the bishop retired from the guardianship and persuaded John Comyn and his supporter Sir Ingram de Umfraville to do likewise in favour of Sir John Soulis as sole guardian. Sir John was connected by marriage with the Comyns but was also a close neighbour of the Bruces and could thus act as a stabilizing factor between the two.[21] Sir John had now to deal with the two-pronged invasion which King Edward launched in July 1301.

His son, the Prince of Wales, was to drive up the coast of Galloway and Ayrshire from Carlisle, supported by ships in the Firth of Clyde, to inhibit any aid from Ireland and so, in his father's words, 'to gain the chief honour of taming the pride of the Scots',[22] while the King himself from Berwick would secure the defensive line of the Forth and Clyde, cut the link between the unsubdued Highlands and the southwest, and then, joining forces with his son, isolate and crush the latter area. This grandiose design was unfulfilled. Sir John Soulis with his forces operated between the two English armies, harrying the flanks of both without ever committing himself to a frontal attack, while

Robert Bruce, after holding out in Turnberry Castle until September, withdrew his men, immobilized the troops who had captured the castle and forced the Prince of Wales by constant forays to retreat to Carlisle.[23] The prince then moved east to join his father at Linlithgow to which the King had retired after his one success, the seizure of Bothwell Castle[24] on the direct route between the Highlands and the southwest. The pincer prongs had never met.

During the winter, while King Edward remained at Linlithgow engaged in building a castle[25] and organizing the shipment of horses, fodder and supplies from England, the King of France negotiated with him a truce on behalf of the Scots, to run from 26 January 1302 to the end of November. Effectively this meant a lull in hostilities until campaigning weather in the late spring of 1303.[26]

At the court of France, King Philip felt a growing ascendancy over the English monarch. Twice in two years King Edward had failed in his Scottish campaigns. Twice in two years he had been forced to accept the French demands for a truce with the Scots which previously he had utterly rejected. His arguments at the Vatican court against the papal bull had been brilliantly demolished by the Scottish envoy, Master Baldred Bisset.* Judgement had been given in favour of the Scots and in the summer of 1301 their abdicated King, John Balliol, had been released from the jurisdiction of the Pope, to whom King Edward had handed him over in July 1299, to dwell as a free man in the kingdom of France.[27]

In Scotland the significance of this move had not been lost. Writs which before that time had been issued by successive guardians as on behalf of King John were now issued as by King John 'to be valid at our will or that of our dearest son Edward or of John de Soulis Guardian of our Kingdom', and a new seal was struck with the name and title of King John on the obverse, and the name and arms of John de Soulis, knight, only on the reverse.[28]

A strong rumour swept through the Scottish kingdom that the King of France was to restore John Balliol to his throne at the head of a powerful French army.

No news could be more unpalatable to Robert Bruce. For five years he had fought for the independence of Scotland, sacrificing his personal

---

* note IV

standing and inheritance in England. In Scotland his lands in the southwest, during the last two years, had been the main object of English attacks and had been ravaged and burned by the invader, while those of the Comyns north of the Forth had been untouched by war. Yet increasingly he had been cold-shouldered by the Comyns and cut off from the inner councils of state. If John Balliol was restored to the throne, John Comyn 'the Red' of Badenoch would in effect become the ruler of the realm and there was no man more jealous of Bruce or more given to outbursts of temper. In 1295, John Balliol had handed over to his relation, John Comyn, Earl of Buchan, the Bruce patrimony of Annandale. If he returned in triumph with a French army at his back, all the Bruce inheritance in Scotland – Annandale, Carrick and Garioch – would be at risk.

King Edward was no less apprehensive of the rumoured threat. On the spiritual and secular plane, he had never been so weak. His designs on Scotland still aroused the grave displeasure of the Pope and the sword of excommunication was rattling in its sheath. The King of France was at peace with all his European neighbours. He had annexed Flanders and had Gascony firmly under control. Now at last he had a secure base from which he could afford to divert his military forces to the support of the Scots.

This threat to both Bruce and King Edward forced an understanding between the two. The truce arranged in January 1302 gave an opportunity for negotiations to be opened, and on 16 February 1302 Robert Bruce, Earl of Carrick, made his submission to the English king on the following terms:

> Be it remembered that Robert Bruce the younger, who was in homage and faith of the King of England for the Earldom of Carrick, rose in rebellion against the said King his Lord, through evil counsel and has submitted himself to the peace and will of the same King, in hope of his good grace, the King for the sake of the good service which Robert's ancestors and family have rendered to the King and his ancestors, and the good service which Robert himself has promised to render in the future, has declared his grace and will in this manner.
>
> That is to say that Robert and his men and his tenants of Carrick will be guaranteed life and limb, lands and tenements, and will be free from imprisonment.
>
> If it should happen that by Papal ordinance or by a truce or by a conditional peace touching the war against Scotland or the war against France, the aforesaid Robert should be at a disadvantage, so that he may not be able to enjoy his own lands, of which he has possession at present

in Scotland, the King promises to take his loss into consideration so that he may have reasonable maintenance, as is proper for him.

And the King grants to Robert that, so far as it lies in his power, he will not be disinherited of any land which may fall to him by right from his father, in England or in Scotland.

And the King grants to Robert the wardship and marriage of the Earl of Mar's son and heir. And because it is feared that the Kingdom of Scotland may be removed out of the King's hands which God forbid and handed over to Sir John Balliol or to his son or that the right may be brought into dispute or reversed or repealed in a fresh judgement, the King grants to Robert that he may pursue his right and the King will hear him fairly and hold him to justice in the King's court. If, by any chance, it should happen that the right must be adjudicated elsewhere than in the King's court, then in this case the King promises Robert assistance and counsel as before, as well as he is able to give it.

And if, after the Kingdom is at peace in the King's hands any persons should wish to do injury to Robert the King will maintain and defend him in his right as a lord ought to do for his man.

And in witness of all these points the King has ordered these letters patent to be made and sealed with his privy seal.[29]

The admission by King Edward of John Balliol's possible restoration underlines how real that danger appeared and the difficult dilemma in which Robert Bruce was placed. He was estranged from his father who had retired to his English estates, but he had many of his brothers and sisters to consider and a new influence had entered into his life. He had fallen in love with Elizabeth de Burgh, daughter of the Earl of Ulster, one of King Edward's staunchest lieutenants. How or when they met is not recorded but it could have been in early days at the English court or in Northern Ireland, where the lands of the two families were adjacent, or at the house of James Stewart, whose wife, Egidia de Burgh, was Elizabeth's aunt.

As soon as Robert Bruce had made his peace with the English King, thus ensuring that he would not become landless, his marriage to Elizabeth took place. Bruce's second marriage was to last through stress and tribulation, separation and reunion until his wife's death twenty-five years later.[30]

The submission of Bruce eliminated one of the bastions of Scottish independence. King Edward, as an experienced strategist, had long recognized that he could not carry out operations north of the Forth so long as the army of Carrick under its brilliant young commander could threaten his communications from the rugged hills of the southwest. In two successive campaigns he had sought to destroy it. But what he could not achieve by force had been brought about by politics and his fertile mind began to contemplate measures to bring to subjection the unsubdued areas of Scotland which it had hitherto been unsafe to attempt.

In January 1303 he obtained the consent of Parliament to exact by various means funds to finance the raising of a new and mighty army which he ordered to assemble in May. In February he dispatched Sir John Segrave, his viceroy in Scotland, and Ralph Manton, his cofferer, to make a reconnaissance in strength towards Stirling with three brigades of armed knights and report back on the condition of the country and the whereabouts and strength of the Scottish forces.

By the evening of 23 February the three columns had reached the neighbourhood of Roslin, south of Edinburgh, and owing to the nature of the ground had each pitched their tents at some distance from each other. News of their advance had reached John Comyn 'the Red' and Simon Fraser, who were hidden with their men in the thickets of Selkirk forest. With a picked force of mounted troops they rode through the night and as dawn broke fell upon the unsuspecting detachment commanded by Sir John Segrave.

Ralph Manton was slain and Sir John Segrave severely wounded and made captive, but a fugitive from the onset alerted Robert Neville who was quietly hearing Mass some miles away. Calling to arms his knights, Sir Robert galloped to the fray and after a sharp struggle rescued Sir John Segrave and drove off the Scots from the plunder on which they had been engaged. The Scots made much of the encounter and spread it abroad as a major victory. It was the last triumph they could claim.[31]

Events on the continent had undergone a startling revolution. Boniface VIII and Philip of France had quarrelled, and the very Pope who had thundered against the pretensions of King Edward in Scotland was now wooing his support and admonishing the Scottish bishops to show to their overlord the obedience and respect which was his due.[32] In Flanders the Flemings had risen in revolt and slain the French garrisons in their towns and at Courtrai on 11 July 1302 the flower of French chivalry, arrogant and contemptuous of their pedestrian foes, had hurled themselves to death in their hundreds against the massed spears of the citizens of Bruges and Ghent.[33] In December of the same year the burghers of Bordeaux, inspired by the Flemish example, expelled the French from their city.[34]

In the space of a few months King Philip's commanding position had been seriously undermined. His feudal host had been decimated, his conquered territories were in revolt, he was embroiled with the Pope and threatened with excommunication. In the bitter struggle with the supreme pontiff, which was to end in the capture and death of Boniface VIII and the move of puppet popes to Avignon, he needed a concentration of his resources. After rejecting year after year the overtures from King Edward for a definitive peace, he now offered to return whatever territory in Aquitaine had been surrendered by the English. King Edward responded with alacrity and in exchange for this restitution sealed on 30 May 1303 a treaty of offensive and defensive alliance, and on the same day the Prince of Wales, by proxy, plighted his troth to Isabel, the King of France's daughter.[35]

In vain a powerful delegation of Scottish nobles including John Soulis, Bishop Lamberton, the Earl of Buchan, James Stewart, Ingram de Umfraville and William Balliol had sailed to Paris to keep the French King staunch to his Scottish alliance. His main objective demanded their sacrifice. Their country was excluded from the treaty and they were left to face alone the full onslaught that King Edward had already planned for their subjection.

Never had his preparations for a campaign been more thorough and elaborate. The latest siege engines were transported to Scotland by sea. Three huge prefabricated bridges were towed to the Firth of Forth so that the English army could bypass Stirling Castle and cross directly into Fife.[36] The Prince of Wales and the Earl of Ulster commanded an army in the west and the King himself in the east.

In the event it was a military parade. Leaving Roxburgh in May 1303, King Edward marched up the eastern route, as in 1296, to reach Kinloss Abbey near Elgin in September without meeting any serious resistance. Only at Brechin Castle was his progress halted. There, with superb defiance, Sir Thomas Maule held them at bay until on 9 August he was killed on the battlements and the garrison capitulated.[37]

The King remained at Kinloss Abbey for long enough to strengthen his hold on turbulent Moray and receive submissions, and then retraced his steps to Dunfermline Abbey for winter quarters from October to February 1304. There the history of 1296 repeated itself. Men and communities flocked to submit. John Comyn 'the Red', who had taken over the guardianship when John Soulis sailed to France, was still at large with a fighting force in Selkirk Forest, but on 9 February at Strathord near Perth he came to terms with the King.[38] The settlement he negotiated 'on behalf of the community of the realm' was very different from the abject surrender of John Balliol and reflected a new approach by King Edward. In the conditions it was laid down that the Scottish people

> should be protected in all their laws, usages, customs and liberties in every particular as they existed in the time of Alexander III unless there are laws to be amended in which case it should be done with the advice of King Edward and the advice and consent of the responsible men of the land.[39]

There should be no disinheritance of the Scottish leaders and forfeited estates could be redeemed by their owners on the payment of varying fines.[40] For some there should be short periods of exile but all in all it was a generous settlement and it is not unreasonable to believe that it was the advice of Robert Bruce which in part persuaded the King that only by a magnanimous gesture could he hope to confirm a peace.

The magnanimity of the monarch was diminished by two vindictive actions. Sir William Oliphant, who held Stirling Castle in the name of King John by order of Sir John Soulis, asked permission to send a messenger to his master to find out whether he might surrender it or whether he should defend it to the last. King Edward refused this reasonable request for no other cause than his determination to test in action the great siege engines he had transported from England.[41] So for three months from May to July 1304, Oliphant and his men, loyal to their commission, were subjected to the battering of every ingenious invention of King Edward's engineers. The *Vicar*, the *Parson*, the *Gloucester*, the *Belfry*, a baker's dozen of engines in all, pounded the castle walls while the English Queen and her ladies amused their idle hours by watching the proceedings from a balcony in Stirling town. Even when the garrison finally offered to surrender unconditionally, King Edward delayed his reply until his latest and greatest machine, the *Warwolf*, had had time to reach him and be tried out in a massive bombardment against the now suppliant defenders.[42]

But even more malignant was his treatment of William Wallace. He had never forgotten nor forgiven that it was this man alone who, in all the successive campaigns against Scotland, had inflicted the one decisive defeat upon the English. In his negotiations with John Comyn the terms for the Scottish surrender contained these baleful words:

> No words of peace are to be held out to William Wallace in any circumstances in our will . . . The Stewart, Sir John de Soulis and Sir Ingram de Umfraville are not to have safe conduct nor come within the King's power until Sir William Wallace is given up . . . Sir John Comyn, Sir Alexander Lindsay, Sir David Graham and Sir Simon Fraser shall exert themselves until twenty days after Christmas to capture Sir William Wallace and hand him over to the King who will watch to see how each of them conducts himself so that he can do most favour to whoever shall capture Wallace with regard to exile or legal claims or expiation of past misdeeds.[43]

For seven years little had been heard of Wallace except a fleeting reference to his presence in Paris and in Rome. Now at the very time when the Scottish nobles were bending their knee to the conqueror, he emerged from the shadow, still defiant, to clash with the English near Peebles in February 1304 and again at the Bridge of Earn in September 1304; then there is silence again until the fateful day of 3 August 1305 when he is betrayed and captured in Glasgow in the house of Robert Rae, a servant of Sir John Menteith.[44]

For four hundred miles along the dusty summer roads, he was led on horseback to London with his legs tied beneath the belly of his beast. On his arrival in the evening of 22 August he was lodged for the night in the house of Alderman William de Leyre in the parish of Allhallows Fenchurch, and from there next morning he was taken in procession by the Mayor of London, the aldermen and the sheriffs, through the thronged streets and jeering crowds to Westminster Hall. There, with his huge frame bound and shackled, he was seated at the south end of the hall to face his judges. A coronet of laurel leaves was mockingly placed upon his brow because of his alleged boast that one day he would be crowned at Westminster. He was not allowed to plead or make defence, but in silence listened to a long indictment of all his crimes against the English, culminating in the charge of treason in that he had been unmindful of his troth and allegiance.

Only then he spoke. He admitted all his acts against the English which he had done in defence of his country against her enemy, but he denied that he had ever been a traitor to the King of England for never had he pledged to him his allegiance. Nevertheless, it was of treason that the court found him guilty and it was for that offence that the King had devised an appalling penalty.

It was inflicted on Wallace the same day. He was chained flat to a hurdle and for the greater entertainment of the populace was dragged by horses along a circuitous route over four miles of cobblestones from Westminster to Smithfield. There he was hanged but cut down half-strangled and still alive. Then he was castrated and disembowelled. His genitals and entrails were burned before his eyes and, after his unspeakable agony had been ended by the headman's axe, his heart was ripped out and added to the flames. His body was then hacked into four pieces. His head was mounted on a pike on London Bridge and the four quarters were distributed to Newcastle-on-Tyne, Berwick, Stirling and Perth to be displayed to the public eye as menacing symbols of King Edward's might.[45]

But the flesh had hardly shredded from his dismembered bones than he had become a legend among the common folk of Scotland. A sense of injustice rankled in their minds. The great nobles had vowed and disavowed their allegiance to an alien monarch and yet had retained their territories and their lives, but a landless man of lesser rank, who had never broken his oath because he had never done homage, was condemned to degradation and a vile death simply for doing his duty in defence of his country. King Edward thought to make an example. He made a martyr instead. The name of William Wallace has echoed down the centuries as a trumpet call to Scotsmen in whatever corner of the globe they dwell.

# 7

By this one act King Edward unravelled for ever the web of cooperation he had sought to create by the conciliatory settlement of 1304 and his subsequent measures.

In the spring of 1305 he had appointed Robert Bruce, the Bishop of Glasgow and Sir John Mowbray to draw up a report on the future settlement of Scotland. Their recommendation was that the community of the realm should be summoned to elect ten persons to attend the next English parliament to help draw up a new constitution for their kingdom. On receiving the King's acceptance, they convened a Scottish parliament at Perth in May, at which the ten were duly chosen. Representing the earls, the bishops, the barons, the abbots and the lay community, the elected members attended the Westminster parliament in September 1305 and in company with twenty English colleagues drew up an ordinance for the government of the land – no longer the realm – of Scotland.

On the surface this appeared to give a form of self-government to the Scots. The viceroy, it is true, was to be the King's nephew, the Earl of Richmond, and the chancellor and the chamberlain were to be English, but they were to be advised and assisted by a Scottish council of twenty-two members, consisting of four bishops, four abbots, five earls and nine barons, among whom were three former guardians, Robert Bruce, Bishop Lamberton and John Comyn the Red. In spite of the number and eminence of these advisory councillors and the fact that, apart from the southeast counties, most of the sheriffdoms in the country were to be held by Scotsmen, the ultimate power was nevertheless concentrated in the hands of the viceroy, who had the authority vested in him to dismiss and replace officials on his own initiative and to maintain in such strategic castles as he thought fit English garrisons and English governors.[1]

However, King Edward believed that the iron fist was sufficiently covered by the velvet glove for the Scots, tamed by their many defeats, to acquiesce in the new arrangements and combine peacefully to put them into operation.

So confident was he that, pending the arrival of the new viceroy, he appointed a committee of four to administer the country in his stead, headed by no other than William Lamberton, Bishop of St Andrews. It was an ironic choice for the bishop was already organizing in secret a combination for the recovery of Scottish independence.[2]

For eight years the Scottish Church had been the coordinating factor behind the Scottish resistance and Bishop Lamberton had been the architect of that coordination. He had supported the Comyns, he had used his powerful influence to reconcile the factions of Bruce and Comyn but his instruments had broken in his hand. When he returned from France after the settlement of 1304 and paid his homage to King Edward, he thought deeply on what potentialities for freedom remained.

During his sojourn in Paris he had realized that, while the French were lavish in their promises, they were too exercised by their own problems to give any active help to Scotland and that their protégé, the abdicated King, John Balliol, had neither the ambition nor the wish to forsake his sequestered rural existence for the hurly-burly of dynastic struggle. Yet in that hierarchical age only a king could inspire and synthesize the deep felt desires of prelate, knight and common man. Wallace had not had the qualifications, the Comyn figurehead was discredited. Only one man remained who had a justifiable claim to the throne and the personality, ambition, skill, prowess and magnetism to achieve that end: Robert Bruce.

Between his surrender to King Edward in 1302 and the fall of Stirling Castle, Robert Bruce had maintained a cautious and diplomatic stance giving lip service to the English monarch but quietly rendering nugatory any demands for his military support. As early as 11 March 1302 he had written to the monks of Melrose Abbey:

> Whereas I have often vexed the abbey's tenants on their grange of Maybole by leading them all over the country in my army of Carrick although there was no summons of the common army of the realm, troubled in conscience I shall never again demand such an army service neither of many nor of few, unless the common army of the whole realm is raised for its defence when all inhabitants are bound to serve.

As a Scottish historian pertinently remarks, 'Bruce's conscience did not trouble him until the beginning of Lent 1302, just in time to ensure that his army would be of less use to Edward than it had been to the Scots.'[3] Again, when asked by King Edward in the spring of 1304 to forward the English siege engines for the attack on Stirling Castle, he duly complied but omitted to include the vital part of the machinery necessary for their function,[4] and yet again when called upon to supply troops for the same purpose, he wrote personally to the King on 4 April 1304 that 'he has been in London and Essex where his lands lie and is still there endeavouring in every possible way to procure horses and armour for himself and his people but . . . has had no success whatever in his attempts to borrow for the purpose or get a penny of his rents'.[5]

During King Edward's invasion of Scotland in 1303 he had been with the Prince of Wales and his father-in-law, the Earl of Ulster, on the western route which was no more than an unopposed military parade and was left in charge of Ayr Castle. From there he was ordered to join Sir John Segrave in February 1304 to make a mounted raid on Wallace and Simon Fraser in Selkirk forest, but it is significant that while some of their followers were captured both these leaders had prior warning and escaped, for which Bruce was gently chided by King Edward with the words 'as the cloak is well made, also make the hood'.[6]

It was a difficult and uneasy role to play, but until the autumn of 1305 it succeeded. Not only he, but members of his family, obtained the favours and dangerous friendship of the monarch. Edward Bruce, his brother next in age, was placed in the Prince of Wales's household and a younger brother, Alexander, after a brilliant career at Cambridge University – 'no one,' wrote a contemporary, 'who read arts at Cambridge before or since his time ever made such progress' – was granted by royal favour the living of Kirkinnen near Wigtown and made Dean of Glasgow.[7] Bruce himself had already been given the guardianship of his young nephew, Earl Donald of Mar, with all the benefits of the great Mar estates in the northeast and the control of the formidable stone-built fortress of Kildrummy, as well as the wardenship of three royal forests.[8] In March 1305 he asked for and obtained the de Umfraville lands in Carrick[9] and in the same month was entrusted in company with Bishop Wishart and Sir John Mowbray to ordain in what manner the guardians of Scotland should organize its defence.[10]

He was indeed 'a favourite son' and it is understandable that he should be so. Long ago, when Prince of Wales, Edward had assessed the fine temper of the family when Bruce's grandfather and father had been his companions in arms in the heat and dust of the Holy Land. Now in their descendant he saw all those qualities that he most admired, sagacity, endurance, courage and skill in arms. So, in his relationship with Bruce there was something deeper than a politic wooing of a powerful Scottish magnate. And on Bruce's side too there must have been a respect for the determination and abilities of the older man, for in his future kingship he was to model much upon the royal pattern he had observed.

So, when his father died in March 1304[11] and, at the age of thirty, Bruce succeeded to the vast family estates in the counties of Essex and Huntingdon, Dumfries and Aberdeen, there was every worldly reason why he should pursue the path of conformity and enjoy the pleasure of married life in the courtly circles of the Crown.

But the Celtic blood of his mother pulled him towards Scotland. The 'Community of the Realm', that conception to which every Scottish document had referred during the years of struggle, had become to him over the past decade a living entity and overriding all affinity to the English King was the profound conviction that he and he alone was the rightful monarch of the northern realm whose mission it must be, when the time was ripe to recover its ancient independence.

After obtaining probate of his English estates in May 1304[12], he travelled north to King Edward's camp outside Stirling Castle at the same time as Bishop Lamberton reached it from France. There King Edward was indulging an old man's vanity by showing off his virile prowess before his young Queen. Mounted on horseback, he rode so close beneath the walls of the besieged castle in order to direct operations that on one occasion a javelin hurled from the ramparts lodged in the steel plates of his armour and on another a huge stone fell so near that his horse reared and overturned with its master, who was lifted up, dazed and shaken, and carried by soldiers to his tent.[13]

When the old friends, prelate and earl, observed or heard of these proceedings, the same thought must have come to them both: the King was an old man who by the hazard of war or by sickness must soon die and when he was succeeded by the Prince of Wales, of whose vacillating character they were both aware, a new opportunity for Scotland's freedom could arise. On 11 June 1304 at the Abbey of Cambus Kenneth they signed a bond:

that they should mutually help each other in all their several businesses and affairs at all times and against all other persons whatever without any deceit and that neither of them should undertake any important business without the other of them. They will mutually warn each other against any impending danger and do the best to avert the same from each other and for the full performance of the agreement they bound themselves by oath and under the penalty of the sum of £10,000 to be applied for the recovery of the Holy Land.[14]

No more was written, but there can be little doubt that from that time plans were quietly being prepared through the network of the Church for decisive action in the event of King Edward's death. One major problem that had to be solved was the attitude of John Comyn 'the Red'. For nearly seven years he had been in the forefront of opposition to the English but, brave and pugnacious as he was, his efforts had been amateur and ineffective and at the end had left the kingdom as much a conquered province as she had been in 1296. Nevertheless, even if he had lost the confidence of the Church, he was still the head of one of the most powerful families in Scotland and either his full support or his elimination was essential to the success of any revolt.

In the late summer of 1305, while the ten Scottish commissioners were making their way to London to attend the September parliament and draw up an ordinance for their country, Robert Bruce and Bishop Wishart, who had deliberately excluded themselves from that body, remained in Scotland. It is reasonable to surmise that during that period parleys with John Comyn began. News in October that King Edward lay sick in bed gave urgency to the proceedings and Bruce offered Comyn a simple choice: Help me to be King and I will give you my estates or give me your estates and I will help you.

John Comyn preferred possessions to the Crown, and an exchange of signed and sealed documents was made between them to that effect.[15]

It is possible that John Comyn would have adhered to his commitments if King Edward had not recovered from his sickness, but unfortunately for all, the monarch regained his health with a mind already burgeoning with suspicion.

Correspondence with certain Scottish nobles had been found on William Wallace when he was seized. Nothing is known of its content but almost immediately the smiling face of the King towards Robert Bruce began to darken. On 15 September 1305 he gave orders, 'Let it be commanded to the Earl of Carrick that he place Kildrummy Castle in the keeping of a man for whom he shall answer',[16] and on 10 October he revoked the gift of de Umfraville's lands to Bruce that he had made six months before and returned them to their owner.[17] Both Kildrummy Castle and the de Umfraville lands were in sensitive areas where resistance to his rule was most likely to erupt. Kildrummy was the key to Moray, in whose mountains the Bishop of Moray still lurked, outside the King's peace, with a body of turbulent followers, and men everywhere in Carrick had a close association with Bruce through his mother's side.

King Edward smelled mischief, but he was too shrewd a ruler to show his hand until he could discover how far the ramifications of conspiracy extended, if conspiracy there was. Robert Bruce and John Comyn still remained on the advisory council for Scotland, and during the winter of 1305–6 Bruce must have visited his English estates for he was at the English court in January 1306.

Whether because he lost his nerve as the King's spies went to work, or out of jealousy of his coeval or in the hope of material reward, John Comyn informed King Edward of the covenant into which he had entered, and told him that he would produce as proof the document signed and sealed by Bruce. King Edward kept his own counsel and, while he was awaiting delivery of documentary proof, assumed again his friendliness to Bruce. But one evening while he was entertaining an inner circle of his friends and the wine was circulating freely, he grew expansive and let fall that on the morrow he had in mind to arrest the Earl of Carrick and try him for treason.

Among his guests was the Earl of Gloucester, whose family had, for generations, been linked in friendship with the Bruces. Hastily he sent the keeper of his wardrobe to Bruce's lodging with twelve pence and a pair of spurs, which the keeper presented to Bruce with the words, 'My lord sends these to you in return for what he on his side got from you yesterday.'

Bruce may have sensed a duplicity in the King and arranged with his friend to give this signal if danger was imminent, or he was quick to take an unpremeditated hint. He handed back the twelve pence with thanks to the keeper and sent his squire secretly to saddle two horses. Then he told his staff not to disturb him as he had much work to do in his chamber and quietly slipped out to join his squire and ride through the night towards his castle at Lochmaben, where his wife and brothers were in residence.[18]

By day and night the two rode northward, and as they neared the border they met a Scotsman travelling south, a rare sight at that time of the year. Bruce stopped to ask to what destination he was bound and something uneasy in the man's behaviour aroused his suspicions. So he had him searched and on his person was found a letter from John Comyn to King Edward enclosing the bond which Bruce had signed and sealed. Having disposed of this ill-fated man, Bruce reached Lochmaben on the fifth day after his departure from London and told his brothers of all that had occurred.[19]

At that time King Edward's justices were holding their sessions in the nearby town of Dumfries to which the local magnates would normally repair. John Comyn was at his castle of Dalswinton nine miles away, so Bruce sent him a message requesting that they should meet on 10 February at Greyfriars Church on their way to the sessions.

When he appeared the two withdrew for privacy to the high altar, and there Bruce drew forth the bond and taxed John Comyn with his treachery. Angry words ensued and daggers were drawn, but Bruce got his blow in first and Comyn fell wounded on the altar steps.[20] His uncle, Sir Robert Comyn,[21] who was nearby, sprang forward and struck Bruce on the breast with his sword, but his blade was deflected by Bruce's armour and he in turn was cut to the ground by Christopher Seton, the husband of Bruce's sister Christina.[22] In haste the two men left the church to join the followers of Bruce who were waiting outside. Calling for his horse, Bruce was about to mount when one of them, Roger Kirkpatrick, seeing his commander's agitation and the blood upon his clothes, asked what had occurred.

'I doubt,' said Bruce, 'that I have slain Red Comyn.'

'Do you doubt?' replied Kirkpatrick, 'then I'll make sure,' and, followed by James Lindsay, he ran into the church and dispatched the wounded man.[23]

The bloody deed was done and Bruce had now to risk his all or run for shelter to his sister's court in Norway. His choice was instant. Hailing his men at arms, he rode so fast to Dumfries castle that the garrison, taken by surprise, surrendered quickly and their constable, Sir Richard Siward, was made captive. The startled justices, who were holding their sessions in the great hall, barricaded the doors, but given by Bruce the choice of having the castle burned about them or a free passage to England, they preferred to preserve their lives.[24]

*　　*　　*

As word spread of Bruce's success, the Scots began to flock to his banner but the odds against him were enormous. The plans on which he and the Church had been working were based on the premise of King Edward's death. Now they had been precipitated by the murder of Comyn and their chances of success were immeasurably diminished. The formidable monarch was still alive and in command of superior forces: the powerful relatives of the dead Comyn were roused to savage vengeance against his assassin and the bloodstains on the altar steps filled with a superstitious terror the simple minds of the common people. All depended upon the reaction of the Scottish Church.

But the Scottish Church was staunch to the single principle which had animated its actions during the years of strife: the independence of Scotland. When Bruce hurried from Dumfries to Bishop Wishart in Glasgow and kneeling before him made confession of his violence, the little bishop shrived him of all his sins and gave him absolution for the sacrilege he had committed.[25] The clergy throughout the country were so informed and adjured in the name of their bishops to rally to Bruce as to a sacred cause.[26] Bruce in return swore a solemn oath to preserve and defend the liberties of the Scottish Church.[27]

Uplifted and strengthened by this spiritual help, Bruce acted with rapidity and strategic skill. The castles of Dunaverty, Rothesay and Ayr, which commanded the Firth of Clyde and could keep open the way for reinforcements and supplies from Ireland and the Outer Isles, were occupied by his supporters through force or by agreement, and those of Tibbers and Dalswinton were seized[28] and, with the castles of Dumfries and Lochmaben already in hand, effectively dominated the western route to Scotland. Orders were issued placing all persons on twenty-four hours' notice of mobilization and a formal demand was sent to King Edward that he should recognize Robert Bruce as King of Scots. The response, not unexpectedly, was that Bruce should return to the English Crown all the castles he had seized, to which in return he replied that he would continue to capture castles until his demand was met and would defend himself 'with the longest stick he had'.[29]

Mindful of his bond with Bishop Lamberton, Bruce had conveyed to him a message that he was to have himself crowned at Scone on 25 March 1306, ten years to a day since the outbreak of war between English and Scots. Lamberton was then at Berwick in his capacity as president of the council acting on behalf of the absent English viceroy of Scotland, to which he had been entrusted by King Edward. Under cover of darkness, when the opportunity came, he slipped away and hastened to Scone to be present at the ceremony.[30] As harbinger of his coming, he had sent secretly to Bruce his young squire, James Douglas. Some time after the boy's father, the irascible Sir William Douglas, had died in the Tower of London and his lands had been given to Lord Clifford by King Edward, the bishop had taken James into his household. Now, as Barbour writes, all alone

he took the road to Lochmaben and near Arickstone he met the Bruce riding with a great company to Scone to be enthroned and made King. And when Douglas saw him coming he rode forward in haste and greeted him and made obeisance very courteously and told him all his conditions and who he was and how Clifford held his inheritance. Also that he came to do homage to him as his rightful King and was ready in everything to share his fortune. And when Bruce had heard his desire he received him with much pleasure and gave him men and arms. For he judged that he would be worthy of his fathers who were brave and able men. Thus they made their acquaintance that never afterwards by any chance of any kind was broken while they lived. Their friendship increased ever more and more for Douglas served always loyally and Bruce so wise, strong and valiant gladly and well rewarded his service.[31]

On 25 March 1306 in the Abbey of Scone, Robert Bruce was crowned King of Scots with all the formality and solemnity that could be achieved. The kingly robes and vestments which Bishop Wishart had hidden in his treasury against this longed for day were brought out by the old man and set upon King Robert, and a circlet of gold was placed upon his head;[32] while the great banner of the kings of Scotland, with its lion and scarlet lilies, that had lain so long concealed, was planted behind his throne. Three bishops, of Glasgow, St Andrews and Moray, were there, and four earls, of Atholl, Lennox, Menteith and Mar; but noticeably absent was the Earl of Fife. He was still a youth and held in England as a ward of court and thus unable to perform his hereditary office in the ceremony. But his nineteen-year-old sister, Isabel, who was married to the Earl of Buchan, now an ally of King Edward and close kinsman of the dead Comyn, got knowledge of the coronation. To her the call of Scotland and her youthful hero-worship of Bruce proved greater than her wifely duty. Seizing her husband's finest horses, she rode with utmost speed to Scone to act on her brother's behalf. She arrived a day too late, but so that the rites of ancient tradition might be served, a second ceremony was performed – on Palm Sunday, forty-eight hours after the first – in which the golden circlet was lifted in her youthful hands and once more placed upon the brow of Robert Bruce, Earl of Carrick, Lord of Annandale, King of Scots.[33]

# PART TWO

# 1306-1314

Great was the task that Robert Bruce took upon himself and unbearable the burdens upon his shoulders. His mishaps, flights and dangers; hardships and weariness; hunger and thirst; watchings and fastings; nakedness and cold; snares and banishment; the seizing, imprisoning, slaughter and downfall of his near ones and – even more – his dear ones no-one now living, I think, recollects or is equal to rehearsing.

But if there were one to tell how with a glad and dauntless heart Robert Bruce triumphed single handed over all the ill-luck and numberless straits through which he went: the victories and battles, where, by the Lord's help, by his own strength and by his human manhood he cut fearlessly his way into the columns of the enemy, now mightily bearing these down and now mightily warding off and escaping the pains of death – then such a one, I deem, would prove that in the art of fighting and in vigour of body, Robert had not his match in his time in any clime.

*John Fordun's fourteenth-century Chronicle
of the Scottish Nation*

# 8

King Edward was about to hold his Lenten court in Winchester when he received the news of Comyn's murder and the revolt of Bruce. A terrible rage possessed him. His clemency had been abused, his trust betrayed. The whole realm of England must be roused to crush a stubborn and ungrateful people. Hoisting his long legs, which had now become unwieldly, into a horse-drawn litter, he was borne to London. From there he issued a proclamation throughout the country that at the Feast of Pentecost, 22 May, he would bestow a knighthood on his son, the Prince of Wales, and that all esquires eligible for that honour should repair to Westminster to be knighted in their turn by their future King and march with him against the perfidious Scots.

On the appointed day, some three hundred of the flower of English youth received their accolade in the Abbey church and then attended a banquet at the Temple presided over by the King. Two swans enmeshed in golden chains were laid before him on the table and all the knights there present swore upon these never to rest until the kingdom of Scotland had been subdued. The King then rose and vowed, 'Before God and the swans', to avenge the death of Comyn and the insult to the Church, and when this had been accomplished never again to bear arms against a Christian but only against the heathen in the Holy Land.

A shout of acclamation greeted his words and the Prince of Wales, responding to the heady enthusiasm of the new-made knights, swore before them all never to sleep two nights in the same place until he had reached Scotland. A great army was set in train and made for Carlisle under his command, while behind him his father followed in slow and painful stages because of his infirmities.[1]

But long before the bizarre pageant of the swans, King Edward had taken more mundane measures. Troops and provisions had been sent to strengthen the garrisons of Berwick and Carlisle against invasion.[2] Aymer de Valence, Earl of Pembroke, cousin of the King and brother-in-law of the murdered Comyn, had been appointed special lieutenant for Scotland and ordered, with Sir Henry Percy and Sir Robert Clifford, to march against the rebels with an army drawn from the northern counties.[3] No mercy was to be shown. All taken in arms and all who had given them shelter were to be executed without trial. All who had been concerned in Comyn's death and those who had joined their ranks were to suffer the ghastly fate of William Wallace.[4]

Armed with these plenary powers and accompanied by a picked body of 3000 mounted men, Pembroke rode swiftly north. Many Scottish nobles related to the dead Comyn joined his forces as he made for the Forth crossing, and without opposition he reached Perth early in June and secured the town with numbers now increased to 6000. His progress was so rapid that he surprised and captured the Bishop of Glasgow at Cupar Castle, Fife, which that churchman 'comme homme de guerre' had recently seized from the English,[5] and hard by in Kinross, the Bishop of St Andrews, after urging his tenantry to join the forces of Bruce, submitted his person. Only their cloth saved them from the gallows. They were sent under escort to King Edward, who cast them in irons into the dungeons of Porchester and Winchester castles respectively.[6]

The loss of two of the three foremost leaders of the Scottish Church was a grievous blow to Bruce, but the clergy remained faithful to his cause and rejected without hesitation the papal excommunication against him which King Edward had asked for and received. The remaining bishop, the Bishop of Moray, who had not sued for peace even during King Edward's massive sweep through Scotland in 1304 but had retreated into the mountain fastnesses of the Cairngorms, now laid his firm hands on the reins of clerical control. Throughout his diocese in the Mounth he never ceased to preach and exhort his flock that 'they were not less deserving of merit who rebelled with Sir Robert to help against the English King and his men . . . than if they should fight in the Holy Land against pagans and Saracens.'[7]

It was to this province that, after his coronation, Bruce made his way, there to recruit an army to make head against an English invasion. His forces were too thin to man the borders. Apart from the four earls who attended his crowning at Scone, only a little over a hundred landed knights had rallied to his call, and of these two-thirds came from the country north of the Forth and Clyde.[8] Even before his coronation Dumfries had been recaptured by his enemies in the heart of his own domain of Annandale. But in the northeast was a complex of support: the men from his own lordship of Garioch, from the estates of the Earl of Atholl in Strathaan and Strathbegie, from the domains of his ward the young Earl of Mar, from the followers of the Bishop of Moray. So, leaving his Queen and her little court of women under the care of Nigel Bruce, his youngest brother, at Kildrummy Castle, he canvassed throughout the area until he had raised a force of some 4500 men. On hearing of the Earl of Pembroke's approach, he moved south and on 18 June drew up before the walls of Perth.

He had neither the numbers nor the siege engines to invest the town so, resorting to an old chivalric tradition, he rode to the city gates and challenged Pembroke either to bring out his men to fight or to surrender the town. Pembroke replied that the day was too far advanced for combat but on the following morning he would accept his challenge.[9]

Bruce must have known the earl at the English court and regarded him as a man of honour, for when he had withdrawn his men to bivouack for the night near Methven,[10] some six miles away, in a wood on the high ground south of the Almond river, he did not trouble to set out pickets, relying on Pembroke's word. He had failed to realize either the intense pressure put on Pembroke by King Edward to capture Bruce or the virulence of the blood feud of the Scottish nobles who were with the earl. In these circumstances honour played no part.

Some of Bruce's men were foraging for fodder, some cooking their supper, some disarmed and sleeping when the English fell upon them in the summer dusk.[11] There was a wild scramble for arms and horses and a desperate hand to hand struggle ensued. At the first onset Bruce engaged the Earl of Pembroke and slew his horse,[12] but in the mêlée he himself was unhorsed, and as he was mounting again Sir Philip Mowbray seized his horse's bridle and, in the words of John Barbour:

> called aloud 'Help, Help. I have the new-made king.' With that Christopher Seton, when he saw the King seized by his foe, came spurring straight, striking to right and left, and dealt Mowbray such a blow that, though he was of great strength, it made him reel dizzily and had sent him altogether to the ground but that he held by his horse. Then he let go the King's bridle, and Bruce, raising his battle cry rallied his men at hand.[13]

But outnumbered and taken unawares his army had no chance. Twice more he was unhorsed and twice rescued[14] until a little group of his knights, the Earl of Atholl, Edward Bruce, James Douglas, Neil Campbell and Gilbert de la Haye, closed round him and in a tight phalanx broke through the cordon of the English and disappeared into the night.

It was a shattering defeat. In a few hours Bruce's only coherent force had been destroyed. Many of his bravest and most devoted followers, Sir Alexander Fraser, Sir David Inchmartin, Sir Hugh de la Haye, Sir John Somerville, Alexander Scrymgeour, the royal standard bearer, and his nephew Thomas Randolph, were taken in the field and others, among them those two stalwart veterans Sir Christopher Seton and Sir Simon Fraser, were rounded up from the castles to which they had fled. A savage vengeance was exacted.

The normal civilities of war by which a knight could ransom his life were brushed aside by a king of England whose hate transcended traditional codes. All who were captured were treated as outlaws and were hanged or beheaded or drawn and quartered without trial.[15] Only Thomas Randolph was protected by the friendship of the Earl of Pembroke and granted pardon in return for his promise henceforth to fight for the English.

The Prince of Wales and his young companions, who had pushed north from Carlisle and captured Lochmaben, spread over the south of Scotland in the wake of Pembroke and dishonoured the vows of chivalry, which they had sworn at the altar in their midnight vigils before they were knighted, by such merciless severity against the lesser folk that even King Edward was moved to restrain their excesses.[16] All the Lowlands of Scotland were cowed into submission.


Bruce and his handful of knights had taken refuge in the mountains of Atholl, and after remaining there for several weeks, comfortless and hungry in the heather, so that stragglers from the battle of Methven could join them, they drew down Deeside to Aberdeen. From there Bruce sent word to his brother Nigel to bring to him from Kildrummy his Queen, the Countess of Buchan, his daughter Marjorie and his two sisters, Mary, wife of his comrade Neil Campbell, and Christina, now twice widowed, first by the death of her husband the Earl of Mar and then by the execution of her second husband, Christopher Seton.[17]

It was essential for him to bring them under his protection, however inconvenient they might be to a fighting force, for, after the battle of Methven, King Edward had ordered his heralds to proclaim throughout the country that all the wives of his enemies were to be treated as outlaws. Any man, as he might wish, could rob, rape or murder them immune from punishment.[18]

Whether it was Bruce's intention to embark from Aberdeen and seek aid from Norway, where his eldest sister Isabel was Dowager Queen, no one knows. He may have been dissuaded by the Bishop of Moray, since subsequent events indicate that he did meet the bishop there and that together they worked out a plan for the renewal of the struggle in the spring of 1307. All that is certain is that the bishop made his way to the Orkneys, which belonged to Norway, and that Bruce and his womenfolk with a force of some five hundred men, on learning that the Earl of Pembroke was advancing towards them, struck east to the mountainous region on the borders of Perthshire and Argyll in an attempt to reach the Western Isles where old friends of the family, the Macdonalds of Islay, held sway.

Early in August Bruce had reached Tyndrum, the head of Strathfillan, beyond Loch Tay, and had camped near the shrine of St Fillan of Glenlochart.[19]

This holy man of the sixth century was the most venerated of early Scottish saints, and it was not without purpose that Bruce had halted his little army beside his tomb. The sacrilege committed in Greyfriars church weighed upon Bruce's conscience and could shake with superstitious fears the faith of his followers. So here, on a spot hallowed by the most ancient of Scottish churches, it is believed that, as his men gathered about him, he knelt for absolution before the Abbot of Inchafray and received his blessing for all to hear. He had little time to spare.

The hillside on which he was carrying out this ceremony was within the domains of the Lord of Lorne, a son-in-law of the murdered Comyn and vengeful for his kinsman's death. When Lorne received news of Bruce's approach, he mustered his Macdougall clansmen, and with other barons of Argyll blocked the head of the pass to which Bruce was making his way. On 11 August, as Bruce and his small band of knights were riding up the narrow defile at Dalry where they had no room to deploy, Lorne launched his attack. The half-naked Highlanders, swarming down from the slopes on either side, slashed at the bellies and legs of the horses with their long Lochaber axes and brought many to the ground. James Douglas and Gilbert de la Haye were wounded and others unhorsed and slain.[20]

Apprehensive of the danger to his women if all his horses should be lost, Bruce gave the order to retreat and for his women to be lodged and defended in a small castle on an island in Loch Dochart which he had passed on his way to Strathfillan.[21]

The route was along a narrow track between a steep hillside and the loch. On this track Bruce stationed himself at the rear of his diminished forces, turning again and again to face and check the pursuing Highlanders. The Lord of Lorne, angry at the manner in which Bruce kept them at bay, ordered a father and two sons from the MacIndrosser clan to race along the hillside and ambush him at a place where the loch and the rock face met so close that a horse could hardly turn. As Bruce passed beneath them, they leapt upon him. One son seized his bridle but had his arm and shoulder cut from his body by the stroke of Bruce's sword. The other son took hold of his leg intending to unseat him, but Bruce spurred his horse forward so that his assailant lost his footing and was dragged along with his hand trapped between horse and stirrup; the father leapt on the horse's crupper and clasped Bruce's cloak so close to his body that he could not use his sword blade, but Bruce, striking back violently with the pommel of that weapon, dislodged him and split his skull as he fell and then cut down the man whose hand was trapped. When the pursuers saw this feat of arms, they were afraid to follow him, and without further disturbance he rejoined his troops and bivouacked for the night.[22]

Bruce had saved part of his force but his losses of men and horses were severe and the risks to his women very great.

Realizing that the only route to the west accessible to them was blocked by his enemies, Bruce altered his plans. Handing over all the surviving horses to his brother Nigel Bruce and the Earl of Atholl, he ordered them to escort the Queen and her companions with as many men as could be mounted back to Kildrummy Castle. When the women had recovered sufficiently from their hardships, the earl should conduct them as best he could to rejoin the Bishop of Moray in the Norway-held Orkneys, while Nigel should fortify and defend the castle against the advancing English to hold them in check as long as possible. Meanwhile Bruce and his remaining followers would take to the heather and bypass his foes to the south.[23]

When the little group of women with their cavalcade of mounted men had disappeared out of sight, Bruce and his companion knights divested themselves of their mail and, armed only with their swords, daggers and bows, made their way on foot by Glen Ogle south to Balquhidder[24] where they lay up in a cave. Bruce's object was now the castle of Dunaverty at the tip of Kintyre peninsula, to which he had sent victuals and arms soon after his capture of Dumfries. If he could cross to the west of Loch Lomond, he would find himself in the country of the Earl of Lennox, his constant supporter, of whom he had heard nothing since the battle of Methven, and from there could pass to the Campbell lands in the mountains, which push like a huge fist southwards between Loch Fyne and the Firth of Clyde, and so by sea to Kintyre.[25]

To this end he sent ahead his brother-in-law, Sir Neil Campbell, with a small body of followers to go to his kinsmen and arrange with them for boats and provisions to be made ready for the sea voyage to Dunaverty, and he appointed a time and a place for their meeting.[26]

Soon after Campbell's departure from Balquidder, Bruce and his little contingent of knights and men travelled southwest by rough tracks through the wooded hillsides, enduring great cold and hunger, reduced to a diet of roots and berries and such small game as they could snare or net. Eventually they found shelter in a cave at Craigroyston under the shadow of Ben Lomond.[27] From there they searched for boats to carry them to the western shore of Loch Lomond so as to avoid the long trek round its northern end which would bring them into the hostile territory of the MacDougalls.

But no boats could be found until James Douglas discovered one sunk among the reeds which, after it was drawn ashore and emptied, was capable of carrying three persons at a time.[28]

Bruce and Douglas were first rowed over and then two at a time the rest were ferried across while Bruce related to those who had landed tales from a French romance.[29] When all were gathered together, Bruce divided them into two parties between himself and James Douglas to hunt for venison, for they were near starvation. As the two parties beat up the quarry towards each other blowing their horns, the Earl of Lennox, who had escaped to his homelands and was also hunting in that area, heard them and, recognizing the note of Bruce's horn, came quickly towards him, and when they saw each other they embraced with tears of joy for each had believed the other to be dead at Methven.[30]

The earl took them to his encampment and gave them food and drink, and when they had finished he went with them to where Sir Neil Campbell had galleys waiting and from there they sailed down the Firth of Clyde, past the Isle of Bute, to Dunaverty where they were welcomed by Angus Macdonald of the Isles.[31]

But the Earl of Lennox, delaying to give final instructions to his thanes before he departed, was almost captured by the galleys of the Lord of Lorne which were searching the waters for Bruce. Hurriedly launching a boat, he only escaped by throwing overboard all his goods except his armour so as to lighten the ballast and tempt his pursuers to pause to collect the booty.[32]

During this time, Nigel Bruce and his party of women had made their way through the mountains of Atholl and Braemar to the castle of Kildrummy on Deeside. When they arrived they were greeted with the news that the Earl of Pembroke was already installed in Aberdeen[33] and was only waiting for the arrival of the Prince of Wales and his army with their complement of siege engines to attack the castle. The ladies therefore continued their journey northwards towards the Orkneys under the guidance of the Earl of Atholl. For some hundred miles they travelled safely, but in Easter Ross their fortune changed. The Earl of Ross, a supporter of the Comyns, heard of their presence and sent a party to apprehend them. They took refuge in the hallowed sanctuary of St Duthac at Tain on the shore of Dornoch Firth. But the power of the saint was unable to preserve them. They were seized and dispatched under an armed guard to the brooding presence of the English King, who had taken up his residence at the monastery of Lanercost.[34]

At Kildrummy matters had fared no better. The castle was one of the most formidable in Scotland, well provisioned and manned and capable in ordinary circumstances of withstanding a long siege. Day after day, Nigel Bruce and his men beat off every attack with such loss to the enemy that they considered abandoning the siege and returning to England.

But what force could not effect was achieved by treachery. Bribed by the promise of English gold, the castle's blacksmith, Osborne, threw a red-hot ploughshare into the corn store. The flames spread from this to the wooden buildings within the castle grounds so that the garrison was driven to the narrow walk along the battlements. The castle gate was burned, the English entered and, after resisting for a night and a day, the defenders, attacked from both sides, surrendered.[35] The blacksmith received his reward. Having covenanted for as much gold as he could carry, the English fulfilled their bargain by pouring it molten down his throat.[36]

King Edward took instant revenge for the wound which the rebellion of Robert Bruce had inflicted upon his pride. Nigel Bruce, known to his contemporaries as 'a young knight of exceeding beauty',[37] and all who were taken prisoner with him, were dragged through the streets of Berwick and hanged and then beheaded. The Earl of Atholl was conducted to Westminster and there, in response to the claim of his peers that in virtue of his royal blood he should be treated differently from other men, King Edward granted this distinction, with sardonic humour, by having him led on a horse rather than dragged to his place of execution, and there suspended from a gallows thirty feet higher than the normal and, when he had been cut down and beheaded, by having his head hoisted on a pole on London Bridge taller than all the other grisly relics erected there for the edification of the populace.[38]

The women were spared death but King Edward conceived for them a punishment peculiarly humiliating to their sex. The Countess of Buchan, whose dash to the coronation of Robert Bruce had caused the English Court to accuse her of being his mistress,[39] and Mary Bruce, whose husband Sir Neil Campbell was still in arms with her brother, were the objects of his greatest displeasure. For them he ordained that wooden cages should be built jutting from the battlements of Berwick and Roxburgh castles respectively,[40] and that within them they should be shut up as animals in a zoo, exposed to the gaze of passers-by[41] with the only concession to their modesty the provision of privies within the walls.[42] There for the next four years these two heroic young women each endured their solitary confinement with no communication except to the English maidservants who brought them their food and drink. A similar cage was prepared at the Tower of London for Robert Bruce's twelve-year-old daughter Marjorie, with the express condition that she should not be allowed to hold converse with any but the constable of the Tower. So savage a sentence against an innocent child must have stirred the pity and sense of outrage of some about the King, for later he revoked the order and dispatched her to a nunnery at Walton.[43] Christina Bruce, whose second husband Christopher Seton had so recently been hanged, drawn and quartered, perhaps for that reason was treated more leniently than her sister and was lodged in a convent at Sixhills in Lincolnshire.[44]

The last and most important prisoner was Queen Elizabeth, wife of Robert Bruce, through whom the greatest hurt could be done by King Edward to the man he now regarded as a viper nurtured in his bosom. But fortunately for her she was the daughter of the Earl of Ulster, a noble so valuable to the King that any offence against him was dangerous and impolitic. She was therefore only placed under house arrest in the manor of Burstwick-in-Holderness. She was allowed two ladies-in-waiting but it was specified that they should be 'elderly and not at all gay',[45] and her conditions were such that she was forced to complain to the King that she had 'neither attire for her person or head nor a bed nor furniture of her chamber'.[46] She was to remain a prisoner for the next eight years.


No news of the fate of his family and friends had time to reach Bruce when he arrived at Dunaverty: only the unwelcome information from Angus Macdonald that Sir John de Botetourt and Sir John Menteith, with powerful English forces, were on their way to besiege the castle.[47] To be cornered in a castle, however strong, on which all his enemies could converge by land and sea was a situation he had, at all costs, to avoid. He needed time, secrecy and mobility in order to gather together the men and ships for the renewal of his struggle. So, after three days' respite, he slipped away by boat across thirteen miles of turbulent sea to the Isle of Rathlin off the north coast of Ireland.[48]

Only six months had passed since he had been crowned King of Scots and now his kingdom had shrunk to a little island six-and-a-half miles long and one-and-a-half miles wide. Against him was arrayed the might and wealth of England supported by some of the most powerful nobles of Scotland. But he had a toughness and determination so strong that he was inspired to undertake one of the most colossal gambles in history.

His one immediate advantage was the support of Angus Macdonald of the Isles, whose fleet of galleys dominated the western seas and gave him the freedom of manoeuvre to seek men and money for his cause. Agents were landed secretly in his earldom of Carrick to collect his Martinmas rents;[49] his younger brothers were instructed to move into Northern Ireland to raise recruits from his estates in Antrim and those of James Stewart in Londonderry, and Bruce himself set sail for Garmoran in the Western Highlands where his sister-in-law by marriage, Christiana of the Isles, held sovereign sway.

Christiana was the widow of Duncan of Mar, brother of Bruce's first wife Isabella and brother-in-law of Bruce's sister Christina. As sole heiress of Alan Macruarie of Garmoran, she became, on his death, mistress of the lands of Arisaig, Moidart and Knoydart and of the islands of Uist, Barra, Rum, Eigg and Gigha.

Throughout the islands and highlands of Western Scotland, the King's writ hardly ran. They were ruled by semi-independent chieftains whose support of Plantagenet, Comyn or Bruce was motivated rather by family relationships and clan quarrels than by the dictates of a central authority.

Robert Bruce throughout his life was attractive to women, and when he came to Christiana to seek her help kinship and inclination alike caused her to place her resources at his disposal. During the winter months, with her support, he toured her islands and her lands[50] and those of her immediate neighbour, MacKenzie of Kintail,[51] and still further north to the borders of Sutherland, with such effect that by January he had returned to Rathlin with a fleet of galleys and many men.

By then the English had discovered that he was no longer, as they had thought, in the besieged castle of Dunaverty, and on 29 January 1307 King Edward sent out orders for a fleet to seek him in the islands.[52] But the orders were too late. Bruce had already left Rathlin to carry out a two-pronged attack on the mainland.

Some time during these months Sir Robert Boyd, who had been captured at Kildrummy with Nigel Bruce,[53] had escaped his guards and found his way to Bruce. He brought him news of the flight of the Queen and her ladies north and of the fall of Kildrummy, but of their subsequent fate he knew nothing.

Now with Sir James Douglas he was sent ahead with a small raiding party to the Isle of Arran. Rowing close inshore along the eastern side of Kintyre peninsula until nightfall, they crossed unperceived to Brodrick Bay below the governor of Arran's castle. There, hiding their galley and tackle close under the cliffs, they lay in wait until the morning.

It happened that the evening before, near to their place of concealment, the underwarden of the castle had arrived with three boats from the mainland, loaded with provisions, clothing and arms and beached them on the shore. At first light thirty or more English began to unload the boats for transit to the castle. At a signal from Douglas, his men fell upon them and killed them all.

When those in the castle heard the uproar below they hastily armed themselves and ran to their comrades' rescue but Douglas, rallying his men, turned on them so savagely that the governor and most of his followers were killed before they could regain the safety of the castle. Douglas and his company now gathered up the arms and provisions and established themselves in a fortified camp at the head of Glen Coy to keep an eye on the castle and await the coming of their King.[54]

Ten days later, Robert Bruce with thirty-three small galleys made landfall at Drumadoon Bay on the west of Arran and reunited his forces preparatory to making a landing on the coast of Ayrshire. Ahead he sent by night a native of Carrick, called Cuthbert, to spy out the land and, if he found the people were willing to rise, to light a fire at Turnberry point on a day agreed between them.[55]

Meanwhile Bruce's two younger brothers, Thomas and Alexander, accompanied by Sir Reginald Crawfurd and Malcolm McQuillan, an Irish chieftain, with several hundred recruits raised from Northern Ireland, set sail in eighteen ships for Galloway to drive inland and threaten the English lines of communication between Carlisle and Ayr and so facilitate the invasion by Bruce to the north. But their plans went badly wrong. On 9 February 1307, as their galleys entered Loch Ryan and tied up in the harbour or beached upon the shore, they were ambushed as they landed by the Macdowalls of Galloway who were allied to King Edward. Some were killed in the woods beyond the shore, some on the shore, many were drowned in the sea. All the rest, except a few who escaped in two galleys that were still seaborne, were captured. Malcolm McQuillan was beheaded on the spot. Thomas and Alexander Bruce and Sir Reginald Crawfurd, who had all been severely wounded, were taken alive to Carlisle and there by the order of King Edward were hanged, drawn and beheaded and their heads placed on spikes above the gates of the town.[56]

At the time of his brothers' expedition, Bruce was waiting in Arran for the signal from his messenger. On the appointed day, about noon, a light was seen from the expected direction. Orders were given for the embarkation of his men, and a little before evening they put to sea and steered towards the fire which shone more brightly as the darkness fell. When eventually the galleys grounded upon the shingle of the further shore, a distracted Cuthbert emerged from the shadows to tell the King that someone else had lit the fire. He had hidden nearby to give warning that Turnberry Castle above them was garrisoned by Henry Percy and a hundred men. Two hundred more were quartered outside, and the English were so thick upon the ground throughout Carrick and so vicious in reprisals that no one dared rise against them.

When Bruce heard this he turned to consult with his companions. To seek to penetrate a hostile country with his tiny force would seem to be an act of unparalleled rashness. But his brother Edward expressed the feeling of them all when he exclaimed, 'No peril shall drive me back to sea. Here I will take my chances, good or bad.' Bruce replied that, if they were all agreed, their best chance of survival was to attack the troops in the village while they were sleeping unaware of the presence of an enemy.

Noiselessly they surrounded the cantonments and at a given signal fell upon the unsuspecting English with such success that all were killed except a single man who escaped to the castle.

In the castle Henry Percy heard the uproar from the fighting outside and called his men to arms but, uncertain in the darkness of the number of the attackers, dared not attempt a rescue. He shut himself up within the walls leaving a rich harvest of booty to the invaders, including his warhorses and his household plate. For three days Bruce remained on the outskirts of the castle and then, dividing the plunder among his Highlanders, disappeared with them into the mountains of Carrick.[57]

Hidden in the glens of the wild hill country he had known so well as a boy, Bruce took stock of his position. He had been brought up in the chivalric mode of combat. War was a sharpened extension of those tournaments in which he had so often excelled. The mailed warrior on his mighty horse thundered against an opponent distinguished only by the escutcheon on his surcoat, and though numbers counted so also did the skill in arms of each individual and a smaller force might overcome a larger if the combatants had more champions among their number. On this premise he had challenged the Earl of Pembroke outside Perth. Now, apart from his immediate companions – his brother Edward, James Douglas, Gilbert de la Haye, Robert Boyd, Neil Campbell and the Earl of Lennox – he had no accoutred knights among his following. He had little money, few chargers, no shock troops, nor could he forsee the time when he could match the long purses, the heavy cavalry and the siege machinery of the English forces. His men were cat-footed Highlanders, swift in movement, apt in concealment, artful in stalking, silent in execution. The whole mould of his military upbringing must be recast and adapted to different skills and different circumstances.

It is a measure of his genius that in his shifting headquarters in the heather he evolved a strategy from which he never willingly departed throughout his life. From now on he taught his nation the virtue of guerrilla warfare. The forest ambush, the sudden raid, the night attack, the scorched earth, the dismantling of fortresses, these were to become the hallmarks of his campaigns.* Meanwhile his immediate problem was to survive in a region where the inhabitants, whatever their instinctive sympathies, were too fearful of the omnipresent English to give him aid.

* cf note V

# 9

As soon as King Edward heard of Bruce's return to the mainland, he poured troops into Galloway and Ayrshire under the overall command of the Earl of Pembroke. Two thousand men were mustered at Carlisle to be under his immediate call. Sir Dugald Macdowall, whose forces had destroyed the invaders at Loch Ryan, moved up from Wigtownshire to the southwest border of Carrick. Sir Robert Clifford was stationed at the key fords of the River Cree to the South. Sir John de Botetourt patrolled to the east along the valley of the Nith, and from the north John of Lorne came hurrying down with his Macdougall clansmen to the town of Ayr to reinforce Sir Ingram de Umfraville, one-time Scottish guardian, and Sir John Menteith, the betrayer of Wallace.[1]

The successful night attack by Bruce against the cantonments at Turnberry must have been magnified by rumour, for he appears to have been credited with a much greater force than he had at his disposal. Henry Percy remained firmly shut up within his fortress until he was relieved by a thousand men from the Carlisle base,[2] and the Earl of Pembroke hesitated to tighten the noose of the different forces he had around Bruce's retreat in the hope that the Scottish King might be provoked into an engagement on ground more favourable to the English than the wild and mountainous country to which he had retired.

But Bruce remained in the high ground, stalking and attacking small parties of the enemy whenever he could, but moving his headquarters from day to day so no one knew where he would strike next. In this he was helped by people of the country who gave him news of the English movements. Among them was a kinsman who brought him trustworthy information but, being taken before Sir Ingram, he agreed to betray Bruce in return for forty pounds' worth of land to be settled upon himself and his heirs.

He knew it was Bruce's custom to retire each morning into a covert out of sight of his men for his private purposes, accompanied only by a page. He and his two sons decided to surprise him as he was about his business. However, Bruce had become intimate with one of the women of the country who had warned him of his kinsman's treachery. When he saw the three approaching, he said to his page, as Barbour relates:

'What weapon do you have, for I fear that these men wish to kill us?'

'I have but a bow and arrow.'

'Then give them to me quickly and stand far back, for if I win you shall have weapons enough, but if I die make haste away.'

As the three men approached, the father with a sword in his hand, one son with a sword and an axe and one with a sword and a spear, Bruce called on them to halt but they still advanced saying that they had come to help him with fresh news of the English. Bruce raised his bow and when they did not stop let fly an arrow that pierced the father through the eye with such force that he fell backward. When the elder son saw his father fall he sprang at Bruce with his axe but Bruce, who wherever he went carried his great sword hanging from his neck, had it ready drawn and cut him down with a single blow. He then turned on the younger son who was running at him with a spear, sliced off its point and dispatched him before he could draw his sword.

The little page, who had been watching the fight from afar, came running joyfully to his master. Bruce said, as he wiped his sword, 'These were good fighting men until they were ruined by their treachery.'[3]

As the days passed and Bruce continued to elude capture, fugitives from the vengeance of King Edward began to find their way to the Carrick hills in twos and threes and little groups, and on one memorable day, threading her way through his surrounding enemies, came his one time mistress, Christian of Carrick*, bringing with her fifteen of her mounted tenants to be put at his service and the promise of money and supplies.[4]

From her he heard for the first time the terrible fate that had

* cf note VI

overtaken his family and his friends: how his wife and sisters and daughter and their attendant ladies were the prisoners of the English King, some put in cages, some in solitary confinement; how the expedition of his two brothers, Thomas and Alexander, had failed and how they had been hanged, drawn and beheaded; how his youngest brother, Nigel, his brother-in-law, Sir Christopher Seton, the Earl of Atholl and many more had undergone the same barbarous punishment.

When he had arranged an escort to take Christian back to her estate, legend has it that Bruce retired to the cave in which he slept and, throwing himself upon his bed of heather, gave way to such grief at the troubles he had brought upon his family and the hopelessness of his prospects that he considered giving up the struggle for Scotland and sailing to the Holy Land with his faithful companions to fight against the Saracens.

But as he lay in perplexity, his eye was caught by a spider hanging from the ceiling on the slender thread spun from its body. With its agitated movements it was trying to swing the thread from side to side until it could create such impetus that it would reach the wall and there affix the end to form the basis of its web. Six times it swung its pendulum but fell short of its objective: but on the seventh it had achieved such momentum that it reached the wall and there made fast its thread.

And when Bruce saw that a little insect, after so many failures, could persevere to success, he vowed that the King of Scots could do no less.[5]

At that time Bruce had some sixty in his company and had posted sentinels around the camp. A little before nightfall one of these came to him and reported a force of the Macdowalls of Galloway, two hundred strong, coming up the valley with bloodhounds nosing the trail. Quietly in the darkness, Bruce moved his men out of the camp across a deep and rushing river nearby and concealed them among the reeds of a swamp. Bidding them lie still he returned with Gilbert de la Haye to the ford by which they had crossed. The ford and the path leading up the steep bank to where they stood were so narrow that two men could not march abreast. By and by Bruce heard the baying of a hound.

He did not know yet whether this was a casual patrol which would pass by on the other side or whether they were on his track. But as the moon came out of the clouds and shone brightly on the scene, he was able to discern clearly a troop of mounted men gathering on the far bank of the river. At this he sent back Gilbert de la Haye to bring up his men while he himself took up his position at the head of the narrow path. The men of Galloway, seeing one solitary figure on the opposite side, plunged into the river but were quickly brought into single file by the narrowness of the ford. As the first horseman came out of the swirling water he was transfixed from above by Bruce's lance, so Barbour tells us, and fell to the ground with his horse beneath him, which was instantly stabbed by Bruce and lay across the ford. As those following piled up behind the barrier, Bruce descended to the river's edge and with his long two-handed sword mowed down in sweeping circles those who tried to climb over the carcass. Gradually the Macdowalls began to hold back and when Gilbert de la Haye, with Bruce's men, appeared over the brow they turned and fled into the woods.[6]

Heartened by the defeat of the Macdowalls, the little band received fresh encouragement from James Douglas, who soon after rejoined them from his foray into Douglasdale. A few weeks earlier he had asked permission from Bruce to spy out the land about his hereditary castle which had been handed over by King Edward to Sir Robert Clifford. Travelling in disguise with two attendants, he made his way to the house of Thomas Dickson, a leading yeoman in the neighbourhood, who had been a loyal servant of Douglas in his youth and of his father before him. When Douglas had made his presence known, Dickson welcomed him into his house and there concealed him, and each night brought to him secretly his foremost vassals until a group of determined men were joined together for an enterprise against the English. It was agreed that on Palm Sunday, when the garrison of the castle marched to the nearby church carrying their palms, some of Douglas's supporters should enter the church along with them with arms concealed, and others assemble in disguise outside.

On the appointed day the English, who believed themselves far from danger, suddenly heard the cry 'Douglas, Douglas', and were overwhelmed within and without the church and were made prisoners or slain. Moving quickly from the church to the castle, Douglas and his men found the entrance open and no one within except the porter and the cook and tables prepared for dinner and meat simmering in the oven. Douglas closed the gates of the castle and with his followers ate the meat intended for others, and when they were satisfied they packed up as much of the armour and weapons, the silver and clothing as they could carry away. But all the stores of malt and corn were heaped in the cellar, the wine casks were staved and the prisoners were beheaded and cast upon the pile. The well was fouled with dead horses and salt and the whole castle set ablaze.

The gruesome bonfire was said to be Douglas's memorial to the faithful Thomas Dickson who had been killed at the first onslaught in the church: but throughout the countryside it was known as Douglas's larder.[7]

When King Edward heard of the despoiling of Castle Douglas and the discomfiture of the Macdowalls he rose from his sick bed at Lanercost Abbey and sent to the Earl of Pembroke a letter of outraged surprise that he had failed to capture Bruce.[8] The earl took counsel with John of Lorne and it was agreed that Pembroke should make a martial parade with his mailed knights along the main route to Cumnock through the mountains where Bruce was lurking, and while Bruce's attention was taken by this cavalcade John of Lorne with his Highlanders should creep through the woods from the opposite direction and fall upon him unawares.

Bruce indeed was on the high ground when Pembroke and his knights rode by in battle array below, and was considering how to attack them by surprise when he himself was surprised by warning from a messenger that the men of Lorne were close to his rear. Quickly dividing his men into three groups under his brother Edward, James Douglas and himself, he ordered them to retreat in different directions to confuse the enemy and to reassemble later at an appointed place.

But John of Lorne had got possession of a bloodhound which had formerly belonged to Bruce and which he had been told so loved his master, who used to feed it with his own hands, that once it was upon his scent it would turn aside for nothing. When it was brought to the spot from which Bruce and his companions had left, it set its nose to one trail only, so that Lorne, ignoring the other two parties, directed all his men after that commanded by the King. Seeing that his party alone was being followed, Bruce ordered his men to scatter in the hope that the enemy would lose trace of him. But the hound, coming to the point of their dispersal, after casting from side to side once more got on the line of Bruce and the foster brother who was with him.

Then John of Lorne chose five of his men to run fast ahead and overtake the fugitives. Bruce saw them coming in the distance and turned to meet them. As his chronicler John Barbour narrates:

> Soon the five came in the greatest haste with clamour and menace. Three of them went at the King, and the other two, sword in hand, made at his man. The king met the three and dealt such a blow at the first that he sheared through ear and cheek and neck to the shoulder. The man sank down dizzily and the two, seeing their fellow's sudden fall, were affrighted and started back a little. With that the King glanced aside and saw the other two making a sturdy attack against his man. He left his own two and leapt at the other two and smote off the head of one of them. Then he went to meet his own assailants who were coming at him right boldly. He met the first so sharply that with the edge of his sword he hewed the arm from the body . . . So fairly it fell out that the King, though he had a struggle and difficulty, killed four of his foes. Soon after his foster-brother ended the days of the fifth.

Bruce and his foster brother were now very weary and drenched with sweat but dared not rest for behind them they heard the hound. At length they came to a wood through which ran a small stream, and after wading along this a great way they climbed out on the further bank and went deep into the wood before they thought it safe to rest.

When the hound reached the stream it wavered to and fro but could not pick up the scent, so that at last John of Lorne decided that it was useless to proceed and returned with his men to join the Earl of Pembroke.

After Bruce and his foster brother had rested, Barbour relates, they walked on in search of a dwelling from which to obtain food. As they were crossing an upland moor they met with three rough-looking men, one of whom was carrying a dead sheep across his shoulders. They greeted Bruce and he in turn asked where they were bound. They replied that they were seeking Robert Bruce for they wished to serve him. Bruce answered then that if they would accompany him he would guide them there. At this the men looked at each other in such a way that Bruce guessed that they had recognized him and were hoping to obtain the reward offered for his death.

'Good friends,' he said, 'as we are not well acquainted, do you go before us and we will follow behind.'

One of them replied, 'There is no reason to think any harm of us.'

'Nor do I,' said Bruce, 'but this I desire until we are better known to each other.'

In that order they continued until they came to a deserted farm house. Here the men proposed that they should stop and roast the sheep, to which Bruce agreed on condition that two fires were kindled, one for himself and his foster brother at one end of the house and one for them at the other. When the sheep had been roasted a half was passed to Bruce and his attendant. Bruce had travelled and fasted long, and when he had eaten he felt such an irresistible desire to sleep that he asked his foster brother if he could keep watch. 'Yes,' he replied, 'while I can hold out.'

Bruce drowsed for a little with drawn sword beside him, sleeping as Barbour writes, 'like the bird on the bough' but from time to time glancing up for he mistrusted the men. Before long, his foster brother, who was as weary as his master, fell into a deep sleep and began to snore loudly. At this signal the three men, drawing their swords, came to kill them. But Bruce, starting awake, leaped to his feet and kicked his foster brother to rouse him. His foster brother rose but so bemused by sleep that he was too late to parry the blow that slew him. Bruce was now alone, one man against three, but his chain mail and his skill in arms were such that he was able to beat off the attack and dispose of his would-be assassins one after the other.

Sad at the loss of his kinsman, he set out alone for the house by Loch Dee where he had agreed to meet his divided forces. When he reached it late at night, he entered and found the housewife sitting by the fire. He told her that he was a traveller passing through the country, to which she replied that all travellers were welcome for the sake of one. He asked who that one might be.

'Our good King Robert the Bruce,' she answered, 'who is the rightful lord of this country.'

Then he said, 'I am that man.'

'But where are your men?' she asked.

'At the moment I have none.'

'This must not be,' she cried, 'for though I am a widow I have three stout sons each by a different husband, Murdoch, McKie and MacLurg, and they shall become your sworn men.'

She gave him food and shelter and the next morning fetched her three sons to do him obeisance, and he, to try their metal and put them at their ease, set a test for their skill with bow and arrow. Murdoch, the eldest, shot at a pair of perching ravens and pierced them both with the same arrow. McKie shot at a raven circling overhead and brought it down, but MacLurg missed his mark.

Some years afterwards, when he was in a position to do so, Bruce asked the widow how he could repay her kindness. She asked for a small holding by the Cree estuary, but Bruce enlarged her request by granting her land some five miles long by three miles wide which was divided between the three sons, Murdoch of Cumloden, McKie of Larg and MacLurg of Kirroughtrie. On the coat of arms of Murdoch and McKie are displayed the ravens transfixed by an arrow and the place where the ravens were shot is still known as Craigencaillie – the Crag of the Old Woman.[9]

As Bruce and mother and sons were sitting at their midday meal, there was a trampling of horses round the house. The four men sprang up and seized their arms and the widow called upon her sons to fight for the King to their death; but the voices of Edward Bruce and James Douglas were heard outside and Bruce went out to welcome them.[10]

Edward and Douglas had brought with them a body of mounted men. In spite of the fatigues and hazards of the previous day, Bruce was impatient to make use of them. He asked where the enemy were encamped and when Douglas told him that as he came over the hill to the rendezvous he saw in a village below some two hundred English a mile or more distant from the main host, he decided on a surprise attack. Guided by James Douglas, Bruce, his brother and the little body of horsemen rode through the night and quietly stationed themselves around the village where the English were quartered, and when dawn broke fell upon them as they slept so that most were cut to pieces and the rest ran naked to the main army. While the alarm was sounding there and the soldiers moving to their posts, Bruce and his men slipped away into the concealing hills.[11]

The problem of commissariat was now affecting both parties. Pembroke decided to return to his base at Carlisle with his main force but leave spies and patrols to check Bruce's movements so that when an opportunity arose he could dispatch a powerful raiding party to surprise him. Bruce, whose growing body of outlaws and dispossessed men were living off the land, moved south deep into Galloway where game was plentiful and as yet untouched. Making his headquarters in Glen Trool, he spread out with his men in search of venison for the deer were then in season.[12]

When Pembroke learned of their hiding place he carried out his plan to come upon them unawares. With a picked body of 1500 knights, he left Carlisle early in April and made a forced march, riding through the night but remaining in cover during the day with such effect that, moving up Creeside, he reached a wood within striking distance of Bruce's quarters without being observed.[13]

At the head of Glen Trool, Loch Trool lies like a sapphire brooch beneath the shadow of Mount Merrick. Beyond it, he could see Bruce's encampment in a rocky valley embraced by bare mountains. Deciding that the ground was so broken by boulders that his knights would be unable to carry out a cavalry attack, he ordered his troops to steal under cover to the wood nearest Bruce's camp and make ready to capture him by a surprise charge over the intervening stretch of open ground.

In the meantime, he sent forward a poorly dressed woman as a spy to enter the enemy's camp on the pretext of seeking food, and ascertain their numbers and state of preparation. She found Bruce unarmed and at ease, but when she was brought before him her nerve failed and she told him of the nearby presence of the English.[14]

Hastily he armed and summoned his 300 men. They had hardly formed up when the English broke out of the nearby wood. Bruce, seizing a bow and arrow from an archer by his side, let loose the shaft at the enemy leader, transfixing him through the throat. His followers, already aghast at finding the Scots armed and waiting for them instead of unaware in their camp, came to an abrupt halt. Bruce, snatching his banner from the standard bearer, cried out, 'Upon them now!' and his whole force rushed forward. The English fled back into the wood and continued their flight as fast as they could. Only a few were killed before they reached cover but their expedition was ruined.[15]

So shameful was this defeat that the English leaders quarrelled among themselves and Pembroke retired in disgust to Carlisle.[16]

The news that Bruce with 300 ragged men had put to flight 1500 English knights spread from mouth to mouth and transformed the attitudes of many who had hitherto remained quiescent. As the *Lanercost Chronicle* gloomily records: 'Despite the fearful vengeance inflicted upon the Scots who adhered to Bruce the number of those willing to strengthen him in his Kingship increased daily.'[17] Men of substance began to join his band and with this additional support Bruce felt strong enough to leave the shelter of the hills and descend into the plains of Ayrshire. Bypassing the town and castle of Ayr, which remained in English hands, he made his headquarters at Galston and brought the major part of Kyle and Cunninghame under his control. Sir Philip Mowbray, who tried to intercept him with a force of 1000 men marching from Bothwell, was ambushed by James Douglas and barely escaped with his life, and this success further encouraged volunteers to flock to the standard of the Scottish King.[18]

Once more Pembroke, urged on as ever by King Edward from his sick bed at Lanercost, gathered his troops together and making the town of Ayr his base advanced early in May against the encampment of Bruce at Galston. Some miles to the east of Galston rises a conical upthrust of rock known as Loudoun Hill which dominates the countryside. To this Bruce withdrew on news of the enemy's approach. Below it the highway then ran along a broad strip of hard ground about 500 yards in width, flanked on either side by deep morasses impassable to cavalry.

Realizing that the span of the causeway was too great for the 600 men at his disposal to make a stand in depth without danger of being outflanked, Bruce had three wide trenches cut in parallel lines from the morasses to the road to lessen the space he had to defend.

Early on the morning of 10 May, as the sun was rising, Bruce could see from his post on Loudon Hill the English army, 3000 strong, advancing in the distance, 'their first squadron coming', as his expressive chronicler John Barbour relates,

> well arrayed in close order and at its back, a little way off, the second following it. Their basnets were all burnished bright and flamed in the rays of the sun and their shields, spears and pennons lighted up all the field. Their bright embroidered banners and horses caparisoned in many hues and many-coloured coat armour and hauberks white as flour made them glitter like angels of the kingdom of heaven.[19]

When Bruce saw them he descended the hill with his men and stationed them across the narrowed front with their long spears forming a barrier of steel.

Pembroke sounded his trumpet for the first squadron to charge but as they neared the Scotsmen at full gallop suddenly they saw the first ditch and, bunching together to avoid it, their line was thrown into confusion and reached the Scottish spears in such disorder that they were shattered at the first impact. More than a hundred were unhorsed or slain and the rest, reeling back, became entangled with the oncoming second squadron. The Scottish ranks, moving steadily forward with their long spears advanced, turned the chaos into rout and Pembroke, with almost all his army still intact, fled incontinently with them to the castle of Bothwell.[20] The Earl of Gloucester, who with a relieving force was attacked by Bruce three days later, put up a sterner struggle, but after severe casualties he retreated to the security of Ayr Castle.[21]

# 10

The cumulative effect first of Bruce's survival against the odds and then of his subsequent successes was having a profound influence throughout the country. By 16 May 1307 a Scottish lord on the English side was writing to a high official in London:

> Sir Robert de Brus never had the goodwill of his own followers or of the people at large or even half of them so much with him as now; and it now for the first time appears that he has the right and that God is openly for him, for he has destroyed all King Edward's power both among the English and the Scots and the English force is in retreat to its own country not to return. And the people firmly believe by the encouragement of false preachers who come from his army that Sir Robert de Brus will now have his will. These preachers are such as have been charged before the justices as advocates of war and are at present freed on bail and carry themselves worse than before, boasting in their malice and deceiving the people by their false preachings . . . For they have told them that they have found a prophecy of Merlin that after the death of 'Le Roi Coveytous' the Scottish people and the Welsh shall band together and have the sovereign power and live together in peace until the end of the world.[1]

This prophecy was soon to be put to the test.

The angry astonishment with which King Edward heard, time after time, that his commanders had failed to capture the elusive Bruce determined him to carry out the task himself. Summonses were sent to all the leading men in England who owed him feudal service to assemble at Carlisle on 8 July together with the Welsh levies. By sheer willpower he persuaded himself that his illness had abated, made a thanks offering in the cathedral of the litter in which he had hitherto been carried, and mounting his horse prepared to place himself at the head of his troops. But the effort was too great. After covering only six miles in four days, he reached the little village of Burgh-on-Sands a few miles north of Carlisle and there, on 11 July, expired.[2]

His last request to his son was that his heart should be conveyed to Jerusalem but that his bones should be separated from his flesh and borne in an urn at the head of his army into Scotland and remain unburied until that obdurate country had been totally subdued.[3]

But ancestor worship was never a characteristic of the Plantagenets and the first actions of Edward II were to dispose of his father's corpse, bones and all, at Waltham Abbey to await a royal burial later, and to recall from banishment his profligate minion, Piers Gaveston, whom that same father had recently exiled. Having carried out these two agreeable tasks, he returned to the army assembled at Carlisle and marched it in leisurely fashion to Cumnock on the borders of Ayrshire. There he remained until 28 August and then, for want of provisions, withdrew it to England without striking a blow.[4] Three years were to pass before he again took the field in person against the Scots.

The Earl of Pembroke was left as Viceroy of Scotland but remained inactive, contenting himself with holding the line of Clydesdale to contain Bruce in the southwest. Early in October he was superseded by the Earl of Richmond.*

The withdrawal of the English forces gave a breathing space to Bruce in which to consider his plans for the future. Hitherto he had been defending himself against two separate enemies united for his destruction: the English and the Scottish nobles of the Comyn faction. Now that King Edward I was dead, the rabid hostility which had concentrated all the energies of England on one objective, the annihilation of Bruce, would no longer operate. Edward II had more pressing matters to deal with at home, and without his impulsion the garrisons in the English-held castles would be more concerned with securing the safety of their own bailiwicks than sallying forth in search of foes.

This allowed Bruce a greater freedom of movement to deal with his other opponents in Scotland. In broad terms these were the Macdowalls of Galloway, the Macdougalls of Lorne, the Earl of Ross and the numerous Comyn supporters under the Earl of Buchan in the rich

* cf note VII

lowlands of the northeast. Even so the undertaking was formidable. Bruce was, in effect, still only the leader of guerrilla bands who depended for their provisions on what they could obtain from the land, for their pay on the loot they could extract from their enemies, and for their very existence on their devotion to their leader personally and to the cause of Scottish freedom.

In the campaigns that follow, Bruce's skill in timing and diplomacy, his daring and determination in combat, mark him not merely as a formidable warrior but as a master of strategic warfare.

His primary objective, as he unerringly grasped, must be the destruction of the Comyns in their own heartlands before the English King could once more turn his attention to Scotland. They were the head and main front of the opposition to his kingship. His lesser foes must be briefly savaged or overawed until this end had been achieved, and for that achievement much depended on the success of the Bishop of Moray in the north.

In accordance with the plans which he had agreed with Bruce at Aberdeen the previous year, the bishop had returned from the Orkneys to the Mounth at about the same time as Bruce was preparing to land in the southwest. There he launched a fiery crusade throughout his bishopric to such effect that the men of Moray began to take down their weapons from the walls of their dwellings, to join in small groups and then in greater groups until the whole area hummed with menace like a hive of bees about to burst out in a swarm at the signal of their sovereign. Sir Reginald Cheyne and other pro-English sheriffs in the region were soon aware of this undercurrent of revolt, and by May were openly declaring

> that if Bruce can get away in this direction or towards the parts of Ross he will find the people all ready at his will more entirely than ever before unless King Edward will send more troops. For there are many who stay loyal to his crown only so long as the English are in power for otherwise, they say, they must come to terms with their enemies.[5]

But it was not until after the death of Edward I and the retreat of Edward II that Bruce was in a position to take advantage of this potential support. When that opportunity arose his first action was to shatter the Macdowalls of Galloway, partly because their lands were nearest and plentiful in cattle, but also to wreak vengeance on Dugald Macdowall who had caused the murder of Bruce's two brothers. With fire and sword he swept through the province so furiously that many peasants fled from their homes and with their livestock found refuge across the border in the Cumbrian forest of Inglewood, while those who remained were given the choice of paying tribute or death.[6]

Leaving the Macdowalls to lick their wounds and Sir James Douglas to remain in command in the southwest, Bruce broke through the English line on the Clyde at the propitious moment when Pembroke was handing over his office to the indecisive Earl of Richmond.[7] Then, marching north through the western Highlands, gathering support as he went, he confronted the Macdougalls of Lorne by land while Angus Macdonald of the Isles, with his fleet of galleys keeping pace through the waters of the Firth of Lorne and Loch Linnhe, threatened· them by sea. Bruce had no time to waste on a minor campaign, so offered to John of Lorne a temporary truce which he accepted for, as he wrote dolefully to Edward II, 'Robert Bruce approached these parts by land and sea with 10,000 men they say or 15,000. I have no more than 800 men . . . The barons of Argyll give me no aid. Yet Bruce asked for a truce which I granted him for a short space and I have got a similar truce until you send me aid.'[8] Either a scribe added an extra nought or John of Lorne was grossly exaggerating the number of Bruce's men. Less than a year later at the important battle of Inverurie Bruce had only 700 men.

Having immobilized the Macdougalls of Lorne, Bruce swept up the Great Glen capturing the Comyn castle of Inverlochy at its foot and Castle Urquhart on the shores of Loch Ness and at last joined hands with the Bishop of Moray.

Reinforced by the bishop's supporters, he seized Inverness Castle, burned Nairn, and after razing all the captured castles to the ground turned in October 1307 to face the Earl of Ross.[9]

The Earl of Ross had been responsible for the capture of Bruce's Queen and his womenfolk, and it would have been understandable if Bruce had sought to ravage his earldom in revenge. But Bruce was King of Scotland and far-sighted enough to subjugate his personal grievance to the future interests of his kingdom. The Earl of Ross was guardian of the young Earl of Sutherland and thus virtual lord of all the north of Scotland from the Moray Firth to Cape Wrath. It was better to win him as a friend than leave a yawning gap in the maintenance of the realm. So Bruce offered him a truce to run until June 1308. For Bruce this left his hands free to deal with the Comyns without danger to his rear, for the Earl of Ross a chance to delay a final decision until he could see how matters would evolve. He accepted the truce, but being a cautious man excused himself to Edward II as follows:

> We heard of the coming of Sir Robert Bruce towards the parts of Ross with great power, so that we had no power against him but nevertheless we caused our men to be called up and we were stationed for a fortnight with three thousand men, at our own expense, on the borders of our earldom and in two other earldoms Sutherland and Caithness and Bruce would have destroyed them utterly if we had not made a truce with him at the entreaty of good men, both clergy and others until next June. May help come from you, our Lord, if it please you, for in you, Sire, is all our hope and trust. And know, dear Lord, that we would on no account have made a truce with him if the warden of Moray had not been absent from the country and the men of his province would not answer to us without his orders, for the purpose of attacking our enemies, so that we have no help save from our own men. Wherefore, dear Lord, remember us and tell us what is your will on these matters of which we have given an account.[10]

So far Bruce's plan of campaign had been a brilliant success. The Macdougalls of Lorne and the men of Ross had, for the time being, been eliminated as a fighting force without a blow being struck. Now Bruce could concentrate his whole strength against the nerve centre of Comyn power: and in his whole strength he could count among his shock troops not only his old comrades – his brother Edward, the Earl of Lennox, Gilbert de la Haye and Robert Boyd – but Sir William Wiseman, Sir David Barclay and other knights of Moray, so that he had a force at his disposal of 700 picked men.

Apprised of Bruce's approach, Comyn, Earl of Buchan, whose great domain stretched over the level lands from Aberdeen along the coast to the Moray Firth, mustered his forces and prepared to oppose him.

Bruce had advanced as far as Inverurie, the chief town of his hereditary estate of Garioch, when he was seized with a violent sickness which drained him of his strength. Fearful of being attacked in the open plain while their leader lay out of action, Bruce's men under his brother Edward carried him in a litter to a strong defensive position of wood and bog at Slioch, 16 miles to the northwest, and there on Christmas day, while the snow lay thick on the ground, the Earl of Buchan caught up with them. For three days there was a running fight and then the earl withdrew to wait for reinforcements.

Bruce's men were in a precarious position for their provisions had given out. Edward Bruce thereupon took the bold decision – and throughout his life he was bold to the point of foolhardiness – to march out in battle array in full sight of the enemy with the sick King in his litter in their midst, and retire in close order to the mountains of Strathbogie where the lord of that area, Sir Lawrence, was a staunch adherent of their cause. So formidable was their attitude that the Earl of Buchan, who was none too sure of the loyalty of his followers, let them depart unscathed.[11]

Slowly Bruce regained his strength and, as the onset of winter began to freeze the mountains, his army descended once more to Inverurie for the milder climate and better provender of the plains.

In the meantime, the Earl of Buchan had received reinforcements from Sir David Brechin and his men from Angus and an English contingent under Sir John Mowbray, and by late January had assembled 1000 men at Old Meldrum.

From there Sir David Brechin made a reconnaissance in strength and, surprising Bruce's outposts, slew some and sent the rest flying back to their main army at the far side of Inverurie. When the news was brought to Bruce he rose from his sick-bed and called for his horse, saying to his servants who remonstrated with him on account of his weakness, 'Their arrogance has made me sound. Therefore, as the Lord wills, I shall either destroy them or they me.'[12]

At the head of his army, animated by the sight of their King on horseback supported by a man on each side,[13] Bruce advanced steadily against the enemy cavalry. These, when they saw so unexpectedly the mounted figure of Bruce with his banners waving, began to back their horses for they knew his reputation as a warrior: and when the foot soldiers and archers saw them falter they turned and fled, and the cavalry seeing them flee turned also in panic and never drew rein until they reached the English-held castle of Fyvie, 12 miles to the north. The King, exhausted by his effort, handed over the pursuit to his brother Edward. The Earl of Buchan and Sir John Mowbray with their men, after a brief respite at Fyvie, continued their flight towards the nearest seaport but were brought to bay by Edward at Old Deer and after a fierce encounter fled in all directions. Buchan and Mowbray escaped to England where Buchan died within the year. Sir David Brechin rode hotfoot to his own castle at Brechin and a few months later transferred his allegiance.[14]

The whole province of Buchan now lay wide open to Bruce and, while he was recovering his strength, he sent his brother Edward to ravage it from end to end so that never again would it become a threat to his throne. The Comyn men were slain, their farms burned, their livestock slaughtered. Not for two generations would the land recover and then only when it was colonized by Lowlanders loyal to the Scottish Crown, and for fifty years men talked of the Herschip (harrowing) of Buchan.[15]

Meanwhile the young James Douglas had been active in the southwest. Broad-shouldered and slim with a pale complexion and black hair, he had a warmth and thoughtfulness of disposition which attracted the love and loyalty of all who were near him. In company he was gentle and courteous, speaking with a slight lisp, but to his enemies the daring of his projects, the boldness of their execution, his sudden appearance in their midst when least expected smacked of the devil.[16] The 'Black Douglas' became, in the popular imagination, a figure of menacing ubiquity at whose mention stout men quailed and with whose name mothers frightened their unruly children into trembling obedience.

Hearing that Sir Robert Clifford had refurbished Castle Douglas and placed in command a seasoned warrior named Thirlwall, Douglas once more threaded his way secretly to Douglasdale and made contact with his local supporters. From them he learnt that whenever farmers moved their cattle within range of the castle, Thirlwall would sally forth with his garrison and seize the beasts. So a few nights later, Douglas hid the greater part of his men in a wood and the rest, disguised as countrymen, he sent forth in the early morning to drive cattle past the gates of the castle. When Thirlwall was informed of their passage by his sentries, he called his horsemen together and set out to plunder the drovers in such haste that his head was unhelmeted. But as he neared the drovers, a little past the wood where Douglas lay in ambush, he heard behind him the sudden cry of 'Douglas, Douglas', and turned to find himself cut off from the castle and outnumbered. Thirlwall and most of his party were slain but a few rode hellbent in time to warn the garrison to bar the gates and man the walls before Douglas could come up with them.[17]

Two governors of Castle Douglas had now been killed and Douglas let it be known that he would take revenge on anyone who dared to take possession of his ancestral home. In England and Scotland it became known as the perilous castle of Douglas and no candidates would come forward for the post.

But by the autumn of 1307 it had been assumed by a young knight called Sir John Webton. The reason for his action was contained in a letter that he carried upon his person in which the young lady whom he had been wooing unsuccessfully promised that if he defended Castle Douglas for a twelvemonth she would become his bride. Her tactful method of disposing of an unwelcome suitor proved successful. He was lured from the castle by a stratagem similar to that which Douglas had previously employed and was slain in the encounter. His garrison was overwhelmed and Douglas, at his leisure, was able, in accordance with Bruce's policy, to raze the castle to the ground.[18]

After this success many of the men of Douglas joined him, and with increased forces he drove eastwards and by the summer of 1308 had gained control of all Douglasdale, Upper Clydesdale and Selkirk forest as far as Jedburgh.[19] In July, just as he was about to move north to join Bruce for his next campaign, he captured Thomas Randolph, Bruce's nephew, near Peebles. Randolph had been taken prisoner by the English at Methven and since then had fought for his captors. When he was brought by Douglas before his royal uncle and reproached for his change of allegiance, he fiercely replied that the King made war like a brigand instead of fighting a pitched battle as a gentleman should.

Bruce had known Randolph as a boy and had recognized his exceptional military qualities. He therefore treated him with an ironic tolerance. Randolph was placed under the close constraint of his captor and within a very short time had so succumbed to the genial personality of his uncle that he humbly begged for pardon and in due course became, after Douglas, the most brilliant of Bruce's commanders.[20]

The campaign which Bruce was contemplating was against the Macdougalls of Lorne. Throughout the spring and summer of 1308 he had moved in the northeast from one success to another. The Comyn castles of Tarradale, Slains, Kinedar, Rattray, Dundarg and Kelly were captured and destroyed; Duffus and Belvenie were wrested from Sir Reginald Cheyne; Sir William Wiseman seized Skelbo Castle. The royal English castle of Elgin was overcome at the third attempt and the other royal castles of Fyvie, Kintore and Aboyne succumbed to their assailants. In July these activities were crowned by the revolt of the citizens of Aberdeen against the English and the surrender of its commanding fortress.[21] Now at last Bruce had a main seaport in his hands from which to re-establish trade with Flanders, the Hanseatic towns and the countries of Scandinavia. All eastern Scotland from the Moray Firth to the Tay had come to his allegiance except for Banff, Perth, Dundee and Forfar, and by the end of the year Forfar had fallen to the enterprise of an Angus man, Philip the Forester, who with others of his countrymen scaled the castle walls by night and put the defenders to the sword.[22]

By mid-August the truce with John of Lorne was due to expire and Bruce made his dispositions accordingly. James Douglas was summoned from Selkirk forest to join him, and Edward Bruce with his freebooters, fresh from their harrying of Buchan, were sent to Galloway to intimidate the Macdowalls, whose pugnacity was being revived by the approach of English reinforcements from Carlisle.

By the end of July Bruce began to march his army westward towards Argyll and by the third week of August was ready to launch his attack. To reach into the heartlands of the MacDougalls of Lorne he had to advance through the Pass of Brander, a narrow and hazardous track reduced to a few yards in width by the precipitous flank of Ben Cruachan on the right and on the left by a sheer drop into the waters of Loch Awe. At this ideal site for an ambush John of Lorne prepared to make his stand. Placing some of the 2000 men at his disposal to block the pass with a barrier, he concealed the more numerous part on the mountainside above while he himself, at that time a sick man, lay in one of his galleys on Loch Awe below.

But Bruce was too experienced in guerrilla warfare to be caught in such a trap. Warned by a scout of John of Lorne's dispositions, he sent James Douglas with a party of light-armed archers to climb by a circuitous route unperceived to a place high on the mountainside above the ambush. When he had received a message that Douglas was in position, he moved with his armoured knights into the mouth of the pass against those who held it and at the same time sent his Highlanders fanning up the hillside.

With a shout of triumph Lorne's men rose to their feet and began to hurtle boulders down on the warriors below, but even as they did so the concealed archers under Douglas let fly a hail of arrows into their backs and then drawing their swords charged down upon them from above. Taken by surprise and assailed from both sides, the men of Lorne tried to make a stand but as one after another fell before the enemy onslaught the rest took to their heels for the only bridge over the River Awe and attempted to destroy it behind them. But the pursuit was too fast. The bridge was captured intact by Bruce's men and his army spread over the land of Argyll, rounding up cattle and gathering spoil.

John of Lorne fled with his galleys and in due course found his way to the English and received from Edward II the resounding title of Admiral of the Western Seas. His father, Alexander, the aged Lord of Lorne, who had remained in his castle of Dunstaffnage, was soon besieged by Bruce and in a short time surrendered and was taken as hostage for the good behaviour of his followers. Bruce then garrisoned and provisioned the castle and placed in charge a warden to overawe with his authority any dissidents among the Macdougalls.[23]

With the glamour of his successful campaign in Argyll fresh upon him, Bruce marched up the Great Glen to Moray to come to a final reckoning with the Earl of Ross. The Earl of Ross, as has already been indicated, was a cautious man. Weighing up the events which had occurred since he entered into truce with the Scottish King, he came to the conclusion that there was little to be gained from reliance on Edward II. His natural inclination for the independence of Scotland, provided it could be indulged in without unpleasant consequences for his security, was increased by the territorial concessions which Bruce was prepared to offer him. Accordingly, on the last day of October 1308 at Auldearn, near Nairn, in the presence of an imposing array of Scottish knights and clerics, he humbly submitted his person to Robert Bruce, King of Scots, and asked pardon for his trespasses.

In the rolling phrases of the deed in which his submission is recorded the earl states:

Because the magnificent prince, Sir Robert by the Grace of God King of Scots, my lord, out of his natural goodness, desire, clemency and special grace has forgiven me sincerely the rancour of his mind and relaxed and condoned to me all transgressions or offences against him and his by me and mine . . . and has graciously granted me my lands and tenements and has caused me also to be heritably enfieffed in the lands of Dingwall and Ferncrosky in the sheriffdom of Sutherland of his benign liberality: I, taking heed of the great benevolence of such a prince and because of so many gracious deeds to me . . . do surrender and bind me and my heirs and all my men to the said lord my King . . . and we will be of a surety faithful to him and his heirs and we will render him faithful service assistance and counsel . . . against all men and women who live or die. And in token of this, I, William, for myself, my heirs and all my men to the said lord my King have made homage freely and have sworn on the Gospel of God.[24]

His promise of faithful service was fulfilled. A friendship grew up between his family and that of Bruce and in due course Hugh Ross, his eldest son, married Matilda, the youngest but one of Bruce's sisters.

In the meantime, Edward Bruce had descended upon Galloway like the Angel of Destruction. Dugald Macdowall, who had gathered together the shattered remnants of his clan after Bruce's whirlwind campaign in the autumn of 1307, joined forces with an English contingent under Sir Ingram de Umfraville and Aymer St John and together, with some 1200 men, they attempted to oppose Edward at a crossing of the River Dee. But though his force was inferior in numbers, Edward, with his usual impetuosity, launched against them on 29 June an attack so furious that they broke and fled and their leaders with difficulty escaped to the nearby castle of Buittle.[25] Dugald Macdowall's family fled to England where they were granted a manor by Edward II[26] and Dugald himself was appointed Governor of Dumfries.[27]

With this main force defeated Edward overran the province, levying heavy contributions of corn and cattle, destroying a number of minor castles and receiving into allegiance the now dispirited inhabitants. He then moved north to link up with Douglas returning south after the battle of Brander Pass, and together they besieged and captured in December 1308 the key fortress of Rutherglen, hard by Glasgow.

He moved south again on hearing that Aymer St John had recruited in England a force of knights and foot soldiers some 1500 strong and was once more in Galloway. On this occasion Edward Bruce was accompanied by those seasoned warriors James Douglas, Robert Boyd and Alexander Lindsay, and was joined by Angus Macdonald with a reinforcement of Highlanders from the Western Isles.

They had pitched camp at the head of a narrow defile when early one morning Edward was roused by a scout who informed him that the English, learning of the Scottish position, had made a forced march to surprise him and were now close at hand. There was a heavy mist that morning so that men could not see as far as a bowshot distance. Stationing his foot soldiers to bar the defile, Edward took the little body of fifty armed knights he had in a detour to the rear of the advancing English and followed their track a short way behind them, concealed in the mirk. His daring intention was to wait until the

English clashed with the foot soldiers and then to charge out of the mist and take them from the rear. Before mid-morning the mist suddenly cleared and Edward and his little posse of knights found themselves exposed to view a short distance from a greatly superior body of cavalry. If they retreated they would be overwhelmed so, as Sir Alan Cathcart who was with them related to John Barbour, Edward gave the immediate order to charge. The English, taken by surprise, had hardly time to turn their horses before the Scotsmen had sliced through them, leaving a trail of blood and slaughter, and before the English could turn again the Scots with exemplary discipline had wheeled round and charged back through the disordered lines, creating such confusion that when they wheeled once more to deliver a third onslaught the English broke and fled.[28]

From that time the hinterlands of Galloway were under the control of Bruce.

The last centre of resistance by Scottish enemies had been eliminated. Henceforward he could devote his energies to clearing his kingdom of English garrisons, ordering his administration and obtaining the recognition of other powers as the rightful monarch of an independent kingdom.

# I I

The astonishing reversal of fortune which within two and a half years had transferred the hunted fugitive in the heather into the ruler of two-thirds of Scotland must in the first place be credited to the man himself. Bruce's physical strength, his cheerfulness in adversity, his resourcefulness in danger, his brilliance in tactics and strategy alike marked him as a leader who could animate the courage and inspire the affection of all who followed him.

But no man can operate in a vacuum. It was because in the second place he had behind him the widespread support of the Scottish Church, whose network provided him with military intelligence and whose preachings with recruits, that the latent goodwill of the community was conjured into positive action on his behalf.

And in the third place the death of Edward I and the subsequent political troubles of his successor allowed him to deal with his opponents in two separate phases.

The character of that successor is depicted with remarkable unanimity by the chroniclers of the age. Edward II, they write, was large, handsome and brave but weak-willed, indolent and frivolous, caring neither for politics, war nor business but only how to amuse himself.[1] The principal provider of his amusement was his boyhood friend and companion, Piers Gaveston, whom he married to his niece and created Earl of Cornwall.[2] This irrepressible young man, who entertained his King by nicknaming the leading magnates of the realm with such epithets as 'Burst-belly', 'Joseph the Jew', 'The Cuckold's bird' and 'The Black Dog of Arden' and compounded his insults by unhorsing them at every tournament, not unnaturally provoked in them a furious resentment.[3] For the five years between the death of Edward I on 7 July 1307 and the capture by treachery and the beheading of Piers

Gaveston on 19 June 1312 at the command of the Earl of Lancaster, both English King and nobles were constantly distracted from the business of Scotland by the struggle of one to retain and the others to remove the favourite from his side.

In November 1308 Philip IV of France, whose daughter Isabella had been married to Edward II in January of that year, sought to help his son-in-law. He sent his eldest son to the English court to suggest that the King should negotiate a truce with the Scots and so leave himself free to concentrate his energies against his rebellious barons. At the same time he wrote to Bruce, expressing his special love for his royal person, reminded him of the ancient alliance between Scots and French and asked for his assistance in a forthcoming crusade: a somewhat ingenuous attempt, it would seem, to divert him from prosecuting his war against England.

Whatever the reason, such a message from the leading power in Europe was in itself of immense importance to Bruce for it not only recognized his claim to be King of Scots but by wooing his friendship acknowledged him as master of his kingdom.

While his lieutenants had been fighting in Galloway Bruce had made a stately progress through eastern Scotland from Ross to Perthshire and from there, freed at last from the pressure of campaigning, had issued the first three acts of government of his reign and on 16 March 1309 convened a parliament at St Andrews to consider among other business a reply to the French King.[4]

The reply was tinged with irony. After thanking Philip IV for his affection for their King, the parliament recalled to him the innumerable ravages which the English had inflicted on their country. Nevertheless, they continued, when 'the pristine liberty' of Scotland had been restored and peace obtained from their aggressors, not only the King of Scots but all his nation would rally behind the Holy Crusade on which the King of France was intent.[5]

Not for eighteen years had a free assembly of parliament been held in Scotland and it was now attended by a notable gathering of noblemen and clergy. The three Earls of Ross, Lennox and Sutherland were there in person. The earldoms of Fife, Menteith, Mar, Buchan and Caithness, whose heirs were in wardship, were represented by deputies from their communities as were the other earldoms of the kingdom with the exception of Dunbar and Angus. Among the knights and laymen were Edward Bruce, who had been created Lord of Galloway by his brother after his successful campaign in that province, the Constable Gilbert de la Haye, James the Steward, Robert Keith the Marischal, who had recently returned to Bruce's side, the King's close adherents James Douglas, Thomas Randolph, Neil Campbell, Alexander Lindsay, William Wiseman, David Barclay, Robert Boyd, Angus Macdonald of the Isles and Hugh, son of the Earl of Ross.

Among the clergy were the Chancellor, Bernard Linton, Nicolas Balmyle, who had been chancellor in 1301 and was now Bishop of Dunblane, the Bishops of Moray, Ross, Brechin and Dunkeld, a representative of the Bishop of Glasgow, Robert Wishart, who had been handed over by Edward II to the Pope the previous December, and the Bishop of St Andrews, William Lamberton who, unlike his compatriot, had been released on parole by Edward II to act as an emissary between the two countries.[6]

This impressive concourse was seized upon as an occasion to proclaim to the world the right of the Scottish people to their independence and of Robert Bruce to be their King.

On 17 March, the day after the reply to Philip IV's letter had been issued, 'the bishops abbots, priors and others of the clergy duly constituted in the realm of Scotland' made a solemn declaration that Robert, Lord of Annandale, 'the Competitor', ought by reason of his superior title, the wishes of the community and the laws and customs of the country to have received the Crown of Scotland and that because of the elevation of John Balliol to the throne, his subsequent deposition and the invasions of England great and manifold evil had fallen upon the kingdom until, by the workings of divine providence, 'the people, not wishing any longer to bear the calamities which had been brought upon them through want of a captain and faithful leader, had taken for their King, Robert Bruce, grandson of the Competitor and had raised him to the throne'. Before concluding with an expression of loyalty to King Robert, they added the warning that

> if anyone in opposition should claim right to the Scottish Kingdom by means of documents sealed in the past and containing the consent of the people be it known that all this was effected by irresistible force and violence, by numberless fears, bodily torture and other terrors which could well pervert the opinions and minds of righteous men and strike dread into the stoutest hearts.[7]

A few days later a similar declaration was made by the nobles, affirming that King Robert was the true and nearest heir of King Alexander last deceased.[8]

In both these declarations the emphasis is on the legitimacy of Bruce's kingship. The coronation of John Balliol is treated as an aberration brought about by overwhelming force. The direct descent of Robert I from Alexander III is clearly enunciated.

On this point Bruce would neither make or would be allowed to make any concessions.

In consequence the negotiations for peace which Edward II initiated in 1309, at the instigation of his father-in-law, first by sending the Bishop of St Andrews, then in March Oliver des Roches, the French ambassador, and finally in August Bruce's own brother-in-law, the Earl of Ulster, to meet with Scottish representatives ended in deadlock.[9] Edward was not prepared to grant and Bruce was not prepared to accept anything less than recognition of his right to be King of an independent realm.

During these protracted negotiations Edward II had been able to effect a temporary accommodation with his barons and to bring back to his side Piers Gaveston who, at their insistence, had been banished to Ireland the summer before. Now with the talks broken off and in response to the recurrent cries for assistance from his English-held castles in Scotland, he put a full-scale invasion in train that autumn.

Two separate armies, under the command respectively of Sir John Segrave and the Earl of Hereford and of Sir Robert Clifford and Sir John Cromwell, were sent to Berwick and Carlisle. No sooner had they reached their headquarters than the prospect of a winter campaign among the sodden hills of Scotland appeared so uninviting that they promptly arranged a truce with the Scots.

When it expired on 14 January 1310 Edward II was once more in trouble with his barons and it was prolonged to 8 March. By then he had been forced to accept the surveillance of a reform committee which gave itself the name of 'the Lords Ordainers' and the truce was extended yet again to June, 'for,' as the *Lanercost Chronicle* sagely remarks, 'the English do not willingly enter Scotland to wage war before summer, chiefly because earlier in the year they find no food for their horses'.[10]

The lull in hostilities throughout 1309 and the early part of 1310 enabled Bruce to visit various areas of his kingdom and deal with administrative matters which needed his attention. He had not forgotten the help he had received from the Western Highlands in the desperate winter of 1306–7 so during the summer and autumn of 1309, with the aura of majesty still about him from the acclamations of the St Andrews Parliament, he made a royal progress along the western seaboard from Ross and Cromarty to the southern shores of Argyll, greeting the Highland chieftains and receiving their allegiance to one who was now a king indeed and not in name only as he had been when they last met.[11]

During this progress or at its end he must have had Angus Macdonald of the Isles in his company and been satisfied by him that he had sufficient control of the western seas to keep open the route between Ireland and Scotland for the passage of goods. For a trade had sprung up with the Irish for the supply of provisions, armour and weapons to the Scots of which they were sorely in need. Since there was no manufacture in Ireland of the latter two commodities, the merchants met the demand by importing them from England and the continent and re-exporting them to Scotland: to such an extent that in January 1311 Edward II had a proclamation made 'in all towns, ports and other places where vessels touch' throughout Ireland prohibiting any trade with the insurgent Scots on pain of the severest penalties.[12]

But because of the dominance of Angus Macdonald and his galleys trade continued virtually unhindered. In the east, his possession of most of the ports on the North Sea gave Bruce the opportunity to obtain similar supplies from Scandinavia, the Hanseatic towns and Flanders through the enterprise of Scottish privateers or shipmasters of those countries who were prepared to run the gauntlet of the English navy. In return they took back timber, hides and in particular Scottish wool which then, as now, attracted a higher price for its quality.

The improvement of Scottish sheep and fleeces had been largely the work of the Scottish Church and at its annual convocation on 13 February 1310 it showed itself no less mindful of its human flock and their shepherd. During the previous year Pope Clement V, a Gascon like Piers Gaveston and friendly to Edward II, had pronounced excommunication on Bruce and all who gave him aid 'for damnably persevering in iniquity' and outlined with relish the horrors that awaited them in the life hereafter if they continued in their frowardness.[13] Now as the clergy of the Scottish realm gathered together they set at rest the apprehensions of the devout by brushing aside the fulminations of the Holy Father and issuing a manifesto 'to all the faithful' in splendid and resonant Latin that Robert the Bruce had been chosen before God and man as the rightful King of Scotland 'ut *deformata reformet, corrigendaque corriget et dirigat indirecta*': that he might reform what is deformed, correct that which needs correction and straighten that which has gone awry.[14]

Though, unlike Bruce, Edward II had the support of the Pope, he was being harassed in every other direction. The Lords Ordainers, twenty-one in number, were preparing restrictive ordinances for him to sign. His favourite was being threatened with violence and a coolness had arisen between his father-in-law and himself. He had discovered that while the dispatches to Robert Bruce from Philip IV which had been shown at the English court had been addressed to Robert Bruce, Earl of Carrick, those which had been handed to Bruce by the French envoy had been addressed to Robert Bruce, King of Scots.

He therefore sent a furious letter to his father-in-law accusing him of double-dealing. Philip IV, who had learned from his daughter that she was being entirely neglected by her husband in favour of his minion, responded by demanding Edward II's presence in Paris to do fealty to him, as his lord, for the lands which he held in France. According to the Monk of Malmesbury who wrote a contemporary history of Edward II's reign, 'The King was convinced that if he obeyed the summons of the King of France and left Piers Gaveston in the midst of his enemies, death, imprisonment or worse might befall him.'[15] He therefore sought to evade the French summons and postpone the reforms which the Lords Ordainers were trying to impose upon him by leaving London for the north, to which he had already sent his favourite, and from there issuing a royal edict throughout the kingdom that all who were bound by feudal duty to join him with a fixed quota of armed men when he went to war should assemble at Berwick on 8 September for an invasion of Scotland.

At the same time orders were issued to the Mayor of Dover and the mayors of forty-one other ports to provide ships for the provisioning of the expedition.

In the event his call to arms was boycotted by all the great barons with the exception of Piers Gaveston, Earl of Cornwall, and the Earls of Gloucester and Surrey.[16] Nevertheless there was a powerful influx of the lesser barons and knights, among them those seasoned veterans of the Scottish wars, Henry Percy and Robert Clifford, and 'a numerous crowd of Welsh and English infantry intent on gain'.

At the head of this army, which compared in numbers with any that his father had launched against Scotland, Edward II in mid-September advanced from Berwick to Roxburgh and then through the forests of

Jedburgh and Selkirk to Biggar[17] on the borders of Lanark and Peebles. Biggar, almost at the centre of southern Scotland, was a strategic point from which he could strike at the Scottish army from whichever direction it might appear. There, from 14 October, he waited in expectation of its approach but waited in vain.

Bruce had received ample warning of the invasion and reacted in accordance with his cardinal military principle: to avoid at all costs a pitched battle. He withdrew his main army beyond the Firth of Forth and left to his lieutenants with small flying columns the task of harassing the lumbering progress of the English army.

Throughout the south of Scotland in that year the harvest had failed and there was widespread famine. The country folk, aware of the English massing on their borders, had gathered up their meagre stock of corn and had retreated with their sheep and cattle into the remote fastnesses of mountain and forest.[18] Edward II and his army found themselves in an empty and silent land.

Breaking camp at Biggar, they moved down the valley of the Clyde to Bothwell which was still in English hands, and as they moved James Douglas and his men, who had known this countryside since their birth, kept pace with them in the forest shadows and took their toll of straggling footmen and foundered food wagons and melted again into the woods.

From Bothwell the English pressed on to Renfrew,[19] presumably to link up with John of Lorne, Admiral of the Western Seas, who since April had been receiving reinforcements of ships at Carlingford Bay in Ulster with orders to sail to Argyll and rouse the Macdougalls once more against the Scottish King.[20] But Angus Macdonald of the Isles must have held them at bay with his fleet, for when the English army crossed north over the estuary near Dumbarton, they found neither friend nor enemy.

They now began to suffer the want of fodder and provisions, and as the knights and barons observed their valuable warhorses grow gaunt and falter beneath their weight, their resentment at this fruitless expedition became vocal. Edward II therefore turned eastwards along the line of the Campsie Hills to Linlithgow[21] and, after resting there for five days, on 28 October retired to his base at Berwick.

Upon this dispirited and retreating army Bruce now let loose, in greater strength, his raiding parties whose morale had been raised by the failure of the English forces to achieve any positive result.

The Monk of Malmesbury writes:

At that time, Robert Bruce who lurked continually in hiding did them all the injury that he could. One day when some English and Welsh, always ready for plunder, had gone out on a raid, accompanied for protection by many horsemen from the army, Robert Bruce's men, who had been concealed in caves and in the woodlands, made a heavy attack on our men. Our horsemen, seeing that they could not help the infantry, returned to the main force with a frightful uproar: all immediately leapt to arms and hastened with one accord to the help of those who had been left among the enemy: but assistance came too late to prevent the slaughter of our men . . . Before our knights arrived up to three hundred Welsh and English had been slaughtered and the enemy returned to their caves. From such ambushes our men often suffered heavy losses. For Robert Bruce, knowing himself unequal to the King of England in strength or fortune, decided that it would be better to resist our King by secret warfare rather than to dispute his right in open battle. Indeed I might be tempted to sound the praises of Sir Robert Bruce.[22]

And as the *Lanercost Chronicle* relates, 'So soon as the English had retired to Berwick Robert Bruce and his people invaded Lothian and inflicted much damage upon those who were in the King of England's peace.'[23]

On hearing of the presence of the elusive Scottish army in Lothian, Edward II again entered Scotland but by the time he reached the province the Scots had once more disappeared.

For the next six months Edward II remained at Berwick[24] with his army still in being, partly to distance himself from the troublesome Lords Ordainers in the south and partly in anticipation of further attacks on Lothian where he had left Piers Gaveston in control at Roxburgh. During this period he was constantly baffled by the behaviour of Bruce, to whom the initiative had now passed.

In mid-December he learned, by what seems a calculated leak from Bruce, that the Scottish King was collecting an army to invade the Isle of Man. Edward hastily ordered the English ships on the eastern seaboard to sail round to the west to defend it.[25] By this action he weakened his own commissariat and at the same time strengthened that of Bruce, who was able to receive into the eastern seaports of Scotland, which the English navy had been blockading, supplies from Northern Europe invaluable in this year of famine.

Yet within a fortnight of this news of an Isle of Man invasion, Bruce was on his doorstep in Selkirk forest prepared to arrange a truce. Two envoys were sent to the Scottish King and after a preliminary meeting a further discussion was arranged at Melrose, but Bruce suspected treachery and did not attend.[26] Instead he moved to Galloway and by February 1311 was threatening to raid the western marches. Rumour had it that reinforcements for the attack were being recruited in the Mounth and Piers Gaveston was sent with a cavalry contingent to Perth to cut the communication between the Mounth and Galloway,[27] but rumour had lied and within two months bitter cold and lack of forage had driven the favourite back to Berwick.

Apart from a foray into the forests of Selkirk and Jedburgh by the Earls of Gloucester and Warwick, a stalemate now ensued.[28] Edward II busied himself with the refurbishing of the English-held castles in Lothian and Galloway from the bases of Berwick and Carlisle. Bruce remained in his ancestral domains of Annandale and Carrick, slowly throttling into submission by land and sea the citadel and town of Ayr and building up a disciplined force to take advantage of the situation which he anticipated would soon arise: the departure of Edward II south to face the demands of his intransigent barons.

That moment came soon after midsummer 1311 when the Lords Ordainers assembled in London to lay their ordinances before parliament and required the presence of their King to declare it open.[29] Compelled by shortage of funds with which to pay his army, Edward II unwillingly returned to his capital after securing the safety of his favourite in the rugged castle of Bamburgh on the Northumbrian coast.

Then, says the *Lanercost Chronicle*,

> Robert the Bruce, taking note that the English King and all the nobles of the realm were in such distant parts and in such discord about the accursed Piers Gaveston, having collected a large army invaded England by the Solway on Thursday before the feast of the Assumption of the Glorious Virgin 12 August and burnt all the land of the Lord of Gilsland and the town of Haltwhistle and a great part of Tynedale and after eight days returned into Scotland taking with him a very large booty in cattle. But he had killed few men besides those who offered resistance.[30]

Bruce had used this raid to test the quality of the resistance he might expect, and having found it wanting he resolved to enlarge the scale of his invasion. Taking his army east to link up with James Douglas and his men in Douglasdale and the forest of Selkirk, he first harried the lands of the pro-English Earl of Dunbar, which lay to the west of Berwick and then, on 8 September, crossed the Cheviot Hills into

Northumberland as far as Harbottle and Holystone. From there, in a wide sweep over the plains to Redesdale, he burned and looted the crops that were ripening for harvest, drove south as far as Corbridge, which went up in flames, and then fanned out along the valleys of the north and south Tyne on his homeward journey, laying waste those parts which he had overlooked before, and returned to Scotland fifteen days after crossing the border.[31]

Observing that the wardens of the marches appointed by the English King were impotent in the face of the numbers against them, the Northumbrians took the only course open if they wished to survive. They sent envoys to Bruce to offer money for a temporary truce.

The Scotsmen were in no mood for moderation. For fifteen years their country had been ravaged and impoverished by the English. Their corn crops had been burned, their livestock slaughtered, their farms destroyed, their people killed and throughout their trading ports and burghs the hum of business had been reduced to silence. Slowly the life blood of commerce was beginning to circulate once more through the body politic but the revenue was pitifully small to meet the demands of government and defence.

When Bruce embarked on the raids into northern England which he continued throughout his reign he had two aims in mind: to obtain the money and supplies for the administration of his country and to keep in fighting trim the nucleus of an army.

Now that he had temporarily regained the upper hand his terms were going to be severe. Immunity was granted to the Northumbrians only to February 1312, and for this brief period they were compelled to pay what was for those days the enormous sum of £2000. A similar tax was imposed on the men of Dunbar.[32] A formidable protection racket was in the making: but the unwritten rules were observed. The monks in Lanercost Abbey, which was situated only a short distance within the English side of the border, had the best opportunity to know what was happening. They record again and again in their *Chronicle* that during these raids it was only those who repelled with force the Scottish demands who suffered death.

Nevertheless the inhabitants of northern England must sometimes have felt that an armed knight on a campaign of blackmail was not the highest example of chivalry. The ideals of King Arthur's knights, to uphold justice and champion the defenceless, were still supposed to be the basic principles of the warrior class. But, even before the War of Scottish Independence, they had seldom been observed in practice.

The habit of violence had taken over throughout Europe as exemplified by Edward I. His barbarous executions of the royal kin and knighthood of Scotland during the course of that war had brought chivalry between the two countries to an end. The northern English were in the unfortunate position of being left unprotected either by a code of honour or a covering armed force, abandoned by the very rulers who had intolerably provoked their next-door neighbours.

Hardly had the truce expired when the Scots attacked the castle of Norham just inside the English border and near to Berwick, burning the town and carrying away many prisoners and cattle. This feat so close to the headquarters of the English command in Scotland was a clear warning to the men of Northumberland and Dunbar that they could look for no defence from England and both areas renewed their tribute.

Meanwhile civil war had broken out in England. Edward II, whose affection for Piers Gaveston, however misplaced, had a depth and sincerity which must elicit respect, had twisted and turned like a fox before the hounding barons in an attempt to protect his friend. At the parliament in August 1311 he had offered to accept all the forty-one articles of the ordinance placed before him by the Lords Ordainers if they would delete that which demanded the banishment of Piers Gaveston. But they were resolute in their refusal. In mid-October 1311 Piers sailed for Flanders, but early in January 1312 he returned secretly to England and was received by the King and taken by him to York for fear of the barons[33] 'and because there was no safety for Piers in England, Ireland, Wales, Gascony or France he tried to arrange for Piers residence in Scotland until the baronial attack should cease.'[34]

The commissioners he chose to treat with Bruce were all Scotsmen, the Bishop of St Andrews, the Earls of Atholl and March, Sir Alexander Abernethy and Sir Adam Gordon, and through them, so anxious was he for his charge, he continually upgraded his offers from truce to lasting truce and 'at length that the kingdom of Scotland itself should be allowed to Sir Robert freely and forever'. To which in chilling terms the Scottish King replied, 'How shall the King of England keep faith with me since he does not observe the sworn promises made to his liege men, whose homage and fealty he has received and with whom he is bound to keep mutual faith? No trust can be put in such a fickle man, his promises will not deceive me.'[35]

Deprived of this last vain hope and denied funds from the exchequer even 'so much as a halfpenny or a farthing'[36], Edward II made his headquarters now in York, now in Newcastle, plundering the country around to pay for his expenses while the Lords Ordainers slowly gathered their private armies together and then marched north. Piers took refuge in Scarborough Castle while his King sought to raise more troops elsewhere, and there, after a siege by the Earl of Pembroke, surrendered on 31 May 1312 in return for the earl's word of honour that his life would be spared. But as he was being conducted to Pembroke's castle at Wallingford in Oxfordshire, he was seized by the Earl of Warwick and on the order of the Earl of Lancaster beheaded on 19 June.

Furious at the execution of his favourite, Edward II joined forces with the Earl of Pembroke, whose honour had been impugned, and marched against Lancaster and his fellow earls.[37]

# 12

Robert Bruce took full advantage of the situation in England. No doubt he was kept informed by the Bishop of St Andrews, William Lamberton. In April 1308 Lamberton had once more pledged his allegiance to the English King and had been released from his dungeon in Winchester Castle on condition that he remained within the diocese of the Bishop of Durham.[1] Edward II had used him on several occasions as his emissary to Robert Bruce, which gave him the opportunity to renew his ancient friendship with the Scottish King. Whatever promises he might make to Edward II, his heart and soul were dedicated to the cause of Scottish independence. For this he believed that peace between the two countries was of paramount importance and exerted all his diplomatic skill to bring it about. But so long as it was not achieved he had no scruple in taking advantage of his privileged position among the English to send to Bruce through the secret network of the Church vital information about his enemies.

Whether it was because of the bishop's reports or of his own assessment, Bruce convened a parliament at Ayr in July 1312 and there decided on a large-scale invasion of England.[2]

Leaving a light force to screen the English-held castles of Dumfries, Dalswinton, Buittle and Caerlaverock, he crossed the Solway with his main army to Lanercost Priory, 16 miles northeast of Carlisle, and there lay for three days sacking the priory buildings and 'doing an infinity of damage'. Leaving Lanercost he marched east to Hexham and Corbridge ravaging the district and taking much spoil and many prisoners, 'nor was there any who dared to resist'. Setting up his headquarters at Corbridge, he sent Edward Bruce and James Douglas on a lightning raid into the county of Durham. Surprising Chester-le-Street at nightfall, they left there a holding detachment and swept on through the darkness six miles south to Durham and fell upon the inhabitants at early light just as they were putting up the stalls for market day. All who resisted were killed and the greater part of the buildings were reduced to ashes while the military defenders of the castle and abbey, too formidable for the Scots to attack, watched timorously from behind their walls the destruction of the city they were paid to protect.

An immense booty of stores, arms, armour and horses was collected and taken to Chester-le-Street and kept under guard by Edward Bruce while James Douglas hurried to Hartlepool on the coast, ransacked the town and returned with a number of wealthy burgesses and their wives to be held for ransom.

Never in the memory of living men had the Peace of the Palatinate been disturbed by foreign foes and a fearful apprehension spread through the peoples of the area at the shock of the Scottish invasion. The Bishop of Durham was in London but the leading men of the city took it upon themselves to visit Robert Bruce in a body and offer £2000 for a ten months' truce to midsummer 1313. This offer was accepted but only on the humiliating condition that the Scots should have 'free access and retreat through the county of Durham whenever they wished to make a raid into England'. The Northumbrians, fearing their turn would come next, hastened to follow the example of their southern neighbours and pay £2000 for the same period of truce while 'the people of Westmoreland, Coupland and Cumberland redeemed themselves in a similar way and as they had not so much money in hand as would pay them they paid a part and gave as hostages for the rest the sons of the chief lords of the country'.[3]

As midsummer 1313 approached emissaries from Bruce were sent to the northern counties to warn them that if they did not purchase a fresh truce he would, reluctantly, have to repeat his punitive raids. The threat was enough. Further immunities to 29 September 1314 were arranged on a cash basis.

Throughout his life Bruce was, within the context of a savage age, a humane man. He was using his power not to butcher aimlessly in revenge but to improve the finances of his bankrupt kingdom. Discipline was maintained and a careful record kept of those who had or had not paid for their immunity, and if any failed in their dues their estates were systematically ravaged. Cumberland was a case in point. By April 1314 they had fallen further and further behind in their agreed payments, but instead of injuring their hostages Bruce sent his brother

Edward with a strong detachment to take over the Bishop of Carlisle's manor house at Rose Castle and lay waste the surrounding district. 'They burnt many towns and two churches taking men and women prisoners and collected a great number of cattle in Inglewood forest and elsewhere and driving them off with them on April 19th, but they killed few men except those who made a determined resistance.'[4]

According to a contemporary account, in the short space of three years Bruce received more than £40,000 from the tributes paid to him by towns, religious houses and local communities.[5]

On their return to Scotland from Durham in September 1312, the Scottish army attempted to take Carlisle by surprise but the garrison were too alert and although the Scots, elated by their successful invasion, made a determined assault upon it they were beaten off with heavy losses, both James Douglas and Gilbert de la Haye receiving wounds. It was no intention of Bruce to settle down for a prolonged siege, and having failed to effect a *coup de main* he continued to Scotland where he had other matters with which to deal.[6]

During his absence in northern England he had sent his chancellor, Bernard Linton, to Norway to iron out certain disputes between the two countries and negotiate anew and reaffirm the ancient Treaty of Perth. Discussion having proceeded amicably, Bruce summoned a Parliament at Inverness and there on 29 October 1312 an agreement was sealed between the King of Scots in person and the envoys of King Haakon V resolving the differences between them and reactivating the settlement of 1266: a conclusion peculiarly satisfactory to Bruce both because of his family relationship with the Norwegian royal family and their overt recognition of his sovereignty of Scotland.[7]

When he rode north from Galloway to Inverness he left behind his brother Edward to harass the English garrisons in the southwest and James Douglas to police the border and raid into Lothian to bring more communities under tribute; but he took with him his third chief lieutenant, Thomas Randolph, and an unexpected addition to his entourage, the Earl of Atholl.

David, Earl of Atholl, was the son of that same John, Earl of Atholl, who had been captured with Bruce's Queen and family in Easter Ross and had been hanged by Edward I on the special gallows in London elevated beyond the normal because of his royal blood. It might have been expected, in view of his family tradition and the execution of his father by the English, that David would have adhered to Bruce but his wife was the daughter of the 'Red' Comyn whom Bruce had struck down in Greyfriars church, and in the subsequent blood feud between the two families he had been drawn in on the Comyn side and had taken the field against Bruce on several occasions. In January 1312 he had been one of the emissaries sent by Edward II under the lead of William Lamberton, Bishop of St Andrews, to request Bruce to grant political asylum to Piers Gaveston.

It was important to Bruce to win over another great earl to his cause and there is little doubt that, during the close contact which these negotiations entailed, the magnetism of the Scottish King and the influence of the subtle bishop were exerted to induce Atholl to transfer his allegiance: a course to which a cold assessment of the odds and his natural instincts might well have inclined him. In any event he rode with Bruce to Inverness and there before the parliament his vast lands were formally restored to him and he was created Constable of Scotland, an office which good, loyal, devoted Gilbert de la Haye, the existing holder, had handed back to Bruce so that his King could use it as a bait to catch the earl.

But Bruce at the same time provided a reinsurance for his generosity to Atholl. Thomas Randolph, who after his youthful effrontery to Bruce when he was captured in July 1308 had proved to his royal uncle his daring in the field and his wisdom at the conference table, was granted the earldom of Moray, an earldom which had remained dormant in the possession of the Crown since 1130. With it he received, with wide powers, the great part of the province of that name which lay between the earldoms of Ross and Atholl and could exert an influence on each.

> By this creation Bruce gave to the warlike men of Moray, to whom he owed so much, a leader of their own and that leader his own nephew. Henceforward it was the banner of Randolph the men of Moray followed in the war: and it was with the men of Moray Randolph performed those exploits which have endeared him to the heart of every Scot.[8]

Judging by the actions which followed on the parliament at Inverness, a progress report and future plan must have been made concerning the destruction of the castles held in Scotland by the English. At the time of Bruce's first parliament at St Andrews in 1309 and after the harrying of Buchan and Galloway, the English still retained of their major castles three north of the Tay: Banff, Dundee and Perth; three on the line of the Firth of Forth and Clyde: Stirling, Linlithgow and Bothwell; six in the southwest: Ayr, Loch Doon, Dalswinton, Dumfries, Buittle and Caerlaverock; and four in Lothian: Edinburgh, Roxburgh, Jedburgh and Berwick, together with numerous second and third rate strongpoints. The possession of every castle gave the English a dominance over the surrounding countryside and a base at which an invading army from England could regroup and refurbish its forces.

The policy of Bruce was to raze to the ground any castle that he captured so that it would never again become a focus of infection. His problem was how to achieve these captures. The odds were heavily weighted in favour of the defenders. Edward I, with the most sophisticated siege engines of the period at his disposal, took three months to capture Stirling in 1304. Bruce had neither the means to buy nor the skilled men to operate these formidable machines. He had to rely on patient blockade or the brilliance and daring of his stratagems.

During the three and a half years between the parliaments of 1309 and 1312 a beginning had been made. North of the Tay, Banff in the winter of 1309–10 and Dundee in the spring of 1312 had been starved into surrender. In the southwest, by the end of 1311, a similar fate had befallen Ayr and Loch Doon. Now, with Edward II still embroiled with his barons and the northern counties of England under tribute, a determined effort was decided upon to deal with the remaining strongholds.

Bruce's first action was to move from Inverness to Perth and there invest the town. Leaving part of his force to prosecute the siege probably under the command of the Earls of Moray and Atholl,[9] he rode south for a daring attempt to capture Berwick by surprise. Berwick was the town nearest to the English border and the headquarters of their Scottish command. The audacity of the project has the touch of Douglas about it and it is reasonable to assume that it was on his initiative that Bruce came to join him in the attack which so nearly succeeded.

'Coming unexpectedly to the castle on the night of St Nicholas,' writes the Lanercost chronicler, that is on 6 December 1312,

he laid ladders against the walls and began to scale them: and had not a dog betrayed the approach of the Scots by loud barking it is believed that he would quickly have taken the castle and, in consequence, the town.

Now these ladders, which they placed against the walls, were of a wonderful construction as I, myself, who write these lines, beheld with mine own eyes. For the Scots had made two strong ropes as long as the height of the wall, making a knot at the end of each cord. They had made a wooden board also, about two feet and a half broad, strong enough to carry a man and in the two extremities of the board they had made two holes through which the two ropes could be passed; then the cords having been passed through as far as the knots, they had made two other knots in the ropes one foot and a half higher and above these knots they placed another board and so on to the end of the ropes. They had also made an iron hook, measuring at least one foot along one limb and this was to lie over the wall but the other limb being of the same length hung downwards towards the ground having at its end a round hole wherein the point of a lance could be inserted and two rings on the sides wherein the said ropes could be knotted.

Having fitted them together in this manner they took a strong spear as long as the height of the wall, placing the point thereof in the iron hole and two men lifted the ropes and boards with that spear and placed the iron hook (which was not a round one) over the wall. They then were able to climb up by those wooden steps, just as one usually climbs an ordinary ladder and the greater the weight of the climber the more firmly the iron hook clung over the wall. But lest the rope should lie too close to the wall and hinder the ascent they had made fenders round every third step which thrust the ropes off the wall. When therefore they had placed two ladders upon the wall the dog betrayed them, as I have said, and they left the ladder there which next day our people hung upon a pillory to put them to shame. And thus a dog saved the town on that occasion, just as of old geese saved Rome by their gobble.[10]

Although the ingenious invention of the hempen scaling ladders failed to bring success on this occasion, it was to prove of inestimable value in the future.

Foiled in this attempt to take Berwick by surprise, Bruce left as swiftly as he had arrived and returned to Perth to take over the control of the siege.

Throughout the wars of Scottish independence the English regarded the town of Perth as of immense strategic importance. Easily provisioned from the sea, dominating the rich cornlands of Angus and Fife, menacing the whole central part of Scotland, positioned as an ample caravanserai for invading armies moving up from the south, it was the most pampered outpost of the English occupation. Its defences were constantly being improved and by 1312 it was girdled by massive stone walls with towers at intervals along the ramparts.

Around its base it was lapped by the River Tay on the east and a deep and wide moat on the other three sides.

At the time of Bruce's approach it was strongly garrisoned by 120 mounted men and a greater number of footmen and archers, all under the command of Sir William Oliphant, the stubborn and courageous knight who in 1304 at Stirling Castle had held the might of Edward I at bay for more than three months. After he had surrendered there he was imprisoned in England for four years and was only released on condition that he fought for the English Crown.

Although the Scots had surrounded the town preventing any access from outside, they had no heavy artillery with which to batter down the walls and after six weeks saw no weakening among the defenders from lack of supplies. Bruce was unwilling to immobilize in a long siege his armed forces, many of whom were Highlanders who do not take kindly to static war. Fertile in resource as ever, he resorted to a stratagem. Secretly by night he had the moat sounded for depth and at last discovered a place 'where men might to their shoulders wade'.

Openly giving orders to call off the siege, he and his men packed up their gear and in full view of the enemy formed up and marched away to the shouts and jeers of the garrison.

When he had reached a concealing wood at a safe distance from Perth he halted his army and set them to work constructing rope ladders long enough to reach to the top of the town's ramparts. After eight days, which he reckoned would be enough to lull the defenders into a sense of security, he set out on the black night of 7 January 1313 towards the sleeping town. Horses and grooms were left behind and his knights and foot soldiers crept stealthily through the darkness to the edge of the moat and there waited in silence. When no sentinels were seen nor heard Bruce himself, with a ladder slung around his shoulders and a spear in his right hand, lowered himself in full armour into the icy water and began to wade across testing the depth with his spear as he went. The water presently reached his neck but then grew less until he reached the other side, and placing his spear in the iron hole of his ladder with his great strength lifted it up and hooked it on the rampart.

Among his company at that time there was a young French knight who, when he saw the King lead the way through the water carrying his ladder as a common man, crossed himself exclaiming, 'What shall we say of our nobles in France who think only to stuff their bellies when so renowned a knight will risk his life for a miserable hamlet?'

He followed the King through the moat and was first up the ladder with Bruce behind him. All the Scots followed and set their ladders to the walls and climbed onto the battlements. Still there was no alarm. Bruce rapidly divided his men into two detachments keeping himself a chosen band to guard the rampart above the ladders and sending the rest to range through the town. The night was suddenly filled with uproar as the Scots, scattering in all directions, 'put their foes to great confusion, who in their beds were or fleeing here and there'. Surprise was complete and resistance negligible. By sunrise the town was in Bruce's hands.[11]

An immense booty was garnered by Bruce's men 'till some who were before poor and bare became rich and mighty with the spoil',[12] but few of the defenders were killed for Bruce had given strict orders to spare all who did not resist. Many of the townsfolk were Scots and Bruce sought always to heal rather than exacerbate the divisions of his countrymen. In his political outlook he was a man of his time, believing in the feudal structure as the basis of his kingdom, and in dealing with the great nobles who had opposed him he erred on the side of magnanimity in seeking to reconcile them to his rule. So now to the Earl of Strathearn, who had been captured at Perth by his own son who was on Bruce's side, he returned all his lands on his vowing allegiance.[13]

Even more remarkable in this respect was his action at Dumfries. After giving orders for the castle and town of Perth to be razed to the ground, he moved to the southwest where his brother Edward had been preventing, as far as he could, any supplies reaching the quartet of castles, Dumfries, Dalswinton, Buittle and Caerlaverock, from the solid English base at Carlisle. Dumfries was commanded by that same Dugald Macdowall who had been responsible for the death of two of Bruce's brothers in 1307, yet when on the verge of starvation the garrison surrendered on 7 February 1313, Bruce allowed Macdowall to go free in the hope that as head of the great Macdowall clan in Galloway he would end their persistent disaffection by accepting the actuality of Bruce's kingship. In this Bruce was disappointed for whatever Dugald may have promised when he surrendered, no sooner was he out of range than he once more threw in his lot with the English.[14]

The castles of Dalswinton, Buittle and Caerlaverock held out a little longer, but by 31 March 1313 all had surrendered and were razed to the ground.

There now remained outside Lothian only two strongholds in English hands, Bothwell and Stirling. Walter FitzGilbert, the Governor of Bothwell, surrounded as he was by the Stewart lands whose young owner, Walter Stewart, was fighting with Bruce, kept studiously inactive awaiting events and could be ignored, but Stirling was the gateway between north and south Scotland and Edward Bruce was given the vital task of bringing about its submission.

Meanwhile Bruce took advantage of the strong Scottish force he had spare to hand in Galloway after the surrender of the castles to link up with Angus Macdonald of the Isles and with his fleet invade the Isle of Man. 'On the 18th May, Lord Robert King of Scotland put in at Ramsay with a large number of ships and on the following Sunday went to the nunnery at Douglas where he spent the night and on Monday laid siege to the castle of Rushen.'[15] Early in June the castle surrendered and the island, which had been so treacherously taken by Edward I in 1290, became once more Scottish. In December 1313 Bruce handed over the lordship of the island to his nephew Thomas Randolph, Earl of Moray, in return for feudal dues of one hundred marks and the provision of six ships each of twenty-six oars. In 1315 John of Lorne temporarily seized the island[16] but was driven out in 1317 by the Earl of Moray and it remained a Scottish possession until 1333 when it passed to England for good.[17]

Bruce returned to Scotland after his successful expedition to be greeted by the heartbreaking news that his brother Edward had committed him to an agreement which threatened to undo all that he had so painfully achieved.

His brother Edward did not take kindly to sieges. He was essentially a cavalry leader, delighting in mobile war, impatient with the dull recurrent routine of blockade. Already he had shown his lack of perseverance when he was conducting the siege of Dundee the year before. There, tired of sitting still, he had accepted from William Montfichet, the governor of the town, an offer to surrender if the castle was not relieved by the English on a certain date. Fortunately for the Scots, Edward II furiously denounced his subordinate's agreement and threatened Montfichet with death if he did not continue his resistance. Dundee had to be starved into submission.[18]

For more than three months Edward Bruce had been camped with his men around Stirling Castle. There was little he could do against the massive fortifications without any engines of siege warfare. He had to wait and wait until the provisions of the defenders failed them. In the end he must have succeeded for he had sealed off all means of access and the King of England was too occupied in his own kingdom to give a thought to the beleaguered garrison.

But Sir Philip Mowbray, the castle's commander, had a shrewd knowledge of Edward Bruce's impetuous character. At midsummer 1313, as he took stock of his diminishing supplies, he offered as one chivalrous knight to another that, 'if by midsummer a year thence he was not rescued by battle, he would yield the castle freely.' Edward fell headlong into the trap, and without consulting their respective monarchs the two men pledged their honour to fulfil the treaty.[19]

Possibly Edward Bruce believed that the King of England was too locked in conflict with his great barons and too outraged by their murder of his favourite to turn his attention to Scotland. But, in view of his knowledge of his brother's policy never to risk a pitched battle against the English,[20] the length of time he allowed for the rescue displays at least an appalling lack of judgement, at worst a selfish desire to be rid of the tedium of a blockade. The challenge to the honour of England was too great and too public to be ignored and nothing was more calculated to compose the differences between Edward II and his nobles than the prospect of settling with Scotland once and for all.

The difficulty for Bruce was compounded by the impossibility of disowning the pledged troth of his brother and there is no wonder that he upbraided him in the words put into his mouth by Barbour:

That was unwisely done indeed. Never have I heard so long a warning given to so mighty a King as the King of England. For he now has in his hand England, Ireland, Wales and Aquitaine, with all under his seigneury, and a great part of Scotland, and he is so provided with treasure that he can have plenty of paid soldiers. We are so few against so many. God may deal us our destiny right well but we are set in jeopardy to lose or win all at one throw.[21]

From now on through the coming year the efforts of Bruce were to be concentrated on capturing the great English castles in Lothian and training his men for the inevitable clash with England.

His lieutenants nobly responded but the lead was taken by a simple countryman whose name still glows in the minds of Scotsmen. He was called William Bunnock and it was his custom to bring to the castle at Linlithgow the harvest from the fields. On a day in September

1313 he sent a message to the garrison that he had for them a load of hay greater and of better quality than any he had delivered that year. Indeed he spoke the truth for eight armed men were hidden beneath the hay and nearby the castle gate others had concealed themselves in the undergrowth.

He drove towards the castle with his wagon of hay and had a stout farm hand with a bill hook in his belt by the horses' heads. As he approached, the porter opened the gate and in the gate's entrance Bunnock halted the waggon. Then with a loud voice he cried, 'Call all, call all', at which the farm hand cut the horses' traces leaving the wagon to prevent the portcullis falling. Bunnock leapt off the driving seat to dash out the porter's brains, the eight armed men brushed out of the hay to deal with the loiterers standing by and the men concealed in ambush rushed from their hiding place through the castle gate with their swords drawn and quickly overcame the unsuspecting garrison. With the castle taken Bunnock sent the news to Bruce, who quickly dispatched reinforcements, had the fortress dismantled and gave Bunnock a rich reward.[22]

The whole province of Lothian, which covered the present day counties of Edinburgh, Haddington and Berwick, the eastern half of Roxburgh, the eastern corner of Selkirk, the eastern confines of Peebles and the southern and eastern portions of Linlithgow, had been seething with disaffection. Their situation was indeed unhappy. Officially they were within the King of England's peace but they got no protection from him and by Bruce they were treated in the same manner as the northern counties of England: they paid tribute or suffered the consequences. Yet when they paid tribute to Bruce the garrisons of the English-held castles which lay so thick upon the ground would sally forth and seize their goods and hold them as prisoners for ransom on the grounds that they had dealt with the enemy.[23]

Their feudal lord the Earl of Dunbar, who had consistently supported the English, and their Lord Chief Justice, Adam Gordon, appealed to Edward II detailing their lamentable plight, but though he reprimanded the governors of his castles, the populace was still oppressed and knew not where to turn. In the words of the *Lanercost Chronicle*,

> the Scots were so divided among themselves that sometimes the father was on the Scottish side and the son on the English and vice versa: also

one brother might be with the Scots and another with the English; yea, even the same individual be first with one party and then with another. But all those who were with the English were merely feigning, either because it was the stronger party, or in order to save the lands they possessed in England: for their hearts were always with their own people, athough their persons might not be so.[24]

Since the hearts of these people were for Scotland, Bruce's lieutenants were able to take risks which only a friendly populace made possible.

On Shrove Tuesday, 27 February 1314, the garrison of Roxburgh were holding a feast before the oncoming of Lent. Taking advantage of this James Douglas approached the castle with sixty picked men. Over their armour they wore black cloaks and went along a path in single file on hands and knees as if they were cows or oxen which had not been herded in for the night.

As they came near the castle they heard one of the sentries on the wall say to his companion, 'The local farmer nearby must be making good cheer, for he has left out all his cattle,' to which the other replied, 'Good cheer tonight but Douglas will have them tomorrow,' and so, laughing, they left the ramparts. Then Douglas and his men came to the walls and hooked up their ladders. The first man up, named Sim of Leadhouse, was seen by a sentry as his head and shoulders came over the parapet, but before the alarm could be given Sim caught him by the throat with one hand and with a knife in the other stabbed him in the heart; then hissed to those waiting below, 'All's well, speed quickly.'

When all were up they went silently in each direction along the sentry walk and it is said by Sir Walter Scott, in his *Tales of a Grandfather*, that Douglas, leading one party, coming round a corner saw a woman sitting on the wall with her back turned singing a lullaby to her baby.

> 'Hush ye, hush ye, little pet ye
> Hush ye, hush ye, do not fret ye
> The Black Douglas shall not get ye'

at which he placed a hand upon her shoulder and growled 'Do not be sure of that', and she turned and saw in horror the Black Douglas beside her: but he promised to protect her.[25]

The garrison were all in the great hall, dancing and singing as the custom was on Shrove Tuesday, when suddenly there was a cry of 'Douglas, Douglas', and the men of Douglas poured through the doors. Although greatly superior in numbers, the English were taken by surprise and fled incontinently in all directions.

Only the governor, William de Fiennes, rallied a few men around him and shut himself in the keep. Although at daylight he saw that the rest of the castle was in the hands of the Scots, he continued to hold out until he received an arrow wound in his face so severe that, after yielding on condition that he and his companions had safe passage to England, he died on return to his home.

Sim of Leadhouse brought to Bruce the news of Roxburgh's capture and was suitably rewarded, and a gang of workmen under Edward Bruce was sent to level to the ground the tower and walls of the castle.[26]

Thomas Randolph, Earl of Moray, was not to be outdone. He and Douglas had been close friends ever since he had been captured by Douglas and had lived with him as his prisoner until he had sworn allegiance to Bruce. In looks there was a striking contrast between the two young men. Douglas was tall, thin and dark; Randolph of medium height, thickset with fair hair and complexion.[27] Their temperaments matched their physical appearance. Both indeed were noted by all for their courteous and modest demeanour. But Douglas remained always the brilliant commando, intense, restless, ruthless and inspired, while Randolph even in his youth was more measured in his approach to his problems with a larger understanding of statecraft, as Bruce had observed and made good use of in placing wide areas under his administration.

But however measured his approach, a comradely rivalry would spur him to feats as dramatic as those of his friend.

When he heard news of Douglas's success as Roxburgh he was lying with his men below the castle of Edinburgh intent on its capture. Perched on its pinnacle of rock the castle seemed invulnerable to all means of attack but the wearing away of its defenders by starvation. Yet weeks of blockade had passed by and no parleys of surrender had been made. So Randolph made enquiries among the citizens and promised a reward to any who should know a way up the face of the crag. By and by a stalwart man, named William Francis, came before him.

'When I was young,' he told Randolph, 'my father was keeper of the watch house at the castle, and since I was young and giddy and much in love with a girl in the town here below, I made a ladder of ropes to hang from the wall of the castle and found a way down the rock so that

I might visit her secretly and without suspicion. Often, I would descend at night and stay with her and when it drew near to day I would climb up again without discovery so that however dark it may be I can find the path aright. If you would make the attempt I can bring you to the wall.'

Randolph told him to make a rope ladder sufficient in length to reach the top of the wall and from his men selected thirty who had knowledge of mountain climbing, of whom there were many among his Highlanders from Moray. Then on 14 March, the night being dark, he arranged for the main body of his force to make an assault on the south gate of the castle which, because of the position of the castle, was the only quarter on which an assault could be made, while he and his thirty followed William Francis up the north face of the rock which was very high and fell away steeply from the foot of the wall.

With finger holds and toe holds in the crevices, they followed William Francis, sometimes near behind him, sometimes held up seeking for a handgrip, clinging to the rock face, knowing that if they slipped they would be broken to pieces on the boulders below. Half-way up the crag they came to a ledge just broad enough on which to crouch, and there they rested to get their wind. As they were sitting there, they heard the officers of the watch, who were doing their rounds, meet on the ramparts above them and stop to talk. One of them, wishing to startle his companions, suddenly threw a stone over the wall and cried, 'Away, I see you all!' There was one ghastly moment for the little party as the stone bounded down the crag before the man moved on with the rest of the watch.

Now the climbers had to negotiate the steepest part of the rock but at last reached the foot of the wall. It was nearly twelve foot high and, without knowing what lay beyond, William Francis hooked on the ladder and was the first to mount it, followed by Sir Andrew Gray and Thomas Randolph. The rest climbed up behind them, but before they were all up the watch heard the clatter of arms and, raising the cry of 'Treason', hurled themselves on the invaders.

Hearing the clamour, Randolph's main force, which had been lying near the south gate in pitch darkness waiting for a signal, rushed forward to batter the doors. Slowly fighting every yard, Randolph and his little band of thirty worked their way towards the mêlée at the gate and while some, meeting the constable of the castle, engaged him in a fierce struggle which ended in his death, others opened the gate to their comrades.

As the main force surged in through the open gate the garrison sought only to save themselves, some slipping through the gate, some sliding over the walls.[28]

The pride of Edinburgh was captured and soon afterwards undermined so that it toppled in a ruin to the ground.[29]

The spectacular capture of Edinburgh came as a climax to the campaign against the castles of Lothian, of which many of the smaller ones had already fallen unrecorded by history. When Edward II led his great army into the province three months later, only Dunbar, Jedburgh and Berwick remained in the hands of the English. Their long predominance in Lothian had at last been destroyed.

# 13

Edward II had begun the marshalling of his great army soon after Sir Philip Mowbray, under the chivalrous grant of a safe conduct, had arrived in London and informed him of the terms of the treaty he had made with Edward Bruce. For him, unlike the Scottish King whose policy had been recklessly contravened, it was a godsent opportunity to bring to battle the elusive Scots and overwhelm them with the superiority of his arms and numbers. 'The relief of Stirling' was a bugle call offered to his uncertain lips with which to rally his nation behind him and bring harmony to his jangling barons.

Throughout the spring and summer of 1313 Prince Louis, brother of King Philip IV of France and uncle of Isabella, Edward II's Queen, had been trying patiently to achieve a settlement between the English King and those of his magnates who had been responsible for the execution of Piers Gaveston. The challenge of Stirling provided the final pressure to bring the two parties together. On 13 October 1313 in Westminster Hall the Earl of Lancaster and his confederates admitted that they were guilty of Gaveston's death and made a humble apology to the King for their misdeed and he, in turn, graciously granted a general pardon to them and to their followers. Two banquets were then given by the King and the Earl of Lancaster respectively to celebrate their accord[1] and the full attention of the hierarchy of England could now be directed to the destruction of Scotland.

The odds in their favour were very great. They could draw on a manpower five times as large as that of their enemy and from a country which, apart from the northern counties, had been untouched by war and was ranked as the most prosperous in fourteenth-century Europe. Ireland and Wales were quiet; the papacy favourable; France for the time being friendly and internally there was such peace as had not been known since the beginning of the reign. Against these advantages Scotland, ravaged by nine invasions and eighteen years of warfare, could only offer the genius of the King and the ardour of his followers.

On 28 November 1313 Edward II wrote to the Earl of Dunbar that he would bring an army north before midsummer.[2] On 23 December he sent out writs to eight earls and eighty-seven barons summoning them to appear with their contingents at Berwick on 10 June 1314. In February 1314 he reiterated to his supporters in Scotland that he intended to lead an army against Bruce. In March he made the Earl of Pembroke once more Viceroy of Scotland,[3] and from 9 March onwards a stream of executive orders for the mobilization of men and supplies issued from the royal headquarters. The Earl of Ulster was deputed to raise and transport troops from Ireland: 16,000 foot were levied from thirteen English counties in the north and Midlands; 5000 archers and spearmen from north and south Wales; numerous ships and sailors from the seaports of England to provide transport for the provisioning and equipment of the land forces; and throughout Europe, by word of mouth, a general invitation for the attendance of all knights in search of chivalric fame or the spoils of fortune.[4]

Early in May an embargo was put on the export of foodstuffs and 106 four-horse and 110 eight-oxen carts were drafted from various sheriffdoms to provide the wagon train of the army.

As Edward II awaited at Berwick the arrival of the different contingents he was in an expansive mood. To Hugh Despenser the younger, the son of his closest adviser Sir Hugh Despenser the elder, he allotted the spacious lands of Thomas Randolph, Earl of Moray, and to others of his following he handed out the patrimonies of Scottish gentry which he was confident would fall into his hands. His optimism was shared by knights and barons in his train, many of whom brought with them tapestries, plate and furniture to furbish the houses which the king had promised them in advance.[5]

The only shadow on his euphoria was the sullen refusal of the Earls of Lancaster, Warwick, Surrey and Arundel to answer to his summons in person. Although, in accordance with their feudal obligations, they sent their quota of cavalry and footmen, they cloaked the personal animosity which had motivated their own nonattendance by claiming that the consent of parliament should have been obtained before making war.[6]

However, the Earls of Gloucester, Pembroke and Hereford were at his side and among the veterans of his father's Welsh and Scottish campaigns were Sir Ralph de Monthermer (formerly styled the Earl of Gloucester before the succession of his stepson to the title), Sir Robert Clifford, Sir Henry Beaumont, Sir Maurice Barclay, Sir Marmaduke Tweng and Sir Giles d'Argentan, described as the third best knight in Christendom.[7] Edward II had recently ransomed d'Argentan from the Emperor of Byzantium who had seized him on his way to aid the knights of Rhodes against the Saracens.

Also serving in his army were Scotsmen who still opposed Bruce, among them John Comyn, son of the murdered 'Red' Comyn, Sir Ingram de Umfraville, one-time Scottish guardian, his brother the Earl of Angus, and a host of knights from France, Brittany, Poitou, Guienne and Germany.[8]

As the contingents from different directions came marching in and set up their tents at Wark-on-Tweed, hard by Berwick, there had assembled by 10 June the greatest army that a king of England had ever commanded. Foremost in splendour and force were some 2500 heavy cavalry furnished by the nobles and knights. Each horseman was clad in chain mail overlaid by a surcoat with his armorial bearings. His horse, thickset and strong as a percheron, had flowing blankets about its body – 'trappings' – to trap and entangle the thrusts of sword and spear, and the rider when he was in the saddle carried with him a twelve foot lance and a battle axe, sword or mace. His squire was in attendance upon him and one, two or three mounted armoured men at arms. The brutal impact of a thousand knights charging in thunder together could appall the bravest and never had the English rank and file had such confident expectation of success as when they saw so great a force of cavalry.

Next in deadly execution, some 3000 in number, were the *corps d'élite* of the Welsh archers who had become so expert in the use of the longbow that they could loose their shafts with such speed that five arrows would be airborne at the same time. And lastly the main body of foot soldiers, 15,000 in all, in quilted coats and steel helmets armed with spear, shield and sword.

Such was the army that Edward II had at his disposal: but if the body, more than 20,000 in numbers, was strong, the single head was weak. Although Stirling had to be reached by 24 June to observe the terms of the challenge, it was not until 17 June that the King began to march from Berwick, with his forces arranged in ten divisions.[9] 'He hastened,' writes a contemporary chronicler, 'day by day to the appointed place, not as if he was leading an army to battle but as if he was on a pilgrimage to St James of Compostella. Brief were the halts for sleep, briefer still for food: hence horses, horsemen and infantry were worn out with toil and hunger.'[10]

By 21 June he had only reached Edinburgh. Here the army was revictualled by twenty-three ships which had sailed up the coast of England to the port of Leith and on the next day, to catch up in time, they made a forced march to Falkirk, 22 miles through the dust and heat of a scorching summer's day. There they bivouacked, parched and exhausted, with still ten miles and thirty-six hours to go in which to meet the provisions of the challenge.

Ahead in Torwood lay the Scottish army.


Torwood was a vast forest with rocky outcrops lying across the ancient Roman road from Edinburgh to Stirling some five miles north of Falkirk. Here by the end of April 1314 Bruce had made his head-quarters and begun to assemble his army.

He called a halt to all subsidiary expeditions and to him came Edward Bruce and his men fresh from their invasion of Cumberland, and Douglas and Randolph with theirs from Lothian, elated by the captures of Roxburgh and Edinburgh. Summonses for military service had been sent throughout the kingdom, and as the days lengthened and the weather became milder, groups of men under their knights, lairds or chiefs or on their own made their way at fitful intervals to the Scottish camp from the farthest reaches of the country. As they came in they were welcomed by the King and allotted for their training to one of the four divisions into which he had ordered his battle array.

Of these the vanguard was commanded by Thomas Randolph, Earl of Moray. At the end of its training period it consisted of about 500 men from his earldom of Moray, from Ross and the far north and burghers from the towns of Inverness, Elgin, Nairn and Forres. The second division, led by Edward Bruce, drew on the men of Buchan, Mar, Angus, the Mearns, Menteith, Strathearn and Lennox, with a small contingent from Galloway, to make up a roll call of 1000. The third division of a similar size was under the nominal command of the High Steward, Walter the son of Bruce's old friend James Stewart who had died in 1309, but as Walter Stewart was a minor the control was actually in the hands of his cousin, James Douglas. Their men came from Lanark, Renfrew and the Borders.

The fourth division had the double strength of 2000 and was commanded by the King himself. Here under his banner were gathered from western Scotland Highlanders from a score of different clans,* muting their feuds beneath his chastening eye and in the face of the common enemy. Bruce's own men from Carrick, Kyle and Cunningham were there and Angus Macdonald with his liegemen from the Western Isles.[11]

Lastly there were 500 light horse under the Marischal Sir Robert Keith and a small company of archers from the Ettrick forest.

Altogether the Scottish army amounted to between 5000 and 6000, little more than a quarter of the English host.

During the two months he had in hand, Bruce's main preoccupation was the training and discipline of his disparate forces. He knew that he had neither the horses, equipment nor numbers to fight the English cavalry with cavalry of his own. His army must fight on foot and be based on the schiltron: the hedgehog of spears. But he realized, and this was his brilliance as a tactician, that the schiltron must not be merely static and defensive but be able to act on the offensive as a mobile battering ram. Considering that the majority of his troops were Highlanders accustomed rather to the wild charge or the ambuscade, the astonishing coherence and control shown in the movement of the schiltrons on the battlefield of Bannockburn argues not only how thorough must have been their training but how remarkable the personal ascendancy of the King for chiefs and people so independent to accept the discipline entailed.

He was helped in this by the different relationship from England existing between master and man in Scotland. The gradations of wealth were less steep. Whereas in England the natural leaders were high on their horses remote from the humble foot soldiers, in Scotland the chiefs, burghers and landowners, with leaner purses, were accustomed to fight side by side with their own men on foot. When they did so they wore lighter armour than when on horseback and their followers steel helmets and steel gloves and either back and breast pieces or padded leather jackets. All were armed with twelve-foot spears and swords or axes.

Like many of the great commanders who followed him in history, Bruce took pains to make himself known to all his men, 'ever, as he met them, he greeted them cheerfully, speaking an encouraging word

* cf note VIII

to one or another and they, seeing their King welcome them in so forthright a manner, were greatly heartened and were ready to fight and die to uphold his honour.'[12]

During this period he selected the site of the battlefield on which he would oppose the English. That which he chose was 'almost the copybook military position for the strategic defence of Stirling Castle'.[13]

About two miles north of Torwood, the Roman road dipped down to the valley of the Bannock burn. Rising in the hills to the west the burn descended through wooded slopes and meadows to the ford which served the road and then plunged into a deep gully by the hamlet of Bannock and cut its way through the boglands in an arc to the northeast to debouch into the Firth of Forth. North of this natural obstacle there was to the left of the road the New Park, a moderate area of undulating grassland backed by thick woods which had been enclosed by Alexander III as a royal forest: to the right of the road a narrow stretch of meadow which ended abruptly at its eastern edge in a steep bank, dropping down into the Carse of Balquiderock, a flat plateau of clayland embraced by the arms of the Pelstream and the Bannock burn. Beyond these, marshlands, intersected by streams, extended to the Firth of Forth.

No advance by the English could be made from the east across this spongy area; nor could they make a detour to the west where the Torwood and the New Park stretched in an unbroken forest. Their only means of approach towards Stirling were along the Roman road through the New Park or somewhat to the east of the gully where by fording the Bannock burn where its banks were lower and taking the public track, they could pass outside the New Park under the lea of the escarpment at the Carse's edge.

Bruce must have reconnoitred the ground on many occasions with his lieutenants for when the time came to take up their positions there the move was made with great smoothness. In the meantime, to prevent the English cavalry deploying onto the open ground either side of the Roman road, if they crossed the ford, he honeycombed the area with pits dug a foot in breadth and knee deep camouflaged with brushwood and grass and had trees felled and placed in barricades across any tracks through the forest which might be accessible to horsemen.

While the work was being carried out he sent James Douglas and Sir Robert Keith with a small mounted patrol to monitor the progress of the English army.

On 22 June they returned with the news, which they reported to the King in private, that the English were on the move from Edinburgh in immense numbers, for the whole landscape was covered by mounted men with waving banners, columns of foot soldiers and archers and lines of wagons stretching into the distance. Never before had they seen such a multitude and splendour. Bruce told them to keep this knowledge to themselves but to spread it abroad that the English were advancing in great disorder so that the men might not be discouraged.[14]

He now gave orders that the camp followers, grooms, 'small folk' and others too ill-armed to be included in his schiltrons should retire with the wagon train of food and equipment to a valley hidden behind Gillies Hill and that the straggling bands who, though adequately armed, had arrived too late for enrolment in his trained formations should accompany them and wait there until summoned.[15]

Next he dispatched the vanguard and the other two divisions to their prepared positions north of the Bannock burn: the vanguard, under Thomas Randolph, to St Ninian's Kirk to watch the track along the Carse, with the divisions of Douglas and Edward Bruce echeloned to his right in that order while he, with his division, remained as rearguard in Torwood to cover their withdrawal. When this had been completed he brought his men across the burn and took his place to the right of his brother's division. The whole army was now in line facing southeast down a gradual slope which gave them observation both of the entry to the New Park and the Carse. And there, after placing sentries, they slept.[16]

Next morning, 23 June, soon after sunrise, the army heard Mass and prayed to God for their cause, and since it was the vigil of St John the Baptist they observed it as a fast, taking only bread and water. And when they had armed and taken their stations the King had it proclaimed to each division that if any were of faint heart let him depart at once, at which a great shout arose from the assembled troops that all would conquer or die.[17]

Meanwhile the English army were approaching from Falkirk and about midday had reached Torwood, where they halted. Here they were met by Sir Philip Mowbray, the Governor of Stirling Castle, who had made a wide detour of join them. He pointed out that there was no need for a battle to take place, for under the laws of chivalry the

Sunday, 23 June 1314

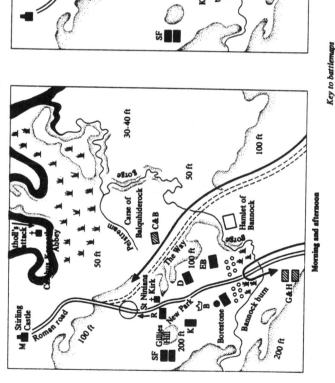

Morning and afternoon

Late afternoon to after midnight

Key to battlemaps

■ Scottish Army    ▨ English Army

A   Airth, Commander Scots Base Depot      K     Keith, 500 light horse
B   Bruce, 2000 foot                       SF    Small Folk
D   Douglas, 1000 foot                     C&B   Clifford & Beaumont, 600 horse
EB  Edward Bruce, 1000 foot                G&H   Gloucester & Hertford Vanguard, 1500 horse
R   Randolph, 500 foot                     M     Mowbray, Governor Stirling Castle

                                           ※ marsh    ooo hidden pits

🙿 boggy

**Monday, 24 June 1314**

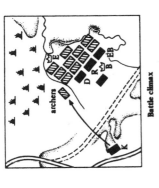

Early morning

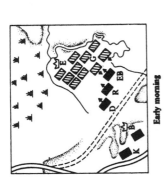

Battle climax

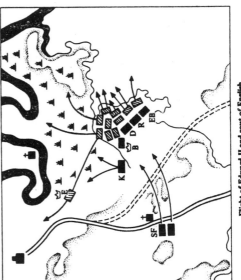

Flight of Edward II and rout of English

English had fulfilled their obligation by arriving within three leagues of their objective and therefore the castle must remain in their hands. [18] But Edward II had not brought his mighty army so many miles to let his enemies once more elude him, but to overwhelm them and march in triumph to the gates of Stirling Castle which he could see in the distance high on its upthrust of rock against a cloudless sky.

A consultation was held among the leaders at which Sir Philip, who had been able to observe the preparations of the Scots from the battlements of the castle, warned that the English could not attack from the western flank as the bridle ways through the forest had been barricaded and that elsewhere the growth was too thick, and that to the immediate front the Scottish forces were drawn up in the New Park. It was decided then that the vanguard should advance along the Roman road under the King's nephew, the Earl of Gloucester, with the expectation that the power of his army would cause the Scots to retire. If not Gloucester would sweep them away with a charge of his heavy cavalry. At the same time, Sir Robert Clifford and Sir Henry Beaumont should take a picked body of 600 knights along the public way at the edge of the Carse and get behind the Scots to cut off their anticipated retreat. Some delay was caused by the intervention of the Earl of Hereford, who claimed that as High Constable it was his hereditary right to lead the army: but this was shortly resolved by making him joint commander of the van with Gloucester.

As the English cavalry emerged from Torwood onto the green meadow which sloped down to the Bannock burn, their many coloured banners and armour glittering in the sun could be seen clearly from across the valley by the Scots who stood to arms.

The English vanguard came down across the meadow and their lines gradually contracted into a column as they approached the ford over the burn with the Earls of Hereford and Gloucester in the lead. The Earl of Hereford's nephew, Sir Henry de Bohun, rode some fifty yards in front, clad in full armour on a powerful horse with his spear in his hand. As he came through the belt of trees on the north bank of the burn he saw on the open ground before him a single rider inspecting the serried ranks of Scotsmen half-hidden in the woodland. He was on a grey palfrey with an axe in his hand and a golden circlet around his helmet. Recognizing the King of Scots, de Bohun without more ado couched his lance and spurred towards him.

Who knows what thoughts passed through Bruce's mind? The prudent course was to fall back within the ranks of his soldiers, but perhaps he was influenced by seeing the crest of the de Bohuns on the surcoat of his assailant. For it was to the de Bohuns that, when he was a fugitive, his lands in Annandale and Carrick had been handed over by Edward I,[19] and it was to the de Bohuns that Edward II had given the Bruce domains in Essex.[20] And then again, how could he, the victor in a hundred tournaments, retreat from such a challenge before the eyes of Scotsmen prepared to lay down their lives on his behalf? So he turned his horse and cantered towards de Bohun, and as the thunderous charge came near swerved to one side and rising in his stirrups brought down his axe with such force on his opponent's head that he cut through helmet, skull and brain and his axe handle shivered in two.[21]

For a minute there was a stunned silence on both sides, and then with a wild cry the Highlanders of the King's division climbed over their fieldworks and charged on the English cavalry who were trying to line up on the open ground below, confused by the hidden pits into which many of them had fallen. The Earl of Gloucester was flung from his stumbling horse and only rescued by his squires and the rest took flight. Bruce stopped the pursuit at once, an eloquent tribute to his training and brought his Highlanders back to their lines.

His brother and his commanders crowded round him and, as far as they dared, upbraided him for so rash an act which might have been the ruin of them all, but he made no answer: only looked sadly at his broken axe handle.[22] Then turning aside from them he scanned the surroundings and almost at once saw the body of horse led by Clifford and Beaumont, which had been riding under cover of the bank along the Carse, appear in sight towards St Ninians Kirk. Roughly he called to Thomas Randolph as he pointed out the horsemen, 'A rose has fallen from your chaplet,' at which Randolph, in consternation, galloped to his division and, marshalling them in a schiltron, took them onto the open ground over which the English would have to pass.[23]

When Sir Henry Beaumont saw the Scots approach he cried, 'Let us halt a little; let them come on; give them room,' meaning that he wished to have space to manoeuvre around them.

Sir Thomas Gray, as his son wrote later, replied, 'Whatever you give them I doubt not that they will have all soon enough.'

'Very well,' exclaimed Sir Henry, 'if you are afraid, be off.'

'Sir,' answered Sir Thomas, 'it is not from fear that I shall fly this day.' So saying, he spurred in between Sir William Deyncourt and Sir Henry and charged into the thick of the enemy. Sir William was killed.

Sir Thomas Gray was taken prisoner as his horse, speared by the pikes, fell headlong and hurtled him to the ground.[24] Observing this, the rest of the squadron approached more cautiously, and surrounding the schiltron attacked it from all sides. But they had been sent as a flying column unaccompanied by archers, and without their hail of arrows, which had been so devastating at Falkirk, they could not break the hedge of spearmen. Every now and then one of these would lunge forward from the ranks and stab a horse so that it fell to the ground leaving its heavily armed rider flat and helpless at his comrades' feet. In frustration the cavalry, circling the schiltron, threw at their assailants battle axes, swords and maces so that a great mound of weapons arose in the hollow centre of the formation. Still the battle went on with the defenders hard pressed, the sun blazing down on them so that they were drenched with sweat and the air thick with dust.

When James Douglas saw how Randolph was surrounded and hidden from sight by the superior numbers of the mailed knights, he went to Bruce and asked if he might not go to his aid; but Bruce, uncertain whether or not the English would renew their frontal attack, forbade him to leave his post. A little later Douglas, with increasing anxiety for the fate of his comrade, came again with his plea to Bruce and this time was given leave to go to Randolph's rescue. So he marched his men to the fray but as he came closer he saw that the English were beginning to waver and, calling his men to a halt, exclaimed, 'The Earl of Moray has gained the day and since we were not there to help him in the battle let us leave to him the credit of the victory.' And indeed Randolph had taken advantage of an opening between the cavalry to drive his schiltron forward so that it split the enemy in half, some flying north to Stirling and some south to join the main host.

When the enemy had fled, Randolph's men sat on the ground and took off their helmets to fan themselves, for they were weary and soaked in sweat; and after a little while they followed their commander to Bruce's headquarters, and there the men of the other divisions crowded round them with their congratulations.[25]

When Bruce saw them all assembled there in so confident a mood, induced by his own exploit and Randolph's victory, he was silent for a little and then spoke to them briefly of the dismay that would be caused among the English by the double defeat of powerful knights by men on foot, but that nevertheless, if they felt they had shown mettle enough and wished to retire, the decision was in their hands. To which they replied, 'Good King, order us to battle tomorrow as soon as it is light for we shall not fail you for fear of death but persevere until our land is free.' So he dismissed them to their stations with the words, 'Sirs, since you will it so, make ready in the morning.'[26]

That evening he held a conference with his chief commanders, whose experience of warfare enabled them to assess the enormous disparity between the two forces, to consider whether he should not, like Kutusov in Russia five centuries later, make it his main object to preserve the only Scottish army in being by retiring to the wild country of Lennox and beyond and leave starvation and the scorched earth to fight for him rather than risk the annihilation of Scotland's manhood. But while they were debating, Sir Alexander Seton, who was serving in the English army, came secretly to him through the night and said to Bruce, 'Sir, if you ever intend to reconquer Scotland now is the time. The English have lost heart and are discouraged,' and he pledged his life on pain of being hanged and drawn that if Bruce attacked them on the morrow he would surely win.[27]

His description of the English was very accurate. Edward II and his army had been so confident that the mere weight of his heavy cavalry would cow the Scots into submission that, when the news spread that a seasoned campaigner like Sir Robert Clifford had been driven from the field by a parcel of footmen, and a champion in the lists had been slain by a man on a pony, the reaction of the rank and file, already dispirited by two forced marches under blazing sun on successive days, was as inordinate as had been their previous assurance. 'From that moment,' according to the *Lanercost Chronicle*, 'began a panic among the English and the Scots grew bolder,'[28] and in the vivid words of Barbour, 'in five hundred places and more the English could be seen whispering together and saying "our Lords will always use their might against the right and when they wage war unrighteously God is offended and brings misfortune and so it may happen now".' So widespread was the defeatism that Edward II ordered heralds to go to and fro throughout the army to explain that the events of the day had been mere skirmishes and that in the major battle to come victory was certain and rewards great.[29]

Sir Robert Clifford had returned to the English headquarters with news of his defeat late in the afternoon, and it was clear that no further action could take place that day. The main problem now facing the English command was where to bivouac for the night, and in particular to water their innumerable chargers, draught horses and oxen as well as their manpower and yet be in a position the next day to deploy their cavalry in the open ground against the Scots. Many of their commanders knew the terrain from previous campaigns, and the decision taken to move from Torwood to the middle reaches of the Bannock burn was a practical one. The foot soldiers and the supply column laagered on the south bank while the cavalry crossed over the burn onto the level carse with open country between them and the Scottish positions. Both the Bannock burn and the Pelstream are tidal rivers, and in the early evening of 23 June the tide was right out[30] so that, with the help of doors and beams from the barns and houses of Bannock, all the cavalry found their way from the boggy areas along the south and east of the burn to the hard clay of the carse. By the time the movement of men and horses had been completed, the short summer night was almost over: there was no time to rest and the knights stood to arms with their horses bitted.[31]

The disposition of the English army was based on the assumption that the Scots would remain behind their fieldworks to receive the cavalry attack. But when Bruce learnt from his scouts the siting of his enemies he made the daring and momentous decision to take the offensive himself. Never before had foot soldiers marched forward to meet the might of chivalry, but it was to this end that he had directed the training of his men and in miniature it had proved its worth under Thomas Randolph a few hours earlier.

The English cavalry were enclosed on three sides by the Pelstream and the Bannock burn, within, as it were, the arc of a bended bow. These streams in the early hours of 24 June would be at half tide and impassable.[32] He would advance his army so that it formed the taut string between the two ends of the bow and would thus confine the cavalry in so cramped a space that they would be unable to manoeuvre.

Accordingly, he called the officers of his divisions together and explained to them the action he was going to take and gave them their order of battle. When he had finished, according to Barbour, he addressed them in the following words:

'Sirs,' he said, 'we have every reason to be confident of success for we have right on our side. Our enemies are moved only by desire for dominion but we are fighting for our lives, our children, our wives and

156

the freedom of our country. And so I ask and pray that with all your strength, without cowardice or alarm, you meet the foes whom you will first encounter so boldly that those behind them will tremble. See that your ranks are not broken so that, when the enemy come charging on horseback, you meet them steadfastly with your spears; and do not let any seek for booty or prisoners until the field is surely ours. Think on your manhood and your deeds of valour and the joy that awaits you if you are victorious. In your hands you carry honour, praise, riches, freedom and felicity if you bear yourselves bravely, but altogether to the contrary if your hearts fail you. You could have lived quietly as slaves, but because you longed to be free you are with me here, and to gain that end you must be valiant, strong and undismayed.

'I know not what more to say. You know what honour is. Bear yourself in such fashion as to keep your honour.

'And I promise you by virtue of my royal power that for those who fight manfully I will pardon all offences against the Crown, and for those who die I will remit all feudal dues upon their heirs.'[33]

The officers then returned to their men to tell them what the King had said and to prepare for the morrow.

On midsummer day, 24 June 1314, dawn broke at 3.45 a.m. to usher in a bright and sunny day. Its first rays touched the plumes and trappings of the English cavalry on the carse and brought a slight warmth to the footsore and sodden infantry who were scattered on whatever firm patches they could find in the marshes beyond the Bannock burn. Westwards it picked out the dark mass of trees in the New Park where the Scots were already astir.

It was the feast of St John the Baptist.

The Scottish priests in each division had celebrated Mass, reading in high tones for all to hear the lesson of the day: 'Comfort ye, comfort ye . . . Speak ye comfortably to Jerusalem and cry unto her that her warfare is accomplished.'

The men had then eaten a slight meal and begun to range themselves in their divisions, carrying many banners as their King had bidden. When they were all assembled he called forth and knighted in the field, as was the custom of the day before a battle, all those who had been chosen for that honour, among them Walter Stewart as knight and Sir James Douglas as knight banneret.[34]

The new knights and the whole host were then blessed by the Abbot of Inchaffray, who held in one hand a casket containing the most sacred relics of the kingdom.

When these ceremonies had been concluded, Bruce gave the order to advance. Three divisions moved off in echelon: first Edward Bruce with his right flank protected by the Bannock burn, then, a little back to his left, Thomas Randolph, and then, in the same manner, James Douglas: all in schiltron formation. The fourth division and the cavalry remained in reserve on the lower slope of the New Park.

When Edward II saw the Scots coming forward on foot over open ground he cried in amazement, 'What, will yonder Scots fight?'

To which Sir Ingram de Umfraville replied, 'Surely sir: but indeed this is the strangest sight I ever saw for Scotsmen to take on the whole might of England by giving battle on hard ground,' and even as he spoke the Scots, who were now some hundred yards away, knelt down and made a short prayer to God to help them in the fight; at which the English King exclaimed triumphantly, 'They kneel for mercy.'

Again Sir Ingram replied, 'For mercy yes, but not from you: from God for their sins. These men will win all or die.'

'So be it,' said the King and ordered the trumpets to sound the assembly. [35]

The Earl of Gloucester, the previous evening, had urged Edward II to rest his army for twenty-four hours before engaging in battle and, in a heated argument, had been accused by him of disloyalty. Now, still smarting from the unjust attack on his honour, he mounted his horse so precipitately, when he heard the summons, that neither his squires had time to put his surcoat over his armour nor his vanguard to saddle and range behind him before he had charged headlong at Edward Bruce's schiltron. Unrecognized, he was slain on their spears far in advance of his van[36] who, following him piecemeal as fast as they could, lost many of their bravest knights, among them the veteran Sir Robert Clifford, Sir John Comyn, son of the murdered 'Red' Comyn, Sir Edmund Manley, steward of the English King's household, and Sir Pain Tiptoft.[37]

Vainly the vanguard tried to break the hedgerow of spears but were no more successful than their comrades the previous day. Many of the horses were stabbed and threw their riders who were trampled in the mêlée, and when Randolph came up on the left of Edward Bruce[38] and attacked from the flank those who were engaged against him, the whole van broke and wheeled back to join the main body of cavalry who were trying to form up for action, setting off a stampede of wounded riderless horses into the thick of the mustering squadrons.

Douglas now came up on Randolph's left[39] so that the three Scottish divisions covered the whole of the front between the Pelstream and the Bannock burn,[40] penning the English cavalry in so narrow an area that they were no better than a seething mass of men and horses effectively blocking any access for the infantry behind them to take part in the battle. Now linked together in serried ranks of spearmen, the Scots pushed forward and became so locked in combat with their foes that the English archers in the rear could not loose their arrows without hitting their own countrymen.

At last someone in command on the English side got the archers over to the north of the Pelstream and there, taking their stance twelve paces apart, they began to pour their arrows into the left of Douglas's division. But Bruce, from his vantage point on the slope of the New Park, saw what was happening and ordered Sir Robert Keith with his 500 light horse to disperse them, which he did with such effect that those who were not cut down fled back among the infantry causing them in turn to begin to flee.[41]

But in the loop of the carse the English knights were fighting desperately against the pressure of the Scottish ranks. 'The battle there was fiercest and so great was the spilling of blood that it stood in pools on the ground. There might be heard weapons striking on armour and knights and horses be seen tumbling on the ground and many a rich and splendid garment fouled roughly underfoot.'[42]

For a long while the struggle continued in silence, broken only by the clashing of steel on steel, the snapping of spearshafts, the groans of the wounded and the screams of disembowelled horses. But gradually the English began to give ground and Bruce, seeing them waver, sent his reserve division into the fight. Turning to Angus Macdonald he exclaimed, 'My hope is constant in thee,'[43] and the Islemen rushed forward to join the ranks on the left of Douglas's division which had been much thinned by the English archers. Now the cry was 'Press on, press on, they fail,' for behind the forward spearmen with their twelve-foot pikes came the added weight from the increased rear ranks, each man leaning on the man in front so that the whole mass formed an immense human steamroller.[44]

The Earl of Pembroke and Sir Giles d'Argentan, who were riding either side of Edward II, realizing that the day was lost and that at all costs the King must not be captured, seized each a rein of his horse and, in spite of his expostulations, for he had been fighting with great courage, dragged him away, and with some five hundred knights of his bodyguard pushed and barged through the hurlyburly to the ebbing Pelstream and there crossed towards Stirling Castle. As they fought their way through the press, Edward's shield bearer was captured with the royal shield and seal. Many Scotsmen tried to seize the King's bridle and the trappings of his horse, but were kept at bay by his flailing mace. His horse was piked but lasted until he was clear of the throng, when another was found for him. It was then that Sir Giles d'Argentan turned to him and said, 'Sire your protection was committed to me, but since you are safely on your way, I will bid you farewell for never yet have I fled from a battle, nor will I now.' He turned his horse and spurring desperately into the Scottish ranks was overborne and slain.[45]

Edward II continued to the castle but was refused entry by the governor, Sir Philip Mowbray, on the sensible grounds that under the terms of his agreement he would have to surrender the castle and the King would become a prisoner; but he deputed to him a local knight to guide him by a detour round the west of the New Park so that he could bypass the battle area on his way to England.[46]

When the royal standard was seen to leave the field, the whole English army began to give way. It was at this juncture that Bruce produced that unexpected intervention by which commanders have so often won victory. A signal was given to the watchers on Gillies Hill and over its crest appeared all the camp followers, servants and those who had arrived too late for Bruce to incorporate them in his formations, rank upon rank in massed array, with broad sheets for banners upon poles and spears. As they came down the hill and saw the battle below them and the English beginning to falter, they gave a great shout of 'Upon them, upon them!'[47]

When the English saw this vast host approaching, they believed it to be a second Scottish army and all hope left them. Their slow retreat disintegrated into a panic-stricken rout and each man thought only how to flee. Never in the history of her wars had England suffered such a humiliation or exhibited such helplessness in defeat. She had men and material enough to make many an honourable stand. Her infantry had not even been engaged and many of her archers were among them: but not a leader emerged to rally them. Every armoured knight who had not been unhorsed or killed put spurs to his steed. The Earl of Hereford, High Constable of England, with some of the foremost barons, fled, to their shame, along the route which their King had taken and made for Bothwell.[48] Others less fortunate, penned in by the Scots, attempted to cross the Bannock burn but got bogged in its muddy depths and were rolled over and crushed by those who were crowding after them. Between its banks the burn became so choked by struggling men and horses that the latest comers could pass dryshod over a causeway of drowned and drowning bodies.[49]

One nobleman alone in this hour of panic preserved his calm and his courage. The Earl of Pembroke, after conducting his monarch to Stirling, threaded his way back through the chaos to where some thousands of the Welsh levies were stationed.[50] These were the men from the territories of his vast earldom and were conspicuous from their custom of going to war half-naked. Marshalling them into columns, he set out to guide them over a hundred miles of wild country to Carlisle. All along the route, they were harried by the natives through whose districts they passed, and many who fell out or straggled were killed but the greater part he brought safely across the Solway to the English headquarters at Carlisle.[51]

But the other infantry had little guidance. Bewildered by the disappearance of the cavalry, they dispersed in all directions. Many of them tried to cross the Forth but were swept away in its swirling currents or sucked into the treacherous swamps within its loops. The majority made for Stirling and took refuge on the crags beneath the castle.

So great were their numbers and so many of the English knights had taken flight in the same direction that Bruce, uncertain of the governor's reaction, kept his men in formation for fear that if they were to scatter, a counter-attack would be launched from the castle.[52]

It was this that enabled the English King to escape: for when news was brought that he had been seen riding south, Bruce dared not release his cavalry in pursuit for it seemed to him beyond belief that so powerful an army as the English, with so many seasoned veterans, would fail to rally and renew the conflict. However, at Douglas's request he allowed him to take sixty horse with which to stalk the King.[53]

This was an enterprise for which Douglas's long experience of guerrilla warfare made him peculiarly fitted.

As he passed through Torwood he met, riding the moor beyond, Sir Laurence Abernethy with four score of men come to join the English, but when he heard from Douglas of the day's work he promptly changed his allegiance and accompanied him in the chase.

They caught up with the King's troop beyond Linlithgow, 500 armed men riding in close order, and decided that they were too many to attack in a pitched battle, but from that moment they shadowed them like hyenas a herd of wildebeest so that if any fell behind for however short a space he was taken or killed. They harried them so closely and unceasingly that it was said that not one Englishman could stop even to make water and that when they reached Dunbar, whose earl was ready to receive the King, they flung themselves off their saddles and rushed through the castle gates leaving their horses outside. With these Douglas returned to Bruce. Edward II was placed on a boat sailing for Bamburgh and from there made his way to Berwick, and in due course his knights reached him one by one by land.[54]

Meanwhile Bruce had moved his army before the walls of Stirling in readiness to attack, but at his approach the fugitives clustered there laid down their arms without a struggle and the governor, in formal surrender, handed over the keys of the castle to Bruce and pledged to him his future allegiance: a pledge which, unlike the Earl of Atholl, he fulfilled to his death.[55]

The Earl of Atholl, marching south apparently to the aid of Bruce, had suddenly attacked, on the eve of the main battle, the Scottish base camp at Cambus Kenneth Abbey and slain its unsuspecting commander, Sir John Airth.[56] This treacherous behaviour was the culmination of the resentment he felt for Edward Bruce who, after seducing the earl's sister, Isabel, and getting her with child, deserted her in favour of the daughter of the Earl of Ross, of whom he became so enamoured that his affection spread to the whole family. It is recorded that when he heard of the death of her brother, Sir Walter Ross, at Bannockburn, this hard and passionate man, for the first time in his life, wept for sorrow.

But he had little leisure for grief.[57] His royal brother, now that all organized resistance had ceased, sent him in pursuit of the English who had been seen streaming towards Bothwell, with the order that if they had already arrived there he should lay siege to the castle. Then Bruce turned his attention to tidying up the aftereffects of his victory.

On that midsummer day he had established without question his brilliance as a general and his authority as a leader: but beyond these gifts he now displayed in the aftermath of his success a consideration and courtesy towards the defeated which they did not easily forget. The fame of his humanity spread abroad and the harshest of English chroniclers paid an ungrudging tribute to the magnanimity of his behaviour.[58]

His cousin, Gilbert Clare, Earl of Gloucester, was carried to a neighbouring church and Bruce himself, for part of the night, kept vigil beside his corpse in honour of the family with whom his own had so many close links.[59] The earl's body and that of Sir Robert Clifford were afterwards despatched to their families at the Scottish King's expense.[60] Thirty-four barons and several hundred knights and squires who had fallen in the fray were given honourable burial in sanctified ground. The remainder of the dead were heaped in communal pits.[61]

Nearly a hundred barons, baronets and knights had been taken prisoner and these were treated as his guests while their ransoms were being arranged. Among them was Ralph de Monthermer who, in the days when he was styled Earl of Gloucester during his stepson's minority, had given to Bruce the vital warning in 1306 which had enabled him to evade the vengeance of Edward I. Now with great gladness Bruce repaid his debt of gratitude by entertaining him at his table and then releasing him without ransom.[62] A second prisoner to whom he granted the same favour, as one brave soldier to another, was Sir Marmaduke Tweng who, seventeen years before in the same area, had fought his way through the men of Wallace across the bridge they were about to destroy to find refuge in Stirling castle. Unhorsed at Bannockburn, he had crawled into the undergrowth. The next day, having hidden his armour in a coppice, he came out to look for Bruce, clad only in his shirt. Surprisingly, none took any notice as he wandered hither and thither in this simple raiment. At last, espying the Scottish King, he fell on his knees before him. 'Welcome, Sir Marmaduke,' said Bruce, 'to what man art thou prisoner?' 'To none would I yield but you,' replied Sir Marmaduke, at which Bruce raised him in his arms and took him to the royal tent.[63]

A more bizarre captive was a Carmelite friar called Baston who had been enrolled in the train of Edward II to immortalize in verse the expected triumph of his master. On being taken and brought before Bruce, the Scottish King with gentle humour promised him his freedom if he revised, in favour of the Scots, the epic that, as a practical journalist, he had already written beforehand. With a few adroit transpositions of names he accomplished this task to the satisfaction of his host and was speeded to the land of his fathers by the ironic cheers of his audience.[64]

But the greatest catch of all was that brought back by Edward Bruce from Bothwell. Sir Walter FitzGilbert, the constable of the castle, had for some time been sitting gingerly on the fence but, up to the Bannockburn battle, with one foot in the English camp. He received therefore into his halls, at their request, the Earl of Hereford, the Earl of Angus, Sir Ingram de Umfraville, Maurice, Lord of Berkeley, John Lord of Segrave, Antony Lucy and fifty of their followers. The remainder of their party, for whom he had no room, continued towards Carlisle and were almost all destroyed in the course of their journey. When Sir Walter heard from his distinguished guests the reason for their presence, his duty immediately became clear. His men removed their arms and made them prisoners, and on the arrival of Edward Bruce at the castle gates, Sir Walter handed them over to his keeping with protestations of loyalty to his brother.[65]

The Earl of Hereford was a prize so great that in return for his release his wife was empowered by her brother Edward II to offer fifteen Scottish captives. Among those who were demanded and received by Bruce were his wife, Elizabeth, his daughter Marjorie, his sister Christina, and Robert Wishart, Bishop of Glasgow, now blind and ailing.[66] His nephew Donald, the young Earl of Mar, was also given the opportunity to return, but a close personal friendship with Edward II decided him to remain in England.

Mary Bruce, who had been captured in 1306, had been released from her cage in 1310 and removed to Newcastle[67] and from there in 1312 exchanged for the brother of Sir Philip Mowbray.[68] The Countess of Buchan had been less fortunate. From her cage in Berwick she had been removed in 1312 to the House of the Carmelite nuns in that town,[69] and in 1313 handed from there into the custody of Sir Henry Beaumont.[70] After that there is silence. As she was not included among those reclaimed by Bruce, it must be assumed, knowing his loyalty to his friends, that by then she had died.

The uplift of morale among the Scots at the presence of so many renowned prisoners from a people who assumed they were a master race was further increased by the prodigious spoil that had been left behind. The whole English baggage train which, according to the Monk of Malmesbury, stretched for twenty miles and was worth £200,000, an astronomical sum in modern currency, was captured intact.[71] Among the contents listed were gold and silver vessels belonging to the English King and his nobility, money chests for the payment of troops, siege weapons, arms, hangings, tents, silk and linen apparel, wine, corn, hay, herds of cattle, flocks of sheep and swine and numerous warhorses and their saddlery. There was scarcely a family in Scotland which did not benefit from the generous distribution of these goods which Bruce made among his men.

# Part Three

# 1314–1329

After the aforesaid victory, Robert the Bruce was commonly called King of Scotland by all men, because he had acquired Scotland by force of arms.

*Chronicle of Lanercost*

# 14

The whole realm of Scotland, with the exception of Berwick, now lay in the hands of Robert Bruce, and no King of Scots before or since has had a greater knowledge from his own experience of the character and condition of his people from the feudal aristocracy, with whom he had been brought up at court and tournaments, to the humblest serf, in whose hovel he had found shelter when a fugitive from his foes.

Whatever had been the driving force of his career at its outset – a desire for personal aggrandizement or patriotism or a compound of them both – Scotland was now in his charge and he would labour for her welfare. For her prosperity he needed peace, for her dignity the recognition of her independence and her chosen king, for her spiritual comfort the removal of the papal interdict. Throughout the remainder of his reign his whole policy was governed by his determination to achieve these ends.

He had no wish to prolong the war. He saw his victory, above all, as an opportunity for reconciliation: with the Scottish nobles who had fought against him, with the English whom he had defeated. Soon after Bannockburn many Scottish barons and knights who had served under the two Edwards offered to him their allegiance and were received into his peace. In November 1314, a parliament convened at Cambus Kenneth adjudged that all Scottish landowners who had failed to do so by that date should be disinherited.[1] But Bruce treated this as an enabling statute only and granted a year's grace before enforcing dispossession. His sole proviso was that those who wished to regain their Scottish lands must do homage to him alone. They could no longer be feudatories in two countries and serve two kings. They must choose their nationality once and for all: a decisive break for the multinational feudal system that had hitherto prevailed. In the event,

the great majority became his subjects and with few exceptions served him faithfully. He was less successful in his relations with England.

In the immediate aftermath of Bannockburn he had returned unasked to Edward II the Great Seal of England and the Royal Shield which had been captured in the battle, in the hope that this gesture of amity might elicit a statesmanlike response from the English King. But Edward II had been too humiliated by his defeat and shameful flight, and too conditioned by his father to abhor the Scots, to rise above a petulant childishness when dealing with that race. The opportunity to restore the amicable relations which had existed between his grandfather and Alexander III, and which could have prevented four hundred years of strife between the two nations, was ignored. He made no concession to Bruce's overture, and soon after was embroiled with the four earls, Lancaster, Warwick, Surrey and Arundel, who had absented themselves from his invasion, and was virtually deprived of his executive powers.[2]

Bruce had no alternative but to try to obtain by force what was denied to civility. His troops, who were filled with that elation which comes to those who have fought in war and against all odds have foiled their enemy, were impatient for action. In August 1314, under Edward Bruce, James Douglas and John Soulis (great nephew of the guardian of that name), they were let loose to sweep through Northumberland, County Durham and into Yorkshire as far south as Richmond, exacting tribute and gathering spoil, and back by Cumberland burning Brough, Appleby and Kirkwold on their way.[3] In December of the same year, Bruce himself carried out a second raid along the Tyne valley, occupying Haltwhistle, Hexham and Corbridge, resuming the lordship of Tynedale which had formerly belonged to Alexander III, receiving from the men of that area a down payment for a truce to midsummer 1315 and their feudal homage to him as their Lord.[4]

Early in 1315 yet a third raid was mounted under James Douglas and Thomas Randolph, Earl of Moray, driving deep into County Durham and sacking Hartlepool.[5] The northern English, unsupported by their King, were completely demoralized and made no resistance. 'A hundred English,' wrote their chronicler Walsingham describing the state of their mind after Bannockburn, 'would not hesitate to fly from two or three Scottish soldiers so grievously had their wonted courage deserted them.'[6]

But however useful were the droves of cattle and ransom monies to Bruce for the needs of his kingdom, he realized that these raids in no way shook the structure of England. The wealth of the country, its shipping, trade, industry, manpower and food production were all in the south and Midlands. The northern counties – pastoral, sparsely populated and remote from the centres of government – could temporarily be sacrificed without halting the pulse of the country, provided that the great fortresses of Carlisle, Berwick and Norham remained in English hands as bases for recovery. To bring his enemy to terms, the Scottish King needed to strike in a more sensitive area and it was this consideration that determined him to open a second front in Ireland.

★　　★　　★

Throughout the thirteenth century there had been a great surge forward in the prosperity and settled habitation of that country under the
Anglo–Norman conquerors, but during the wars of Scottish independence Edward I had made it one of the main sources of supply for his
army in Scotland.[7] Irish troops were responsible for much of the
western marches and Irish ships for the provisioning of the Galloway
castles. By the end of his reign the forces and exchequer of Ireland had
been so denuded by his demands that its Lord Lieutenant could no
longer prevent the spread of lawlessness and disorder.[8]

Edward II made several half-hearted attempts to repair these
deficiencies, but once again the requirements of his armies against
Scotland caused him to claw back more than he had supplied and the
situation grew worse.[9] His defeat at Bannockburn by a mainly Celtic
army roused the expectation of his subject Celts. The recovery of their
independence no longer seemed a chimaera.

Taking advantage of this new mood, Bruce, early in 1315, sent
envoys to Ireland carrying with them the following message:

> The King sends greetings to all the kings of Ireland, to the prelates
> and clergy, and to the inhabitants of all Ireland, his friends.
> Whereas we and you and our people and your people, free since
> ancient times, share the same national ancestry and are urged to come
> together more eagerly and joyfully in friendship by a common lan-
> guage and by common custom, we have sent over to you our beloved
> kinsmen, the bearers of this letter, to negotiate with you in our name
> about permanently strengthening and maintaining inviolate the special
> friendship between us and you, so that with God's will your nation may
> be able to recover her ancient liberty. Whatever our envoys or one of
> them may conclude with you in this matter we shall ratify and uphold in
> future.[10]

A desired response came from the O'Neills, the royal line of Ulster,
who sent emissaries to Robert Bruce asking for military aid against the
English and offering the throne of Ireland to his brother Edward.[11]
The moment was propitious. Throughout his career Robert Bruce
had maintained close links with the men of Ulster and was well aware
of the disintegrating state of the country. From the strategic point of
view a friendly Ireland, offering a base from which to threaten the
west of England or to combine with an insurrection of the Welsh,
could provide a powerful bargaining counter against the English.
From the personal point of view it would be a welcome relief if the
savage energy of his brother could be afforded employment at a

distance, for his jealous ambition was already threatening the tranquillity of the state. According to one chronicler he had declared that Scotland was too small to contain both Bruces, and according to another that he could not live in peace with his brother unless he was granted sole rule of half the kingdom.[12]

Bruce had gone some way to soothe his discontent. In April 1315 a parliament was held at Ayr to consider the succession to the throne. Separated from his wife for eight years, Bruce had no legitimate son. His heir presumptive was his daughter Marjorie, about twenty years old, recently returned from England and soon after betrothed and married to Walter Stewart. On the grounds that the continuing peril from England demanded an experienced man at the head of affairs, Marjorie, on her father's advice, agreed to waive her rights as heir in favour of her uncle Edward, described in the entail as a man 'strenuous and skilled in the arts of war'. If Robert Bruce should die without a legitimate male heir, the crown should pass first to Edward, then to his heirs male, then, failing these, to Marjorie and her heirs. If the succession fell to a minor, Thomas Randolph, Earl of Moray, was to act as regent.[13]

At the same parliament the appeal from Ireland was considered and a decision taken to send there an expeditionary force under the command of Edward Bruce. No man was readier for action. He was one who, like the hero of the *Chanson de Geste*, would have declared, 'If I had one foot in Paradise I would withdraw it to go and fight.' Now his craving for the clash of steel and the glitter of a crown could be satisfied in full, while, at the same time, he would be carrying out the strategic objective of his royal brother: to harass England in her most vulnerable quarter. So important was this to the Scottish King that he put at Edward's disposal 6000 veteran soldiers and, knowing the headstrong and reckless character of his brother, designated to accompany him Thomas Randolph, Earl of Moray, on whose combination of judgement and courage he could rely.

On 26 May 1315 the Scots landed at Larne near Carrickfergus in Ulster.[14]

Within a month of their landing, they defeated the Anglo-Irish barons of Ulster at Moiry Pass in Armagh and, after concluding a truce with the defenders of Carrickfergus castle, drove south to Dundalk and on 29 June 1315 put the inhabitants to the sword.[15] Taking advantage of the dissensions between the Anglo-Irish leaders, they defeated piecemeal the Earl of Ulster at Connor on 10 September

1315 Roger Mortimer at Kenlis at the end of December, and on 1 February 1316 routed Edmund Butler, the Lord Lieutenant of Ireland, at the battle of Skerries in Kildare. The road to Dublin was open. But the devious behaviour of the native Irish chieftains who, on two occasions by treachery, involved the Scots in situations from which they extricated themselves with difficulty,[16] decided Edward Bruce to retrace his steps to Carrickfergus to capture the castle and make certain of the base from which he could maintain his supply line to Scotland.

Once again his success in open warfare was almost annulled by deceit. While investing the castle he agreed with the governor that a truce should be observed over the holy week of Easter so that men might spend their time in penance and prayer. But on the night of Easter Eve fifteen ships from Dublin, loaded with armed men under the command of Sir Thomas Mandeville, slipped into the bay and entered the castle by a seaward gate. The Scots, with no thought of treason, were scattered about the countryside or in lodgings in the town below, leaving only Neil Fleming and sixty men to watch the castle gate which fronted on the town.

At first light the garrison of the castle and their newly arrived reinforcements let down the drawbridge and burst upon the unsuspecting Scots. When Neil Fleming saw them he sent a messenger in haste to warn Edward Bruce, and then with his little band pressed forward to hold the enemy at bay and fought them hand to hand until all his company were killed. The respite occasioned by this defence gave Edward Bruce and the twelve knights who were in his quarters enough time to arm and make for the battle with their followers. As soon as they joined the mêlée they drove towards Sir Thomas Mandeville and, one of them felling him to the ground with his axe, Edward turned him over and dispatched him with his dagger. Meanwhile the scattered Scots, as fast as they could arm, hurried to the fray, some to the castle gate and some to the ships, until their opponents, disheartened by the death of their leader, fled back within the castle walls.

When the fighting was over, Edward Bruce looked among the fallen for Neil Fleming. He found him scarce alive with his followers in a heap on either side. He stayed by him until he died and at his death he wept. In all his life this was only the second time he had been known to weep.[17]

Three weeks later, at Dundalk on 2 May 1316, Edward Bruce was crowned High King of All Ireland.

*　　*　　*

A crucial factor in the success which had attended the Scottish invasion of Ireland was control of the narrow seas between the two countries.[18] In the summer of 1314, while Bruce was engaged in the defence of his country against England, John of Lorne, who after his defeat at the Pass of Brander had been appointed by Edward II Admiral of the Western Seas, landed on the Isle of Man and ousted the Scottish garrison. From there he began to canvass the petty chieftains of the Outer Isles and the seagoing men of Argyll to form a maritime opposition to the Scottish King.

Bruce was not slow to realize the danger to his strategy. As soon as the ships which had transported Edward Bruce and his army to Ireland had returned, he made an expedition to the Western Isles accompanied by his son-in-law Walter Stewart. Sailing up Loch Fyne, he bypassed the long beat around the Mull of Kintyre by laying pine trees side by side across the narrow neck of land which separates the lochs of East and West Tarbet and taking his ships over them partly by manpower and partly by hoisting their sails to catch the strong wind that blew from the east. So unexpectedly did he break into the open sea beyond that the men of the isles recalled the ancient prophecy that whoever should sail across the isthmus should have dominion over them. One by one they came to do him homage. John of Lorne was left without supporters and retired to England 'impotent in body and his lands in Scotland totally destroyed', there to receive a pension from Edward II until his death in 1318.[19]

A swarm of island privateers, under the protection of the Scottish King, now threatened the coastal towns of England and the merchantmen who plied between them and Ireland. Chief of these marauders was Thomas Dun, who on 12 September 1315 with four Flemish sea-captains sailed into Holyhead, captured an English ship and overawed the island of Anglesey.[20] A rumour spread that Edward Bruce was about to cross from Ireland and restore the ancient liberties of Wales, and the Welsh rose in revolt under Llewellyn Bren. Edward II had to countermand the Welsh levies who had been summoned to join the army he was preparing against Scotland, and when the French King requested the aid of the English navy against the Flemings, he had to reply that all its ships were required for the defence of Ireland.[21]

So far Bruce's strategy was proving successful. The English were too occupied in dealing with their Celtic subjects to reinforce their northern strongpoints, and gave an opportunity to Bruce to attack them. On 22 July 1315, after ravaging the surrounding districts and driving in the cattle to feed his army, he laid siege to Carlisle. For the first time the Scots had been able to acquire and bring with them siege artillery. But their single stone-lobbing machine was no match for the eight employed by the defenders. The high tower they proposed to wheel up to the walls sank in the swampy ground before it reached its objective. The shelter they built to protect their sappers while they undermined the fortifications suffered the same fate. Nor under the hail of arrows from the battlements could they fill the moat with sufficient bundles of brushwood to form a causeway.

In a last attempt to win success Bruce reverted to the element of surprise. On 30 July he assaulted the eastern side of the city with the greater part of his army, while James Douglas with a picked force of nimble men set up exceptionally long ladders against the western wall where the height and difficulty of access was regarded as adequate defence. But the garrison contained a large contingent of archers, and when the first assailants were observed in that quarter they directed their fire and picked off all who appeared above the parapet. The Scots had been foiled.

On 1 August Bruce cut his losses and returned to Scotland, leaving his siege equipment behind.[22] This was the first English success for a number of years, and the Governor of Carlisle, Andrew Harclay, received one thousand marks from Edward II as a mark of his appreciation.

Six months later Bruce and Douglas made a surprise attack on Berwick on a black night in January 1316, but the moon came out as they approached the uncompleted wall by the harbour and they were repulsed.[23]

Nevertheless, the inhabitants were in a precarious situation. The Scottish fleet was cutting off supplies. From the autumn of 1315 a stream of letters was sent to the English King complaining that men were dying of starvation and that even the horses were being eaten.[24] In February 1316 a party of the defenders under the King's Sergeant at Arms, Sir Raymond de Calhoun, a Gascon knight, against the orders of the governor, went foraging throughout Teviotdale, saying that it was 'better to die fighting than to starve'.[25] News was brought to Douglas in Selkirk forest that there was only a handful of skirmishers rustling cattle, and he set out after them with the few men he had about him. When he came up with them at Scaithmoor he found that there were a vastly greater number of knights and their followers than his own. But it was not in his nature to turn back. It was, he said afterwards, the hardest fight he ever fought. But he won it by concentrating his attack on the enemy commander. His little bunch hewed their way to close quarters with Sir Raymond, and when Douglas dispatched him hand-to-hand the rest lost heart and fled.[26]

The fugitives from this encounter excused their flight from so small a force by ascribing it to the demonic power of the Black Douglas. A Northumberland baron, Sir Robert Neville, whose character was encapsulated in his sobriquet 'the Peacock of the North', provoked by these reports of the invincible valour of the Scottish knight, challenged him, at his peril, to appear before the walls of Berwick. Douglas immediately marched to that neighbourhood, shattered Sir Robert's forces, slew him with his own hand and took his three brothers prisoner.[27] The considerable ransom he received in return for their freedom went to defray the expense of the hunting lodge he was having built at Lintalee in the forest of Jedburgh.[28]

While these activities were taking place, Bruce had returned to his family. His daughter Marjorie was expecting a child in the spring. This was a matter of some moment as his own wife Queen Elizabeth had not conceived since her return from England. On 2 March 1316, when near her time, Princess Marjorie was thrown from her horse and killed. The surgeons who were sent for, conscious of the succession, at once cut open her abdomen and delivered a son from her dead body. Crippled throughout his life from the injury of his birth, the boy, fifty-four years later, became King of Scots as Robert II, the first of the royal line of Stewarts.

When the obsequies of his daughter were over, the King in person, hearing that a muster of an English army was in train, led a raid in force deep into Yorkshire. By midsummer he had reached Richmond, into whose castle the nobles and gentlemen of the surrounding country had ridden for refuge. They offered a very large sum to be left unharmed, which he accepted. He then turned west, leaving a trail of pillage for sixty miles, into the Furness district of Lancashire. There he laid his hands on the accumulated stock of iron ore and had it brought by captives to Scotland where it was in short supply.[29]

Three months after his return, Randolph came to him from Ulster with the news that Carrickfergus castle had fallen and that Edward Bruce was only waiting for the arrival of his royal brother, with further troops, to complete the conquest of Ireland.[30]

&#42; &#42; &#42;

To the end of his life Bruce remained sensitive to the danger from Ireland if it was in unfriendly hands. For him the short sea passage between Ulster and his vulnerable western seaboard was a boundary to be protected no less than the borders themselves. If now there was an opportunity to break the power of the English in Ireland he was prepared to take a calculated risk. A secure base had been established. He had confidence in Randolph's judgement. An attack on Scotland from the south while Edward II and the Earl of Lancaster were at loggerheads could be discounted. Leaving James Douglas and Walter Stewart as regents of his kingdom, he crossed to Carrickfergus in the autumn of 1316 at the head of a considerable army.[31]

There was an ancient custom that whoever became High King of Ireland should make a royal progress through all the provinces of Ulster, Meath, Leinster, Munster and Connaught.[32] To conform to this usage and thereby stamp the legitimacy of Edward Bruce's coronation on the minds of the native Irish chieftains and win their adherence, it was decided that the two brothers should 'make their way with their whole host through Ireland and from one end to the other'.[33] In February 1317 they left their base at Carrickfergus moving south in two divisions, Edward Bruce commanding the van and Robert the rear.

Almost at the outset the impetuosity of Edward nearly brought disaster. The Anglo-Irish barons under the Red Earl of Ulster had had hidden their men in an ambush along the route. Edward, who by then had pushed recklessly ahead without maintaining contact with his brother, they let pass by and prepared to take the rearguard by surprise. But two archers, stepping from the woods to fire at Robert's men, alerted the King to the possibility of a trap and he ordered his troops to halt and take up fighting formations. His nephew Colin Campbell, with youthful enthusiasm, started to charge toward the archers. He was quickly overtaken by his uncle, who gave him a resounding buffet that made him reel in his saddle and a sharp rebuke for disobeying orders. It was well that he had been checked, for within minutes hundreds of the enemy came out of the woods on either side greatly outnumbering the Scots.

It was the bitterest encounter in all the Irish war, and if Bruce's military instinct had not caused him to marshal his men in time, they must have been overwhelmed. Not for nothing had he been named one of the three greatest knights in Christendom. This time he was in the thick of the fight. With Randolph, scarcely less renowned, and other tried companions beside him and a body of veteran soldiers, he gradually gained the ascendancy. Although they were eight to one against the Scots, it was the Anglo-Irish who gave the order to retreat and make in haste for Dublin.[34]

Their arrival there roused the inhabitants to a frenzy of activity. For months they had been demanding the authorities to put the defences of the city in order. Now, with the knowledge that the Scots were only eight miles away, they took matters into their own hands. They clapped the defeated earl in gaol as a traitor, set fire to the suburbs of wooden houses, burnt the bridges across the Liffey and tore down the belfry of St Mary's Church to provide stones to repair the breaches in the walls. Their spirited defence had its effect. As Bruce watched the flames rising around the city from his camp at Castleknock, he doubted, after the losses he had suffered, that he had the men or the time to succeed in a siege against resolute opponents.[35]

He had with him one of the Irish chieftains, Brian Ban O'Brien, whose clan was powerful in the southwest. O'Brien promised that if the King rode into Munster there would be a general uprising in his favour. So Bruce decided to bypass Dublin, march south by Naas in Kildare and Callen in Kilkenny, ravaging the lands of the Anglo-Irish on the way, and then turn west towards Limerick. But when the Scots reached the Shannon hoping 'to effect a junction with the whole Irish army at Saingrel', they were grievously disappointed. As happened more than once throughout the campaign, clan feuds overrode the Irish desire to be free of the English yoke. Brian O'Brien's clan rival was Murrough O'Brien. Automatically, he supported the opposite side and when Bruce reached the river, Murrough's 'Army of Thomond' was mustered on the farther bank 'with intent to strike'.[36]

Bruce was already anxious about his expedition. The great European famine of 1315–17* had spread to Ireland and was at its worst in the southwest. Even without clan quarrels the rallying of Irish chieftains for concerted action was virtually impossible while famine gripped their domains. News, too, had reached him that Sir Roger Mortimer, newly created Lord Lieutenant of Ireland, was consolidating the forces raised by his predecessor, Edmund Butler, in Cork and Waterford to cut off his return to his Ulster base.[37] He gave the order for retreat. The troops were ready to set off when he heard a woman's shriek. Asking the reason for this, he was told that it was the cry of a

* cf note IX

laundress who was in the pangs of childbirth and must be left behind.

At this he halted his army, saying that no woman in such a state should be deserted, and he gave orders that a tent should be pitched and that other women should stay beside her until her child was born, and that arrangements should be made for mother and child to be carried with the troops. Only when this was done did he give the order to move.[38] Their journey north was a long and painful progress through famine and plague-stricken lands, with the horses weakening from lack of forage or killed to provide food for the soldiers. As they crossed the boglands of County Tipperary they were harassed by Edmund Butler and his levies and everywhere along their route they were pestered by the starving Irish peasants who had been reduced to cannibalism.[39]

When they reached Trim in County Meath they rested for four days. The Ulster border was only thirty miles away. Here at last was the first flush of spring grass for their remaining horses and food for the men. So the gaunt and ragged band could pull itself into shape and march into Ulster as soldiers who had completed a mission.

It was time for Robert Bruce to return to his kingdom. Leaving many of his men with his brother Edward, he sailed for Scotland with the Earl of Moray while the passage of the seas was still open, landing late in the month of May 1317.[40]

As soon as it had been known in England that Bruce was intending to join his brother in Ireland, Edward II and the Earl of Lancaster, representing the Lords Ordainers, agreed to mount an invasion of Scotland, but the relations between them were not conducive to efficiency. According to a contemporary, 'Whatever pleases the Lord King the Earl's servants try to upset and whatever pleases the Earl the King's servants call treachery: and so . . . the Lords by whom the land ought to be defended are not allowed to be of one accord.'[41] In the event, the Earl of Lancaster and the barons of his party assembled their forces at Newcastle in October 1316 to await the arrival of the King. But the King had not forgotten Lancaster's refusal to join him in 1314 and took his revenge by failing to appear. The Earl of Lancaster returned home in dudgeon and the troops were disbanded.[42]

The Earl of Arundel, however, hearing that James Douglas was to hold a housewarming on the completion of his hunting lodge at Lintalee in the forest of Jedburgh, gathered together his followers, each armed with a wood-axe, and with a number of other knights and esquires who wished for action, set out, several thousand strong, with the intention of cutting down the forest and destroying the lodge. But Douglas had enough warning of their coming to muster fifty mounted men and a great body of archers, for which that part of the country was famous.

At one point on their line of march the English had to pass between two woods which converged together to form a bottleneck. When he knew the enemy was near, Douglas placed his archers in ambush in a hollow on one side and his mounted men at the far end, and plaited the young birch trees along the edges of the ride so that it was difficult for a horse to break through. Then, as the English closed together to enter the narrowing way and had almost reached its end, he gave his war cry of 'Douglas, Douglas'. The archers poured their arrows into the crowded flanks of the English cavalry and Douglas and his horsemen charged them head on with such force that the leading knights were bowled over and their horses, struggling and kicking, and those behind which had been brought down by the hail of arrows created such confusion that the English turned back into the open space behind and fled in panic.

Their van had been led by Sir Thomas Richmond, whose custom it was to wear a fur hat around his helmet. He was borne down at the first onslaught, and before he could rise Douglas had jumped from his horse, slain him with his dagger and taken his fur hat to wear as a token.

Three hundred of the enemy had missed their route and unexpectedly came across Douglas's new lodge. Finding it unoccupied but with provisions all ready for his feast, they sat down to eat, thinking that he would be too much engaged elsewhere to disturb them. But his success had been so swift that he came back among them while they were still at table, and few survived.[43]

Another party of English knights who, after the disbanding of the army at Newcastle, sought action against the Scots, took ship and sailed north into the Firth of Forth. The sheriff of that area, when he saw the ships approaching, gathered a force of five hundred men and as the ships sailed along the coast kept pace with them on the shore to prevent them landing. But the ships beached at Inverkeithing near Dunfermline before they could come up with them and disembarked so many knights that the defenders, seeing them in formation, lost heart and began to stream away inland. William Sinclair, Bishop of

Dunkeld, with sixty horsemen met them as they fled. He asked the sheriff what was their hurry. The sheriff replied that the English had landed in such force that they could not oppose them. At this the bishop, after saying contemptuously that he should have the gilt spurs hewed from his heels for such cowardice, called out 'Let him who loves his King and country turn smartly and follow me.' With that he cast off his bishop's robe, beneath which he was in armour, and seizing a stout spear rode towards the enemy.

The Scots, shamed into action, drew up behind him. When they neared the English the bishop, who was a big and mighty man, cried out 'Now spur your horses, men, and we shall override them', and like an avalanche they charged the opposing ranks and scattered them in confusion. Many went down before the Scottish spears and others retreating to the ships crowded the nearest so thickly that they over-turned and all were drowned.

When Bruce was later told of how the bishop saved the day, he took him in his arms and called him ever after 'my own bishop'.[44]

The failure of his armed forces decided Edward II to enlist the weapons of spiritual warfare. His opportunity now arose. Pope Clement V, his country's friend, had died soon after Bannockburn. For two years the electoral college had been unable to agree on a successor. At last in August 1316 their choice had fallen on John XXII, a French-man from the English fief of Guienne. The abiding ambition of the new Pope was to launch a crusade against the infidel.[45] The English envoys at his Holy See in Avignon, in the absence of any Scottish representatives, who were debarred by the wholesale excommunica-tion pronounced by his predecessor, easily persuaded him that only the obduracy of the Scots prevented them from offering the whole of their military might for the recovery of Jerusalem.

Accordingly he issued the bull 'Vocatis Nobis' commanding a two-year truce between Scotland and England, and sent a powerful embassy to London under the Cardinals Guacchini and Luca to see that the papal instructions were delivered to both parties. The cardi-nals arrived in the autumn of 1317 and handed over to Edward II the sealed letters they had brought with them. At the same time, they despatched two envoys, the Bishop of Corbeil and the Archdeacon of Perpignan, under safe conduct to the Scottish King with similar letters for his perusal.[46]

A confidential report made to their masters on the completion of their mission has an especial interest, for it is the only contemporary account of a meeting with Robert Bruce in person. From it emerges the portrait of a man of great charm and dignity, calm, assured, with a lively sense of humour and a beguiling courtesy.

He received them, they wrote, with smiling affability. No man, he declared, was more anxious to secure a true and lasting peace nor was more conscious of the Holy Father's benevolence in making efforts to achieve it. But when they handed him the letters he pointed out that they were addressed to 'Our dearest son in Christ, Edward II, illustrious King of England, and to our dear son, the noble Robert Bruce, acting as King of Scots'. 'There are,' he said mildly, 'several gentlemen in Scotland who have the name of Robert Bruce.' It would have been highly indelicate for him to open letters which might be intended for one of these. Only if they had been addressed to the King of Scots would he have felt sure that they were meant for him, and since they were not he had no option but to refuse them.

The envoys, in some confusion, pleaded that the Holy Father could not employ denominations which committed him to one side or another in a temporal dispute. 'But that,' said the king, 'is exactly what he has done by depriving me of the title of King which is acknowledged throughout my realm and by which I am addressed by foreign rulers. Our Father the Pope and our Mother the Church of Rome would seem to be showing partiality among their own children. If you had brought letters addressed in this manner to other kings you might well have received a more savage reply.'

When they begged him to waive protocol and in the interests of humanity bring a halt to hostilities, he answered that this was a matter for his parliament and he could not expect their decision for some time. His tone had remained friendly but firm throughout the interview, but when they retired from his presence the forcible expression of his councillors left them in no doubt of the indignation aroused by the insult to their King.

They returned therefore to the cardinals with the sealed letters undelivered. But the cardinals were unwilling to credit the discouraging report of their envoys and appointed another emissary. The unfortunate man they selected was Adam Newton, Superior of the Berwick Franciscans. Well aware of the delicacy of the situation, he prudently left the papal communications at his friary until he should be confirmed of a safe conduct. After a hazardous journey he found the

King of Scots in a wood near Old Cambus, a hamlet some twelve miles from Berwick, busily engaged in preparing siege engines for an assault on that city. Newton obtained a safe conduct from Sir Alexander Seton, the King's deputy seneschal, returned to Berwick for his papers and once more made his way to Old Cambus.

He was refused a royal interview but his letters were delivered to the King who, observing that they were still not addressed to the King of Scotland, had them handed back with the brusque rejoinder that so long as his royal titles were withheld he would accept no truce but would make himself master of Berwick. Fearful of the fury of his superiors, the friar nerved himself to declare in public, before a gathering of barons and their followers, that the Pope demanded an instant application of a truce. A menacing growl of anger greeted his pronouncement and he was with difficulty hustled away from the place and ordered to find his own way home.

His troubles had not ended. On his road to Berwick he was waylaid by four armed ruffians, robbed of his papal documents, among which were bulls excommunicating the King of Scotland, stripped of his clothes and sent naked on his way. 'It is rumoured,' he wrote in a letter addressed to the cardinals, 'that the papers entrusted to me are now in the possession of King Robert.'

The failure of the papal efforts and the news of the Scottish preparations against Berwick determined Edward II to order a mobilization for the protection of that town, but he was forestalled by Bruce. For some time the citizens of Berwick and the military had been at odds. In June 1317 Edward II received a complaint that the commandant was defrauding the Treasury by 'drawing double pay for his retinue, starving the garrison, committing peculations in stores and totally neglecting the King's interest'.[47] In consequence Edward handed over the control of the town's defences to the mayor and burgesses to be administered on an annual grant of six thousand marks.[48]

Inevitably disputes arose between soldiers and burgesses. Among the latter one Peter Spalding was much offended by the insults he received from the military on account of his marriage to a Scotswoman. In revenge he sent word to Sir Robert Keith, Marischal of Scotland, to whom his wife was related, that, on a certain date on which it was his turn to keep watch over a section of the wall, he would admit the Scots. Sir Robert took the message direct to the King, who decided to risk the possibility of a trap.

Sir Robert was ordered to keep his information secret and to assemble his men at Duns Park. To him there the King would send James Douglas and Thomas Randolph with a small body of picked men, and only then was he to reveal the plot to the other two leaders.

On the night of 1 April 1318 Douglas and Randolph with their scaling party left their horses at Duns Park and marched through the darkness to where Spalding was waiting. There they set their ladders and mounted the walls unseen. Their orders were to hold that part of the walls with their main body until Bruce should arrive with reinforcements, but to send a few throughout the town to cause panic.

When daylight came the prospect of plunder proved too great for Douglas and Randolph to be able to restrain their men, who dispersed through the streets pillaging and killing. This almost proved fatal to the enterprise. Many of the citizens escaped to the castle with their arms and swelled the garrison. By noon, the governor of the castle, Roger Horsely, seeing the holding party on the walls reduced to a handful, made a sally with his increased forces and nearly overwhelmed them. Never was the disproportionate effect that could be achieved by veteran champions more clearly shown than on this occasion. Almost single-handed Douglas and Randolph repelled the attack, ably assisted by a new-made knight, Sir William Keith of Galston, whose name has come down to posterity for his action that day. The English were driven back to the castle.

Bruce arrived with his army soon after, secured the town and within a short time starved the castle garrison into surrender.[49] Conscious of the immense trading value of the greatest seaport in his kingdom, Bruce made an exception from his policy of demolishing all captured fortresses. He repaired and improved the battlements: provisioned the castle with stores for a year and placed town and castle under the command of his son-in-law Walter Stewart. Neither he nor his son-in-law had any illusions that the English would allow Berwick to remain undisturbed. Walter Stewart sent for his friends and followers till he had with him, besides archers, spearmen and crossbowmen, five hundred gentlemen who quartered the arms of the Stewart. He enlisted also John Crab, a Fleming and an expert in the construction of siege weapons, who assembled for him along the ramparts catapults both large and small for the discharge of huge stones or iron darts and installed hoses to emit Greek fire.[50]

When, by May 1317, these precautions had been put in train, Bruce took his army south, captured the castles of Harbottle, Wark and Mitford and then drove deep into Yorkshire, burning Northallerton,

Boroughbridge and Knaresborough.[51] Ripon was spared on the promise of a thousand marks. Six burgesses were taken as hostages to ensure payment.[52] Two years later the unfortunate wives of these men, when the bulk of the debt was still outstanding, petitioned Edward II to compel their fellow citizens to make good their undertaking so that they could once more enjoy the comfort of their husbands.[53] The plunder from this expedition was very great especially in terms of livestock. 'They made men and women captive,' says the *Lanercost Chronicle*, 'forcing the poor folk to drive a countless quantity of cattle before them, carrying them off to Scotland without any opposition.'[54]

The Archbishop of York responded to this incursion into his diocese by proclaiming once more the excommunication of the King of Scots. His opening salvo was followed by a powerful barrage from the Pope. In June 1318 he published a sentence of excommunication not only against Robert Bruce but all his accomplices. Scotland was placed under an interdict, and in September it was ordered that in every church throughout England a service of commination should be held thrice daily in which curses should be pronounced against Bruce, Douglas and Randolph.

# 15

After the departure of his brother to Scotland in May 1317, Edward Bruce, who could never stay still, became involved in the politics and skirmishes of petty Irish chieftains in an attempt to rally them under his royal standard.

His efforts were understandable. By the close of 1316 the English had realized that they must regain control of the Irish seas and cut his lifeline to Scotland. Additional ships were commissioned in December 1316[1] and May 1317[2] to join the fleet at Dublin, and on 13 July 1317 Sir John Athy, with a strengthened naval force, captured Thomas Dun, the Scottish admiral, worsted his ships and destroyed the ascendancy of the Scots.[3] Reinforcements to Edward Bruce could no longer be assured. Local support had become increasingly important.

He was helped in obtaining this by the Minorite Friars and other religious orders whose activities in the cause of Irish independence played somewhat the same part as their brethren in Scotland.[4] To harness still further the patriotic devotion of the Church, Donald O'Neill in December 1317 sent a remonstrance to the Holy See. Styling himself 'King of Ulster and true heir by heritable right to all Ireland', he touched on the evil practices of the English who counted the death of a dog as of more importance than that of an Irishman, and declared that since the Kings of Scotland derived their blood from that of Ireland he was willing to renounce his right to the throne in favour of Edward Bruce, 'a pious, prudent and modest man of ancient Irish descent, powerful enough to redeem the Irish from their house of bondage'.[5]

Few adjectives could be less applicable to Edward Bruce, as he was to demonstrate in his last campaign. In October 1318, when his horses and men were in prime condition after the harvest, he set out with two thousand Scotsmen and a number of native Irish to attack Dundalk. Newly arrived reinforcements from his brother were to follow. On hearing of his approach, Richard Clare, Lord Lieutenant of Ireland, gathered together a force of armed knights many times greater and took up his position across the route to the town.

Edward Bruce had arranged his men in three columns – vanguard, mainguard and rearguard – but had briefed them so badly that none kept contact with their following body. They were strung out at such a distance that the first column was annihilated before the second came up, and then the second before the third.[6]

Edward was in command of the third. He had sent before him as scouts three veteran soldiers: Sir John Soulis, Sir Philip Mowbray and Sir John Stewart. When they saw what had happened to the first two columns and the greatly superior force of English, they advised their commander to turn back. Edward angrily replied that he would fight were the enemy three times as many.

'My brother is near at hand with fifteen hundred men,' said Sir John Stewart, 'let us not fight in such haste', and all three begged Edward to wait for their arrival. The Irish chiefs offered to delay the advance of the English by sending their men on a series of hit and run attacks until Stewart's brother arrived, but were not prepared to take part in an immediate set battle while the Scottish numbers were inferior. But Edward Bruce would listen to no reason. Headstrong as ever, he flew into a rage and swore that no man, while he lived, should ever say that an enemy had made him give way.

To this the Irish coldly replied that in that case they would withdraw their forces and watch the battle from afar. But his three knights, true to their code, answered 'So be it then, we shall take what God sends', and went to arm.

Edward, with a belated onset of self-preservation, dressed as a simple knight. His royal coat of armour he gave to Gib Harper, a stalwart warrior from his estate. But it was of no avail. At the first onslaught the pitiful handful of Scots were overwhelmed. Edward Bruce was cut down by Sir John Bermingham. Sir John Soulis, Sir John Stewart and Gib Harper were slain. Sir Philip Mowbray fell stunned to the ground but, recovering his senses as he was being dragged away by two of the enemy, broke free and managed to join John Thomson, leader of the men of Carrick, who was retreating with his contingent towards the troops of an Irish chief of his acquaintance.

There they were received loyally into safety and made their way back to Carrickfergus.

The English searched among the dead for Edward Bruce. Finding Gib Harper in resplendent mail, they thought he was his master. Showing little regard for the manners of chivalry which distinguished Robert Bruce after Bannockburn, they quartered his body for public display throughout Ireland. His head was cut off and salted in a bucket and in due course was presented by Sir John Bermingham to Edward II. In reward he was created Earl of Louth.[7]

The death of Edward Bruce ended the attempt by the Scots to establish a sister regime in Ireland. But their invasion had to a large extent achieved the object of Bruce's strategy. The authority of the English government had been shattered. Throughout the remainder of the Middle Ages it shrunk within the confines of the Pale. The greater part of the island reverted to its customary chaos of feuding kinglets. Never again could it be used by the English as a base from which to mount an attack on the western seaboard of Scotland.

Edward Bruce had died without legitimate issue and thereby rendered irrelevant the 1315 settlement of succession. Accordingly, at a parliament assembled at Scone in December 1318, a fresh act was passed settling the crown, in the event of the King having no legitimate male heir, on his infant grandson Robert Stewart with Thomas Randolph, Earl of Moray, again to be regent and after him Sir James Douglas.[8]

Much other legislation was enacted at this parliament, some of it recapitulation of ancient laws for the protection of the Church, equal justice to rich and poor and a close season for salmon; but the majority were innovating reforms for the security of tenants and freeholders, the rights of inheritance and especially for the calling up and administration of the armed forces.

Robert Bruce, with his experience of both English and Scottish armies, his grasp of strategic and tactical considerations and his awareness of the relative poverty of his country, realized that his military organization must differ from that of England. In broad terms the English relied on paid foot soldiers and bowmen and a heavily armed cavalry provided partly from the feudal service of magnates but increasingly in return for pay. Scotland could not afford a paid army nor obtain from knight service a cavalry of comparable weight. The main deployment of her military must be on foot.

Bruce maintained the feudal principle of armed service but shifted the emphasis. As early as 1309, when granting or regranting tenure, he required from the lessee, instead of the provision of one knight the provision of ten archers, and continued in this manner in varying degrees from that time on. Unlike the French, whose lack of comprehension caused them to suffer the devastating defeats of Crécy, Poitiers and Agincourt, he understood the efficacy of the long distance weapon.

For his hand-to-hand fighters he made sure of a national reserve by ordaining in the statutes of the 1318 Parliament that every layman possessing £10 in goods must provide himself with a padded leather jerkin, steel helmet and gloves of plate, and that small folk having in goods the value of a cow must own a good spear or a good bow and a sheaf of arrows. It was made incumbent on sheriffs to carry out inspections and, if this law had not been obeyed, to deprive the culprit of his saleable goods and hand the proceeds half to the king and half to his lawful superior.[9]

Determined to knit the whole community together in defence of the country, and knowing too well the disaccord which can arise between civilians and military from the commandeering habits of the latter, he laid down that all leaders bringing their men to the assembly point of the army should bring adequate provision with them or money to pay for it. This attention to martial matters was soon to be justified.

The quarrel between Edward II and the Earl of Lancaster, which in the last two years had almost brought civil war to England, had by August 1318 been patched up by the Earl of Pembroke. An uneasy kiss of peace had been exchanged between the two opponents on a bridge over the River Soare near Loughborough. But the more compelling impulsion to harmony was the loss of Berwick to the Scots. The national prestige was at stake. By June 1319 the forces of King and earl had joined muster at Newcastle, and from there with 12,000 men Edward II marched on Berwick, leaving his Queen Isabella at York.

Every English baron of note had been summoned to join in the assault, and as they came up were allotted their own section opposite the walls of the town so that the whole landward side between the Tweed and the sea was surrounded by a multitude of men, horses, stores, siege engines and tents to form a city greater than Berwick itself. Outside this broad ribbon of besiegers was laid out a defensive system of trenches and earthen ramparts to block a relieving force, and in the estuary of the river an English fleet lay anchored. When all these precautions had been taken, a detailed plan of attack was prepared. Each baron was appointed a place where he should strike. His men were provided with scaling ladders and scaffolding. Companies of archers were allotted to give covering fire and sappers with pickaxes to undermine the walls.

Early on the morning of 7 September the English trumpets sounded and a general assault began from the landward side. Although the battlements were as yet little more than a spear's length in height, the defenders throughout the day held their own, hurling down the scaling ladders and directing their catapults with deadly effect on the massed enemy below. Walter Stewart with a troop of reserves rode from place to place to see where help was needed, dropping off men to fill the gaps where the enemy pressed hardest. Meanwhile, at noon when the tide was full, the English ships came up the river. The leading ship had been so prepared that her boat, filled with armed men, had been drawn halfway up the mast with a bridge of planks to let fall from the boat to the battlement. But she failed to get close enough for the fall bridge to reach it and was left stranded by the ebbing tide. At which the defenders made a sally, set fire to the ship, killed some and captured others, among them an engineer famous for his skill.

All day the struggle continued without the English achieving a breakthrough, and when evening came they sounded the retreat and retired to their quarters.[10]

For the next five days, within eyesight of each other, the two sides prepared themselves for the next assault. The English constructed a huge machine on wheels, roofed with strong planks to contain beneath its canopy sappers to undermine the walls and armed men to burst through the breach when it had been made. Because of its shape it was called a 'sow'. At the same time a number of ships were fitted out in the same manner as that which had been burnt but with strengthened topcastles to be filled with archers. Under the deadly discharge of their arrows, men would drag the vessels across the narrow strip of shallow water which separated the river from the walls and allow the drawbridge to rest upon the parapet.

The Scotsmen, under the direction of John Crab, wheeled the huge catapult he had built into position opposite the sow, and next to it a movable crane against which were stacked bundles of faggots mixed with pitch and tar, bound like casks in bands of iron.

At dawn on 13 September the English once more assailed the town. Under a hail of arrows, the foot soldiers advanced with their scaling ladders while others slowly pushed the sow towards the wall. The English engineer who had been captured was brought to the spot and threatened that if he failed to shatter her to pieces he would surely die. In fear for his life he manned the catapult and, aiming, pulled the trigger. The first stone went straight over the sow and fell behind her. The second flew forth 'with a whizz and a roar' but landed close in front.

For the third time the engineer bent over his catapult and aimed. This time the huge stone went straight to the sky and then, plunging down, crashed through the roof of the sow, shattering the main beam in its descent. As the men inside crawled from the debris a shout went up from the Scotsmen that 'the sow has farrowed'. John Crab let grappling irons down from his crane to hold the sow in place, and then lit his bundled faggots and, swinging them over the wall, burned it to ashes.

With the tide flowing, the English ships were once more making towards the town. The engineer and catapult were hurried to the seaward side and he was warned again, on pain of death, to show his skill. This time at the first shot he landed a stone in the hoisted boat of the leading ship and the men were thrown out turning over and over in the air, some stunned and some dead. No other vessel then dared approach.

But on the landward side the attack still continued with the losses mounting and the women and little children taking over from the fallen, gathering up arrows in armfuls and carrying them to the men on the walls. Walter Stewart, riding inside the battlements with a hundred armed men, found so many places where the defenders were dead or badly wounded that by the time he had made the circuit and filled the gaps, he had but one man left. It was at this moment the news was brought him that the English had stormed the outworks of the Marygate and set the gate on fire. Having no men spare from the fighting on the walls, he called out the garrison of the castle, the last defence if the town fell and, flinging open the gate from within, drove the attackers back and, after stamping out the fire, held the entrance until the enemy withdrew. So for the second time night fell with Berwick unsubdued. [11]

Robert Bruce had taken the measure of his opponents. He would relieve the town but he had neither the army nor the intention to try to break through the entrenchments the English had so painfully created to guard themselves against his attack. By concentrating on Berwick they had left the whole of the hinterland unprotected. He conceived the daring project of seizing the Queen of England from her residence near York and, with her as hostage, dictating the terms of peace.

A flying column under Douglas and Randolph was sent posthaste to Boroughbridge to link with Scottish agents in the city of York. By ill luck one of these was apprehended and under torture revealed the plot. When the archbishop was advised of his story, he could scarcely believe that the two most famous warriors of Scotland would have come a hundred miles out of their country when the English were on the doorstep. But the spy swore that he would lay his head on the block if his report was proved untrue.[12]

The Archbishop of York and the Bishop of Ely gathered together a great concourse of citizens and yeomen, priests, clerks, monks and friars to bring the Queen into the city, and from there despatched her by water to Nottingham. On the next day, having been told that the Scots were few in numbers and hidden in a wood near Milton,[13] some twelve miles north of York where the Swale joins the Ouse, the archbishop decided to attack them, and with his motley following set out at a leisurely pace in that direction. After pausing for their dinner, which the archbishop had served on silver plate, they began to cross the bridge that spans the Swale.

'As men unskilled in war,' says the *Lanercost Chronicle*, 'they marched all scattered through the fields and in no kind of array.'[14] The Scots when they saw them coming set fire to a large amount of hay which had been gathered there, and in the drifting smoke their enemies lost all coherence.[15] As the smoke cleared, the English saw the Scots drawn up in a single schiltron which advanced towards them with a shout so terrifying that they lost all faith in divine protection and took to their heels. Then the Scots, breaking up the schiltron in which they were massed, mounted their horses and pursued the fugitives, killing both clergy and laymen, driving many to drown in the Swale and capturing others. If the battle had not been fought in the late afternoon and brought to a close by night, not an Englishman would have escaped. Three hundred priests were left dead upon the field and for this reason the skirmish was thereafter called the 'Chapter of Milton'.[16]

The Scots now spread throughout Yorkshire, burning and destroying, driving away the cattle and leaving the blackened farmsteads to mark their progress through the land. No fewer than eighty-four towns and villages are noted in the English records as burned and pillaged in this raid.

When news was brought to Edward II of the massacre at Myton and the widespread destruction caused by the Scots, he called his whole council together to decide whether it was better to continue the siege of Berwick until it was taken or march back to England to protect their countrymen. There was bitter disagreement between the barons from the south and those from the north. The former wished to complete the capture of Berwick, the latter to break off and rescue their kinsmen. The King inclined to the former against the advice of the Earl of Lancaster, who then in dudgeon marched off with all his followers. Since these made up a third of the army, Edward II had no option but to raise the siege. He attempted to cut off Douglas and Randolph from their home base, but their intimate knowledge of the northern counties made it easy for them to elude him.[17]

From that time rumours began to spread that the Earl of Lancaster was in league with Robert Bruce, and men pointed out that when the Scots swept across the border only the lands of the earl were left unravaged.[18]

Edward II had hardly disbanded his army when on 1 November 1319 Douglas returned to England to carry out his most savage raid on the counties of Westmorland and Cumberland. The harvest had just been gathered in and for the first time, after two years of famine, the barns were filled. But all were put to flames and the livestock driven back to Scotland.[19]

Ever since Bannockburn the Scottish King had offered peace in return for the recognition of his royal title and the independence of his kingdom, and evidence of his sincerity is recorded in the following letter of unknown date:

> To the most sincere prince, the Lord Edward, by God's grace, illustrious King of England, Robert by the same grace King of Scots sends greetings in the name of Him by whom the thrones of rulers are governed.
>
> Since while kindly peace prevails the minds of the faithful are at rest, the Christian way of life is furthered and all the affairs of holy mother church and of all kingdoms are everywhere carried on more prosperously, we in our humility have judged it right to entreat of your

highness most earnestly that, having before your eyes the righteousness you owe to God and to the people, you desist from persecuting us and disturbing the people of our realm, so that there may be an end of slaughter and shedding of Christian blood. Everything that we ourselves and our people by their bodily service and contributions of wealth can do, we are now and shall be prepared to do sincerely and honourably for the sake of good peace and to earn perpetual grace for our souls. If it should be agreeable to your will to hold negotiations with us upon these matters, let your royal will be communicated to us in a letter by the hands of the bearer of this present letter.[20]

But Edward II, remote from his northern subjects and little aware of their increasing sacrifices as a result of his obduracy, had rejected all overtures. Now, after his failure at Berwick, the anger of his northern barons, the lamentations of his decimated clergy and the evidence from his own eyes of the devastated valleys of Yorkshire persuaded him to open negotiations for a truce. Envoys from both countries met at Berwick on 22 December 1319 and agreed terms. The truce was to last for two years from 1 January 1320.[21] Edward II undertook to destroy Harbottle Castle on the River Coquet and Bruce not to build any castles on the Scottish side of the border – a face-saving clause for Edward as the policy of the Scottish King had always been to demolish any castle he captured.[22] Ironically, Bruce would in any event have ceased his raids. A severe outbreak of scab had occurred among the sheep in northern England[23] and he had issued stringent regulations against the movement of livestock.[24]

What Edward conceded with one hand he tried to recoup with the other. Within a month of the truce being signed, his representatives at the Holy See had persuaded the Pope to renew his fulminations against the Scots. In a bull of unprecedented rancour, the supreme pontiff summoned the Scottish King and prelates to appear at Avignon to answer for their misdeeds. On this occasion his term of address was to 'Robert Bruce, governing the Kingdom of Scotland' – a slight improvement on the 'Robert Bruce, acting as King of Scots' which he had previously used, but not enough for the King to accept the document. In retaliation for its rejection, the Pope commanded the Archbishop of York and the Bishops of London and Carlisle to repeat the notices of excommunication against Bruce and his companions on every Sabbath and feast day throughout the year, and a little later included the Bishops of St Andrews, Dunkeld, Moray and Aberdeen in the same interdict.

The papal invective at last provoked a noble remonstrance from the Scottish nation. Known as the Declaration of Arbroath, it is believed to have been written by Bernard Linton, Chancellor of Scotland and Abbot of Arbroath. It was sealed with the seals of eight earls and thirty-one barons, and in the name of the community of the realm it was handed to Sir Adam Gordon and Sir Edward Maubisson on 6 April 1320 for safe delivery to the Pope at Avignon.

It began by relating briefly the history of Scotland from earliest times: how their people had been converted to Christianity by St Andrew and had received from the predecessors of the Pope security and privileges as the especial charge of the brother of St Peter. Beneath this protection they had dwelt in freedom and quietness until the King of England, Edward I, pretending to be their friend, had invaded their country when it was without a king and inexperienced in war. The letter then related the cruelties and hardships endured by clergy and laymen under English rule, and continued in phrases of mounting eloquence:

> At length it pleased God who alone can heal after wounds to restore us to liberty from those innumerable calamities by our most serene prince, King and Lord, Robert who for the delivering of his people and his own rightful inheritance from the enemies' hand did like another Joshua or Judas Maccabeus, most cheerfully undergo all manner of toil, fatigue, hardship and hazard. The Divine providence, the right of succession by the laws and customs of the Kingdom (which we will defend till death) and the due and lawful consent and assent of all the people made him our King and prince. To him we are obliged and resolved to adhere in all things, both upon his right and his own merit, as being the person who has restored the people's safety, in defence of their liberties. But, after all, if this prince shall leave these principles he has so nobly pursued and consent that we of our Kingdom be subjected to the King or people of England, we will immediately endeavour to expel him as our enemy and as the subverter both of his own and our rights and will make another King who will defend our liberties: for so long as there shall be but one hundred of us remain alive we will never give consent to subject ourselves to the dominion of the English. For it is not glory, it is not riches, neither is it honour, but it is freedom alone that we fight and contend for, which no honest man will lose but with his life.

Quietly then the letter reminded the Pope that he was the viceregent of one who makes no distinction between Jews nor Greeks, Scots nor English, and begged him to instruct the King of England to be content with what he possessed and 'suffer us to live in that narrow spot of

Scotland, beyond which is no habitation, since we desire nothing but our own.'

The letter ended with both a promise and an admonition:

God (from whom nothing is hid) knows with what cheerfulness both our King and we would go to the relief of the Holy Land if the King of England would leave us in peace and we do hereby testify and declare it to the Vicar of Christ and to all Christendom. But if your Holiness do not sincerely believe this and remain too trustful of the English tales and favour them to our destruction then we must believe that the Most High will lay to your charge all the blood, loss of souls and other calamities that will follow between us and them.

We commit the defence of our cause to him who is the Sovereign King and Judge, we cast the burden of your cares upon Him and hope for such an issue as may give strength and courage to us and bring our enemies to nothing. The most High God long preserve your Serenity and Holiness for his Holy Church.[25]

Few men could fail to be stirred by this Declaration of Scottish Independence comparable to that of the United States 426 years later. The impact on the Pope was immediate. His fulminations ceased. Touched in his most tender spot by the offer of support for his long-desired crusade, he sent a stern letter to Edward II exhorting him to make peace with the Scots so that the forces of both countries could be directed against the paynims.

A flurry of diplomatic activity ensued. The English King appointed commissioners headed by the Archbishop of York to treat with the Scots for a permanent peace. Two papal nuncios were sent by the Holy See and two envoys from the court of France, whose King offered to mediate between the two parties. Negotiations dragged on into the spring of 1321 at Newcastle, Berwick and Bamburgh without any move by the English towards recognition of Scottish independence and were then abandoned.

The English, who had the advantage of representatives attending the Pope, persuaded him that the breakdown was entirely the fault of their ungodly opponents. In consequence in February 1321 he fired a salvo of no fewer than six bulls against the Scots, directing that *all* invaders of England should be excommunicated, that the Scottish bishops should appear before the Pope and that Robert Bruce should once more be doomed to Hell.[26]

Yet the hand of God seemed not to have been removed from the King of Scots: for in the previous year his Queen, six years after their reunion, had at last shown that she was capable of conceiving by giving birth to a daughter,[27] and he himself had survived a plot against his life. A hint of its existence was given by the indiscreet chatter of the Countess of Strathearn, and as suspicion began to grow, Murdoch of Menteith, a Scottish nobleman long resident in England and believed to have been one of the original conspirators, decided to journey to Scotland and reveal the whole matter to the King. Its object was to kill Robert Bruce and place Sir William Soulis, hereditary seneschal of Scotland, on the throne.

Sir William's father, Sir John Soulis, had been one of the unsuccessful claimants to the throne in 1292, tracing his descent from the illegitimate half sister of Alexander III. Sir William's mother was the daughter of Alexander Comyn, one-time Earl of Buchan. Agnes Comyn, Countess of Strathearn, was his aunt. The others said to be involved were four barons, Roger Mowbray, Patrick Graham, Eustace Maxwell and David Brechin; two knights, Gilbert Malherbe and John Logie; and one esquire, Richard Brown. The plot would appear to be the last dying paroxysm of the old Comyn–Bruce feud.

Sir William Soulis was seized at Berwick where he had been gathering about him a group of young squires, and the others were swiftly rounded up. A parliament, later known as the Black Parliament, was summoned at Scone on 4 August 1320 to try the conspirators. Sir William Soulis made confession of the whole plot and he and the Countess of Strathearn were imprisoned for life. Graham and Maxwell were acquitted. Malherbe, Logie and Brown were found guilty and executed. Roger Mowbray had died before the parliament met, but his corpse was brought before the judges on a litter. Under an ancient law the sentence of treason involving disinheritance of land, execution and dismemberment could only be pronounced upon the body of a convicted person, alive or dead. On the intervention of Robert Bruce his corpse was spared mutilation and allowed a decent burial.

Sir David Brechin claimed in his defence that the conspirators had sworn him to silence and then revealed the plot: that he had refused to join them but could not break his word. This delicacy of conscience matched ill with the pattern of disloyalty in his career. After his defeat by Bruce at Inverurie in 1309 he had sworn allegiance to him as King of Scots, yet by 1312 he had reverted to the English and was in receipt of a pension from Edward II. He fought against the Scots at Bannockburn and was taken prisoner. Once more he vowed his service to Bruce and was one of the signatories of the Declaration of Arbroath, yet now, by his silence, he had placed his monarch's life in jeopardy. He was condemned to be drawn behind horses through the streets of Perth and then hanged and beheaded.

Sir Ingram de Umfraville, one time guardian of Scotland and famous warrior, had been captured after Bannockburn where he had fought at the side of the English King. He had made his peace with Bruce, received his Scottish estates and affirmed his intention of settling there by affixing his seal to the Declaration of Arbroath. But David Brechin had been his friend and in anger at his death he renounced his fealty to Bruce. With characteristic generosity, Bruce allowed him to go free, attend his friend's funeral and have time to sell up his Scottish estates before departing for England where Edward II, under the polite fiction that he had never changed his allegiance, restored to him his English lands.

The circumstances of the conspiracy have remained obscure but that Robert Bruce, who was a humane man, allowed the severest penalty to be exercised on a knight whose service against the Saracens had earned him the title of 'The Flower of Chivalry' argues that it was a much more dangerous threat than can be deduced from the brief records that exist. Murdoch of Menteith was rewarded for his information by a grant of lands forfeited by the conspirators, and in 1323 was granted the earldom of Menteith which had become vacant when his niece Mary of Menteith, for whom it had been held in trust, resigned her interest.[28]

# 16

The truce signed in December 1319 held throughout 1321 and the northern counties had a short reprieve from the ravages of the Scots. But elsewhere in England events moved towards civil war. Hugh Despenser the younger, who after the death of Piers Gaveston had become the chief object of Edward II's affections, roused the anger of the Marcher Lords by his territorial aggrandizement in Wales. Taking to arms, they joined forces with the Earl of Lancaster and, marching on London, intimidated the King into sending the favourite and his father into exile. Their triumph was short-lived. Five months later their opposition had lost cohesion. Edward II, seizing his opportunity, raised an army, recalled the Despensers and advanced against the Marcher Lords. Some surrendered without a fight: others, under the Earl of Hereford, fled north to join the Earl of Lancaster at Pontefract. The final clash between King and earl was now to take place.[1]

The earl had already entered into negotiations with the Scots for their support in dethroning his cousin, offering in return a permanent peace and full recognition of Scottish independence. It is unlikely that Bruce took these overtures seriously, but anything which weakened England was to his advantage and he gave Randolph and Douglas leave to arrange a meeting with Lancaster and Hereford to discuss details.[2]

This in no way altered his military plans. No sooner had the two-year truce ended on 1 January 1322 than he sent Randolph, Douglas and Walter Stewart on a powerful raid over the border: Randolph to Darlington, Douglas to Hartlepool and Walter Stewart to Richmond, plundering or taking ransom. In vain the northern knights appealed for help to Lancaster who was stationed with his army at Pontefract, 'but he feigned excuse,' says the *Lanercost*

*Chronicle*, 'and no wonder seeing that he cared not to take up arms in the cause of a king ready to attack him.'[3]

The English King, indeed, was on his way. Gathering his forces at Coventry, he bypassed Burton-on-Trent, where Lancaster and Hereford had posted their army to block his passage of the river, and made for their headquarters at Pontefract. The earls hastily retreated northwards, hoping to link up with the Scots. But Andrew Harclay, the governor of Carlisle, by a brilliant move raised the levies of Cumberland and Westmorland and, avoiding the Scots in Teesdale, took up a position at Boroughbridge covering both the ford and the bridge by which the rebels would have to cross the River Ure. Mindful of the lessons of Courtrai and Bannockburn, he posted his pikemen in schiltron formation opposite the bridge and ford supported by archers on both flanks.

On 16 March Lancaster advanced to the attack, sending Hereford and the infantry to seize the bridge while he himself with the cavalry attempted to cross by the ford. Hereford was killed on the bridge as he led his men and Lancaster repulsed by the hail of arrows that decimated his horses. The next morning, with most of Hereford's men deserting, he surrendered to Andrew Harclay. He was taken before Edward II at Pontefract who, without holding Parliament or consulting his peers, had his head cut off as ten years before the earl had done to Piers Gaveston.[4]

Edward II was now like the bullfrog in the fable, fullblown with success. He had achieved his long deferred revenge, freed himself from the bonds of the Lords Ordainers and, as he wrote exuberantly to the Pope requesting him to worry no more about the truce with the Scots, 'determined to establish peace by force of arms'.

In furtherance of this resolution he issued orders for the muster of an army with was to excel in number that which he had led to Bannockburn. Besides the heavily armed cavalry supplied by his supporting barons under feudal service, crossbowmen and mounted spearmen were summoned from as far away as Aquitaine. Every village in England was ordered to furnish one foot soldier fully armed. Taxes were levied on the clergy, cities and towns for the hiring of archers and infantry. Sir Robert Leybourne was placed in command of a naval squadron to attack the west coast of Scotland[5] and Sir Robert Bataille of a fleet to escort the transport ships along the east coast into the Firth of Forth loaded with provisions for the army.[6] When all was ready, Edward II in the early days of August set off for Newcastle towards the border at the head of an enormous force.

Robert Bruce had observed these preparations with almost contemptuous indifference. His strategy for dealing with invasion had long been decided, so much so that on 1 July, while the English were still lumbering towards their assembly area in the east, he entered England on the west. Passing through Cumberland, plundering as he went, he rode across the Duddon Sands to Furness Abbey where the abbot paid ransom for immunity. Still making use of the sands at low tide, he moved swiftly along the coast to Lancaster which he sent up in flames. There he was joined by Douglas and Randolph and together they drove south as far as Preston, which suffered the same fate as Lancaster, and by 12 July they were back on the outskirts of Carlisle after a penetration of eighty miles into England. They encamped near Carlisle for five days, trampling and destroying as much of the crops in the neighbourhood as they could with the herds of cattle they had rounded up, and re-entered Scotland on 24 July.[7]

Bruce had assembled his army at Culross on the north side of the Firth of Forth. He had given orders that all the southeast between the border and the Forth should be left bare of man, beast, crop and habitation.[8] The inhabitants of that district had become used to such evacuations. They built their dwellings by affixing poles in the ground, filling the gaps between with turf and stones and covering the roof with brushwood and turf. To these they set fire on the approach of the English and drove their livestock into the forests and broken uplands, returning after the invasion was over to re-erect their simple homes.

Edward II marched through the scorched landscape of the Lothians unopposed. At Edinburgh he waited three days for the arrival of his provision ships but these had been delayed by contrary winds and the stores he had brought with him had begun to be exhausted. Foragers were sent into the countryside but returned to the King empty-handed except for one lame cow which had been found grazing in a field near Tranent, at which the Earl of Surrey exclaimed, 'This is the dearest beef that ever I saw.' By late September hunger had forced Edward II to withdraw his famished army into his own country where the crops had now been gathered in. His starving soldiers fell upon these with such avidity that an outbreak of dysentery attacked their weakened frames and their dying bodies littered the roads by which the English retired to Yorkshire.[9]

Such was the invasion which Edward II had boasted to the Pope would accomplish the final conquest of Scotland. The only positive actions achieved by this mighty force were the sacking of the abbeys of Holyrood and Melrose and the burning of that of Dryburgh:[10] results that can have brought little consolation to the supreme head of the Church.

Meanwhile north of the Firth of Forth Robert Bruce had collected an immense host from all parts of his country, 'all the power of Scotland, of the Isles and the rest of the Highlands'.[11] On 1 October 1322, as the English King retreated across the border in the east, the Scottish King led his army across the fords of the Solway in the west. Taking the familiar route along the Eden valley and Wensleydale, with a horde of refugees fleeing before his pillagers, he reached North-allerton on 12 October.[12] Here his scouts informed him that Edward II and his Queen were lodged in Rievaulx Abbey fifteen miles to the southeast.[13]

In an attempt to surprise them, Bruce made a forced march through the night of 13 October, but as dawn broke on 14 October he found his direct route blocked by an English force under the Earl of Richmond posted at the western edge of Scawton Moor on the heights of Sutton Bank. The single access up the steep hillside was a rocky pass manned at the summit by the enemy advance guard under Sir Thomas Uhtred and Sir Ralph Cobham. To make a frontal assault appeared suicidal, but the only detour was a fourteen-mile circuit by Helmsley and the chance of capturing Edward II would be lost.

After consulting his commanders, Bruce decided on an immediate attack believing that many of the English, after their recent experiences, were demoralized. The desperate task of scaling the pass was given to Douglas supported by a major part of the army. As he was ordering the ranks, Randolph came running to join him with three of his esquires and the two comrades-in-arms advanced side by side towards the enemy. Sir Thomas Uhtred and Sir Ralph Cobham, reputed to be two of the bravest knights of England, held the narrow gorge, and their followers above and behind discharged a hail of arrows and boulders on the ascending Scots.

Progress was painfully slow, so Bruce released his reserve of agile Highlanders to scramble up a precipitous cliff on his flank hidden by a shoulder of the hill. The last few to reach the top had hardly time to get their breath before they saw the Earl of Richmond coming over a fold of the plateau with reinforcements for his advance guard. With a wild cry the Highlanders charged and the English knights, taken by surprise, 'fled like hares before greyhounds', as Sir Thomas Gray scornfully reports, leaving Richmond and Henry de Sully, Grand Butler of France, in the hands of the Scots.

The advance guard was now assailed from front and rear and all resistance crumbled. Uhtred and Cobham yielded up their swords. The pass was cleared and Douglas and Randolph, joining forces with the Highlanders on the summit, moved against the main army which retreated in disorder. Walter Stewart with five hundred troopers pressed swiftly on to capture the English King. But Edward II, warned just in time, leaped on his horse, leaving behind for the second time in eight years the Great Seal of England and his royal baggage and treasure. Walter Stewart and his men pursued him from Rievaulx to Bridlington and from Bridlington to York, but the King outpaced them and when they reached the gates of the city they found them bolted and barred.

They returned to Rievaulx, where Bruce had made his temporary headquarters to deal with the immense booty abandoned by the English and to sort out the prisoners.

The Earl of Richmond was the first of these to be brought before the Scottish King and was received with extreme coldness. Whether because he had spoken slightingly of Bruce or insulted Bruce's Queen when she was captive in England or for some other reason, Bruce referred to him, in the presence of all, as a caitiff, had him imprisoned closely for two years and only released him in return for the prodigious ransom of £20,000.

In marked contrast he received Henry de Sully and the other French lords with great courtesy. Conscious of the advantage of winning the goodwill of the King of France, he assured them that he was well aware that they took part in the battle not from personal enmity to him but, as honourable knights should, in support of their host. He offered them his hospitality for as long as they should wish to remain, and in due course returned them to their country free of ransom.[14]

This politic gesture brought its reward. Henry de Sully, the leading French prisoner, acted as a skilful go-between in the negotiations which led to the Anglo-Scottish truce of 1323. During the course of these negotiations, Bruce had occasion to write a letter to de Sully which reveals both his own unruffled good humour and the perverse refusal of his royal opponent to face reality.

Robert, by God's grace, King of Scotland to the most noble Henry, Lord of Sully, Knight, his good friend, affectionate and loving greeting. You will recall, my Lord, how it was stated in our letters sent to the King of England and how also we informed you by word of mouth, that we desired and still do desire at all times to negotiate with the King of England on a final peace between him and us, saving always to us and to our heirs our realm free and independent, and also the integrity of our allies. If the English King had been agreeable we were willing to make a truce until Trinity [22 May]. Regarding this, my Lord, we have received your letters and transcripts of letters from the King of England declaring that he has 'granted a truce to the people of Scotland who are at war with him'. To us this is a very strange way of speaking. In earlier truces, even though the English King has not deigned to call us King, we have at least been named as principal on one side, as he has on the other. But it does not seem to us advisable to accept a truce in which no more mention is made of us than the humblest man in our kingdom, so that we could demand no more than any other if the truce were to be infringed wholly or in part.[15]

But if Edward II would not appreciate the weakness of his situation, others could.

The Scots had returned to their country by 2 November 1322, adding to the spoils of their victory at Old Byland near Rievaulx by extracting ransom from the town of Beverley still further south.[16] Soon after their departure Andrew Harclay, Governor of Carlisle, reached Edward II at York. He found him 'all in confusion and no army mustered'.[17]

Harclay was a man of strong character, a stern administrator and a brave and able soldier. For eight years he had maintained his city inviolate while the countryside around went up in flames before the invading Scots. During the barons' revolt he had, by sheer personality, drummed up within a few weeks a scratch force from the disheartened populace of Cumberland and Westmorland and inspired it with the resolution to defeat the mighty Earl of Lancaster and save the King of England. For this he had been created Earl of Carlisle and Warden of the Western Marches.[18]

Now when the Earl of Carlisle perceived that the King of England neither knew how to rule his realm nor was able to defend it against the Scots, who year by year laid it more and more waste, he feared lest at last the King should lose the entire kingdom: so he chose the lesser of two evils and considered how much better it would be for the community of each realm if each King should possess his own kingdom freely and peacefully without homage instead of so many homicides and arsons, captivities, plunderings and raidings taking place each year.

Returning to Carlisle, Harclay disbanded his levies and on 3 January 1323 went secretly to Robert Bruce at Lochmaben. There, after protracted discussion with Thomas Randolph, Earl of Moray, a treaty was signed between the King of Scots and the Earl of Carlisle. Pointing out that both kingdoms had prospered so long as each had a king from its own nation and was maintained with its own laws and customs, the signatories agreed that Robert Bruce and his heirs should be upheld as sovereign rulers of an independent Scotland and that they in turn should do all that they could for the realm of England.

For this purpose there were to be twelve commissioners, six to be chosen by the community of Scotland and six by the Earl of Carlisle, and these would work out the details for the common profit of both countries. If within a year the King of England consented that the King of Scotland 'shall have his realm free and quit for himself and his heirs', then the King of Scotland would found an abbey for the souls of those slain in the war and endow it with 500 marks a year, and would pay to the King of England 40,000 marks at the rate of 4000 a year and would grant to that King the right to choose a wife from his own family for the male heir of Scotland, provided the twelve commissioners consider that this would redound to the common advantage of both countries.[19]

Andrew Harclay made no secret of this treaty. On returning to Carlisle, he summoned the chief men of his earldom who endorsed his action, while 'the poor folk, middle class and farmers in the northern parts were very content that the King of Scotland should freely possess his Kingdom on such terms that they themselves might live in peace.'[20]

But however statesmanlike the solution presented by Harclay and however welcome in the north, he was impinging on the prerogative of the Crown and aroused the fury of his King. Too weak to attack him in his earldom, Edward II had him taken by stealth through the treachery of a friend[21] and, after a summary trial on 3 March 1323, degraded him from his earldom and knighthood and condemned him to be drawn, hanged, disembowelled, beheaded and quartered.

The Earl of Carlisle, 'with most steadfast countenance and bold spirit, as it seemed to the bystanders, went to suffer all those pains . . . then under the gallows, whole in body, strong and fiery in spirit and powerful in speech, he explained to all men the purpose he had in making the treaty with the Scots and so yielded himself to undergo his punishment.'[22]

So died the most resolute and capable of Edward II's lieutenants who, by his own efforts, had raised himself from obscurity to the highest rank of chivalry. It is impossible to believe that he had not intended to present the treaty to Edward II with a plea for its endorsement: but he was never given the chance. Four times before his death he made confession to different priests, the last to the Warden of the Minorite Friars, and all 'justified him and acquitted him of intention and taint of treason'.[23] He was not the first nor the last to learn by experience how frail can prove the friendship of princes.

Andrew Harclay's bold initiative and grisly death were not in vain. A little over two months later the English government, conscious of the popular support his proposals had received and the risk of a leaderless Carlisle falling to the Scots, concluded at Bishopthorpe, near York, on 30 May 1323 a truce for thirteen years. This was ratified by Bruce at Berwick eight days later under the style and appellation of King: a ratification which Edward II accepted and in so doing tacitly acknowledged the royal title he affected to deny.[24]

Apart from clauses to improve peaceful relations between the two countries, the main concessions by the English were an undertaking not to oppose a Scottish approach to the Pope for the removal of his interdict and to concede a neutral status to ships trading between Scotland and other countries, whether at sea or driven to the shores of England by the stress of weather.

The latter clause was particularly relevant in view of the change of affairs in Flanders. The Count of Flanders had long been a friend of Scotland, and as recently as 1319 had snubbed Edward II when he asked him to break off relations with that country. By the summer of 1322 this friendship had become so marked that the English feared Flemish naval attacks on their coast.[25] But in September 1322 the Count of Flanders died. His heir was a child and the regents of Flanders, won round by English diplomacy or gold, on 18 April 1323 expelled all Scots from their land.[26] A valuable source of supply and convoy protection was suddenly removed and the merchant ships to and from Scotland exposed to greater harassment by the English fleet. As a result of the treaty such anxieties were abated.

Freed from the opposition of the English Crown, the opportunity had now been given for Scotland to seek return within the pale of Christendom. Although her Church had nobly supported Bruce in spite of papal wrath, there were yet tender consciences among all classes which would receive consolation from the relenting of the Holy See. It was decided to send Thomas Randolph on an unofficial mission to ascertain the temper of the Pope. In the closing months of 1323 he made his way to Avignon accompanied by Henry de Sully, Grand Butler of France.

Henry de Sully during his residence with Robert Bruce after the battle of Old Byland, evidently conceived a great liking for his host. He acted as his intermediary for the Bishopthorpe truce, and it would appear that it was by his good offices that Randolph was received in audience by the Pope, for Sully was present throughout.

The details of this interview on New Year's Day 1324 are given in a letter sent by the Pope to Edward II later in January. They reveal with what skill the veteran soldier manipulated the Pope to his purpose. He began by humbly asking his permission to go and fight in the Holy Land in fulfilment of a private vow. The Pope replied that he was unable to grant this to one whom he had excommunicated, and in any event the impact of a single warrior would have little effect on the heathen. How different it would be if Randolph could bring about a permanent peace between Scotland and England and so release their armies for this great enterprise. Randolph, in answer, said that Scottish ambassadors had already been appointed to appear before his Holiness to plead for reconciliation so that this might be brought about, and he asked that safe conducts might be issued for their journey to Avignon.

The Pope regretted that it would be unseemly for him to grant credentials to excommunicated persons but, having so salved his conscience, promised to make their travel possible by requesting the rulers through whose territories they would pass to give them protection.

Randolph then explained that it was the dearest wish of his uncle, the King of Scots, to join with the King of France in a crusade to the Holy Land and, even if the French King was prevented, to send a Scottish expedition headed by himself or his nephew. The Pope answered that he could not give his blessing to such an expedition while Randolph's uncle was still unreconciled to Holy Church.

To this Randolph replied that no man was more aware of his obligations to Holy Church than his uncle, nor more anxious to prove his obedience if he would be shown how. Unfortunately, owing to clerical errors, he had been prevented from knowing the wishes of the

Holy Father: but, said Randolph, offering as it were a helpful suggestion from a private individual, these difficulties could be overcome by the simple method of addressing a letter to him by the title of King.[27]

Put in these terms it seemed clear to the Pope that if he could improve the prospects of a crusade by a mere technical alteration, it was his duty to consent.

However, a subsequent uneasiness caused him to write to Edward II in apologetic tones.

> I remember to have told you [he wrote] that my bestowing the title of King on Robert Bruce would neither strengthen his claim nor impair yours. My earnest desires are for reconciliation and peace: and you will know that my Bull issued for attaining these salutary purposes will never be received in Scotland if I address it under any appellation but that of King. I, therefore, exhort you in your royal wisdom that you would be pleased patiently to suffer me to give him that title.[28]

Edward II replied angrily that to give his opponent the title of King could not be regarded as a matter of indifference in that 'the Scottish nation would naturally conclude that the Pope intended to acknowledge the right where he had given the title', and, in spite of his promise in the Bishopthorpe truce not to inhibit a rapprochement between the Scots and the Holy See, he sent a powerful mission to the papal curia with the chief purpose of widening the breach between the two parties. Claiming that the Scots had incurred the suspicion of heresy, he demanded, through his representatives, that the Pope should refuse to sanction the election of Scotsmen to episcopal office in their own country 'because the Scottish prelates are they who cherish the nation in its rebellion and contumacy'.[29]

The Pope reasonably replied that this would deprive the flock altogether of their religious shepherds as no Englishman could receive admittance to Scotland.[30] But though refusing this demand, he remained sufficiently intimidated by English pressure to take no further steps to lift his interdict. On the specious excuse that Berwick had been seized by the Scots in contempt of a papal truce, he claimed that absolution could not be granted unless they handed back the town. The Scots preferred to remain excommunicate.

Nevertheless the papal recognition of Bruce's right to be addressed as King of Scots was a diplomatic triumph which the English could not gainsay. It came at an opportune moment: for two months later, on 5 March 1324, Queen Elizabeth gave birth to a boy who was christened David in honour of his great forebear David I, who had summoned the Bruces to Scotland.[31]

Edward II, as a calculated slight, celebrated the event by inviting Edward Balliol, the son of 'Toom Tabard', from his paternal estates in Normandy to the English court: there to disparage by his presence the legitimacy of the Bruce kingship.[32]

But throughout Scotland there was widespread rejoicing that the good King Robert, as he had now become known, had at last a son and heir. The Chancellor, Bernard Linton, composed a graceful tribute in Latin verse.

Few can have rejoiced more thankfully than the Queen herself. She had not had an easy life. Married in 1302 while still in her teens, she had spent the next four years on and off at the court of Edward I with a husband daily at risk for his secret plans of revolt, and a monarch whose savage temper was as unpredictable as a bull's; then the escape to Scotland and the hard and hazardous days as a new-crowned Queen; the flight to the heather after Methven; the struggle through the ice and snow in the bitter winter of 1306 to St Duthac's shrine; the capture, the eight weary years of house arrest, often not knowing whether her husband was alive or dead, the forced moves from the Yorkshire manor of Burstwick in 1308 to Bistelsham in Oxford-shire,[33] from that to Windsor in 1312,[34] from there to Shaftesbury[35] and then again to Barking Abbey in 1313,[36] and finally to Rochester prison in 1314,[37] allowed only the attendance of a few elderly ladies and often short of food and furniture. After that came the reunion with her husband who, after so many years of separation, must have seemed a stranger, and then the frustrating six years when all looked to her for an heir and she remained barren, and even her stepdaughter was snatched away by death. But now she was the mother of a prince and one born at a time when at last a rest from strife seemed possible.

It is true that negotiations held at York in November 1324 to translate the truce into a final peace ended in the usual stalemate, but there was no resumption of hostilities. She was at last granted the comfort and relaxation of a domestic life; for the King her husband, after years of nomadic existence, in 1325 put in hand the building of a manor house for his family. He chose for the site the village of Cardross on the north side of the Firth of Clyde, close to Dumbarton. It was in no way a fortified castle but a substantial dwelling with hall, King's chamber, Queen's chamber, chapel, kitchen and larder. The roofs were thatched and it had the luxury of glazed windows. There was a garden, a hunting park, an aviary for the royal falcons and a slipway for the King's yacht. The land was bought from the Earl of Lennox and its situation is significant both of the king's love of the sea and of the importance he attached throughout his reign to the security of the western approaches.[38]

By this time he had so arranged matters that the whole seaboard of the western Highlands was in friendly hands, from his son-in-law, Hugh Earl of Ross, in the north at Wester Ross, down through the lands of Thomas Randolph, Earl of Moray, on the Sound of Sleet, those of his sister-in-law by marriage, Christiana of the Isles, and her half-brother Ruairi Macruarie at Garmoran, and of Sir Neil Campbell, his brother-in-law, and Angus Macdonald in southern Argyll, to both of whom he had made grants from the forfeited lands of John of Lorne and the Macdougalls. From all these, as part of their feudal service, he could call for the supply of a varying number of twenty-six oared galleys to keep open communications to Northern Ireland and maintain control of the Hebridean seas.[39]

For himself he had built 'a great ship' and other vessels. The Clyde became the natural centre of his western navy. From his new home it would be under his personal supervision and for its protection, contrary to his usual policy of dismantling fortresses, he left intact the royal castle of Dumbarton near his manor, repaired and victualled the castle of Skipness in Kintyre and, most remarkably, in 1325 built a new royal castle at Tarbert. Across the mile-wide isthmus between its east and west lochs, he cut a track for the haulage of galleys, giving a quicker passage between the open sea and the sheltered waters of the Clyde estuary.[40]

To encourage commerce with Ireland, which had proved in the past an entrepôt between the continent and Scotland when the trade routes across the North Sea had suffered blockade or harassment from the English navy, he created two new royal burghs, one at Ayr and the other alongside the castle at Tarbert, and as a final gesture towards his strategy in the west, in 1328, when he knew his life was nearing its end, he called on Bernard Linton, his wise and brilliant chancellor, to leave his abbey at Arbroath to become the bishop of the Isles and watch over the area which his King had built up and nurtured with such care.[41]

The peaceful years from 1323 to 1327 gave Bruce the opportunity to deal with political and economic matters in other directions.

On the political side his approach was conservative, conforming, as far as possible, to the pattern which had been established by his predecessor, Alexander III. The problem of rewarding those who had supported him from the earliest years, without disturbing existing landowners and creating centres of disaffection, was happily resolved by having at his disposal lands forfeited by a small group of irreconcilables: the Earl of Atholl, John Balliol, John Comyn of Badenoch, John Comyn Earl of Buchan, John Macdougall and Dugald Macdowall. From these estates and the royal demesne he was able to make munificent grants to his two outstanding lieutenants, Thomas Randolph and James Douglas, and other grants, in varying degrees, to his companions in the dark days of 1306 and 1307: Sir Gilbert de la Haye, the Constable, Sir Robert Boyd, Sir Robert Keith the Marischal and Angus Macdonald of the Isles. Apart from these his largesse went to his close relatives: his son-in-law Walter Stewart, his brother-in-law Sir Neil Campbell, married to Mary Bruce, and Sir Alexander Fraser who married her after Sir Neil's death, and to his sister Matilda's husband, Hugh, Earl of Ross.

In short the transfers remained within the baronial class and, contrary to the usual outcome of civil war and chaos, no new men of humble origin emerged to join the ranks of nobility. The fabric of society retained its traditional texture and gave stability to his realm.[42]

On the economic side his difficulties were less easy to overcome. In Scotland it was held that the king must 'live of his own'. His kingdom was, as it were, a vast private estate from which he had to obtain the means to pay for its administration, protection and upkeep. It followed that in times of war his revenues were doubly hit by the need to purchase mounts and munitions and the falling off in the proceeds of trade and agriculture as men were drawn into the forces. Bruce partly resolved the problem by his recurrent raids into England. These were as much for the subsistence of Scotland as to compel the enemy to sue for peace.

It is significant that the export of wool from Scotland in 1327 was the highest from that country throughout the fourteenth century.[43] This was due partly to farmers along the borders and in the Lothians turning from arable to pastoral agriculture as standing crops were too vulnerable to hostile raids, but also because for ten years the Scots had turned the northern counties of England into a huge backyard from which to augment their stock of sheep, oxen and horses.

The consequent increase in the export of wool and hides brought much needed income to the King from the duties that had to be paid before the goods were shipped. Goods could only be shipped legally on the production of an export licence to which had been affixed a special seal (a coket) by the customs officer. Throughout his reign Bruce encouraged the merchants of Scotland by the creation or revival of royal, baronial and ecclesiastical burghs with their complex of guilds, but it was only to the royal burghs, among which the most important were Berwick, Edinburgh, Aberdeen, Dundee and Perth, that he granted the use of the coket with resultant prosperity to their inhabitants: on this prosperity he was soon to draw.[44]

It was natural that he should wish to recompense the Scottish Church for all the support he had received in his struggle for independence, but his generosity so far exceeded the expectations of reward that it would seem that he retained throughout his life remorse for his sacrilege in the Friary church at Dumfries and sought expiation by his veneration of the saints and the endowment of their shrines. St Fillan, St Thomas, St Cuthbert and St Andrew were the special objects of his benevolence. He was the first king to acclaim St Andrew as the patron saint of Scotland. On 5 July 1318, accompanied by a concourse of magnates, clergy and common folk, he attended the consecration of St Andrew's Cathedral, begun in 1162 and completed during the bishopric of his old friend William Lamberton, and endowed the cathedral priory with an annual sum of one hundred marks.

An annual rent of forty marks was granted to the Franciscan friars of Dumfries and twenty to each of the other Franciscan houses in Scotland. Melrose Chapter was the recipient of an annual rent of £100 on 26 January 1326, and in March of that year of the very large sum of £2000 for the reconstruction of its abbey.[45] Payments were made for masses to be said daily for his brother Nigel Bruce and his brother-in-law Sir Christopher Seton, nor did he forget to provide for a candle and lamp to burn perpetually on the altar of the Blessed St Malachy in the Abbey of Coupar-Angus.*[46]

This beneficence played its part in creating a crisis in the royal finances. On 15 July 1326 the King summoned a parliament at Cambus Kenneth Abbey and reported to the assembled prelates, earls,

*cf note X

barons and burghers that 'the lands and rents which of old used to pertain to his Crown had been so diminished by divers gifts and transfers occasioned by the war that he did not have means of maintenance befitting his station.' He asked that in recognition of the hardships that he and his family had borne in the fight for the freedom of them all they should make provision for an increase in his income. Admitting that his request was 'reasonable', they passed a resolution granting him for his lifetime a tenth of all rents and profits throughout the realm, while he in turn conceded that he would limit the requisition of goods and food to which he was entitled under an ancient royal prerogative.[47]

At the same parliament a new Act of Settlement was passed, by which the King's son David, now two years old, was designated successor to his father in precedence to Robert Stewart, and all present swore fealty to the infant child.[48]

Robert Stewart's father, Walter, had died three months earlier to the general grief and in particular to that of his father-in-law, the King. For he had trusted him with responsibility from an early age as a stripling at Bannockburn, as a governor of Berwick, as a cavalry leader at Old Byland, and had never found him wanting.[49] His mourning coincided with that for the Queen's second son John, who died in infancy: but as some compensation the royal family were rejoiced by the marriage of Bruce's sister Christina, widow of the Earl of Mar and of Christopher Seton successively, to Andrew Moray, son of the patriot hero of Stirling Bridge, an inheritor of great estates and soon to become a guardian of the realm.[50]

# 17

Since the beginning of Edward II's reign, England had been at peace with France, but in November 1323 a local clash at Saint Sandos on the border of Gascony occurred between the English and French. The ineptitude of Edward II's brother, the Earl of Kent, whom he sent as ambassador to Charles IV, the newly crowned King of France, to smooth over matters, caused a frontier incident to expand into a threat of war. Unwilling and ill-prepared for such an event, Edward II was persuaded to choose his Queen, Isabella, as the most likely person to negotiate a settlement with her brother Charles IV. Landing in France in March 1325, she had managed by the middle of the summer to induce her brother to restore the provinces of Gascony and Ponthieu, which he had seized on condition that Edward II came to pay homage for them.[1]

Edward II was at that time entirely under the influence of his favourite, Hugh Despenser, whose administrative and financial reforms have excited the admiration of historians but whose greed had antagonized a formidable section of prelates and barons within the kingdom, and whose intimacy with her husband had earned the bitter hatred of the Queen. Conscious of his precarious position if Edward II left the country, Despenser accepted with alacrity the artful suggestion she made that the Prince of Wales should be sent to France to pay homage on behalf of his father. Once she had her son by her side, both she and her brother revealed their true intent. Charles IV refused to return Gascony and Ponthieu and Isabella repaired to the court of the Count of Hainault, who promised her men and money for an invasion of England in return for the offer of her son as husband for his daughter Phillipa.[2]

It was while matters stood thus that Bruce, who had been following events, judged that the moment was ripe for an offer of alliance to the

French. A deputation, headed by Thomas Randolph, was sent to the court of France, with full powers of negotiation. They returned with the diplomatic triumph of a defensive alliance between Scotland and France. By the treaty of Corbeil signed in April 1326, both countries bound themselves to come to the aid of the other if either was attacked by England. Scotland was no longer isolated but linked to the most powerful and opulent nation in Europe.[3]

Through the succeeding months Queen Isabella's invasion of England was daily expected. Ships were hastily ordered by Edward II to Portsmouth, but mutiny broke out and they never left harbour. On 24 September 1326, unopposed by an English fleet, Isabella and her lover, Sir Roger Mortimer, landed at the port of Harwich and, accompanied by the Earls of Norfolk and Leicester, advanced on London. Edward II and Hugh Despenser fled to the west as their followers melted away and took ship for Ireland, but contrary winds drove them back to Cardiff. Captured in Glamorgan on 16 November, Hugh Despenser was executed and Edward II imprisoned in Kenilworth Castle.[4] Bullied throughout December and January, he finally succumbed to the threat that if he did not abdicate the people of England would repudiate not only him but his son also. On 1 February 1327 the Prince of Wales was crowned Edward III.[5]

Donald, Earl of Mar, nephew of the Scottish King, who had been brought up with Edward II and remained his close companion, made posthaste to Scotland on the approach of Isabella's army to enlist his uncle's aid on behalf of his friend. Bruce, who had known him as a boy when he was his guardian, received him with great generosity, restored to him his earldom and gave him encouragement in his plots to raise a Welsh force for the release of the captive King.[6] As a result of these efforts, Edward II escaped from Berkeley Castle, to which he had been removed from Kenilworth, but was captured and once more immured.

The discovery of another conspiracy to free him and the near success of his previous liberation determined his wife and her lover to end his life. Systematically he was ill-treated and starved in the hope that this would bring about his decease, but when his robust constitution failed to succumb to this treatment, a marrow bone was thrust up his rectum and through it a red hot poker to cauterize his entrails so that his body could be displayed to the public gaze without sign of injury, the victim of natural death.[7] On 21 September 1327 Edward III was informed that his father was dead.

*   *   *

Throughout 1326 Bruce had been vexed by the attacks of English ships on his trading vessels to the Low Countries and Hanseatic towns in contravention of the Bishopthorpe truce. In some cases Scottish merchants and their womenfolk had been murdered at sea and their cargo seized, in others Scottish seamen putting into English harbours for shelter from pirates had been arrested and clapped into prison. His complaints had been unheeded.[8]

The abdication of Edward II automatically released him from his truce, and he made the point sharply by attacking the castle of Norham on the day that Edward III was crowned. The attack was beaten off but the English Council of Regency hastily passed an act prolonging the truce on their side of the border,[9] and on 6 March 1327 made a unilateral declaration that it was still in force.[10] Commissioners were appointed to renew negotiations for peace, but as they failed to address their communications to the King of Scots it must be assumed that they were playing for time, for even before the talks broke down Isabella and Mortimer had begun the mobilization of an army.

Bruce's response showed all his accustomed skill. Taking advantage of the disorders in Ulster stemming from the death of his father-in-law the Red Earl, he landed in Antrim soon after Easter 1327 and by July of that year had forced Sir Henry Mandeville, the Ulster Seneschal, to sign a humiliating truce to last one year from 1 August 1327.[11] While he was engaged in rendering the English in Ireland ineffective, three flying columns under Douglas, Randolph and Donald, Earl of Mar, crossed the English border through the Kielder Gap on 15 June and fanned south to Weardale, wasting the country as they went.[12]

Queen Isabella and Sir Roger Mortimer as regents, with Edward III the young King of England, had assembled an army of vast proportions at York, including a crack contingent of 2500 heavy-armed Flemish cavalry under John of Hainault hired by the English treasury for the sum of £14,000 and a spectacular new weapon, the gunpowder cannon.[13] After a splendid feast arranged by Queen Isabella for the Hainaulters and other foreign knights from as far away as Bohemia, which infuriated the xenophobe English and led to a riot,[14] the huge army with its long column of baggage wagons left York on 10 July and moved slowly to Durham. There on 18 July they had the first evidence of their enemy from the distant sight of smoke rising from farms and homesteads burnt by the Scottish raiders.

For two days they trundled across boggy moorland in pursuit but never came in view of their quarry, for they were dealing with men skilled in mobile warfare, as has been vividly described by Le Bel:

These Scots are exceedingly hardy through their constant wearing of arms and experience in combat. When they enter England they will in a single day and night cover twenty-four miles; for they ride on sturdy horses and bring no wagons with them. They carry no provisions of bread and wine: for their abstemiousness is such that they will live for a long time on stewed meat and drink river water. They need neither pots nor pans for wherever they invade they find plenty of cattle and use the hides of these in which to boil the flesh. Each man carries under the flap of his saddle an iron plate and behind the saddle a little bag of oatmeal. When they have eaten the stewed meat they place the plate on the fire and when the plate is hot they spread on it a little paste made of oatmeal and water and make a thin cake in the manner of a biscuit which they eat to comfort their stomachs. So it is no wonder that they can travel farther in a day than other soldiers.[15]

It became apparent to the English leaders that moving in heavy marching order with all their camp gear they would never come up with their opponents. On the mistaken intelligence that the Scots were heading for the Tyne to cross the ford at Haydon Bridge by which they had passed southwards, orders were given for the baggage train to be left behind and for the rest of the army, unhampered by provision wagons but with each man carrying a loaf of bread slung at his back, to make a forced march to the northern bank of the river to cut off the retreat of the enemy.

Setting out at daybreak on 20 July, they reached their objective at dusk. All night they stood to arms, with the knights resting on the ground beside their horses with the reins in their hands ready to mount at a moment's warning. But the Scots did not come and the rain began to fall. It fell and fell without a break for eight days and nights while the English waited for the Scots. The river waters rose and their encampment became a sea of mud. Their scant provisions were soon exhausted and little could be obtained from the nearest towns of Carlisle and Newcastle and even less from the ravaged countryside. There was no shelter: few fires could be kindled from the green and sodden wood and the very leather of their saddlery rotted from the continuous downpour.

As their discomforts increased the murmurs of mutiny grew louder so that in desperation the word was given to recross the river and make for their base camp. But before they left a proclamation was made throughout the army offering, in the King's name, a knighthood and a landed estate to any man who could locate the Scots.[16]

Sixteen squires set off in different directions. Four days later, when the army had reached Blanchland, one of these, named Thomas Rokeby, came galloping into the camp. He had been taken prisoner by enemy scouts and brought before Douglas. When Douglas heard of his mission he sent him back to gain his reward and to tell the King of England that for more than a week they had been waiting to give him battle.[17] The English army was thereupon drawn up in formation and having heard Mass, was guided by Rokeby to where the Scots awaited them. About midday on 31 July they came in sight of their enemy posted on a rocky ridge south of the River Wear which, after the rains, was rushing in spate at the foot of their position. Attack was impossible. The English therefore sent heralds to ask the Scots either to come over to their side of the river or allow them to cross unhindered to the Scottish side so that they could have a stand-up fight. To which the Scots scornfully replied, 'We are here in your kingdom and have burnt and wasted your country. If you do not like it then come and dislodge us for we shall remain here as long as we please.'[18]

Noting that their army lay between the Scots and their native country, the English leaders conceived the idea that, although half-starved themselves, they could blockade the Scots into surrender by remaining static in front and sending probing pincers on either flank. Some success attended both opponents. Douglas lured one of the flanking attacks into an ambush and destroyed some and captured others, but in turn the English circumvented Randolph's position and surprised and killed a large body of his men who were resting in a wood behind.

Aware from prisoners of the English plan, the Scots presented a façade of roistering festivity on their rocky eminence with fires blazing and 'such blasting and noise with their horns', as Froissart relates, 'as if all the devils of Hell had come there.'[19] Under cover of this commotion they quietly removed themselves to a stronger position in a wood called Stanhope Park, two miles off, with a marsh protecting their rear and the turbulent river still in front.[20]

It almost seemed as if Douglas was playing games with his enemy. The English army shifted its ground and the blockade recommenced, but no sooner had they erected their bivouacs than Douglas with two hundred picked followers fetched a wide circle over the River Wear during the night and rode openly up to the far side of the English camp. A sentry challenged him but, roundly dressing down the man for slackness, he was let pass and swept with his two hundred through the lines of tents, slashing their straining ropes left and right until he reached the pavilion of the young King Edward. Only the suicidal gallantry of the royal household enabled the King to escape and for troops to gather against the marauding Scots.

But Douglas blew his horn for retreat to the river and charged through the thickening mass of his enemies into the black night. By the arranged path to the river's edge he waited to check his men as they passed. After a little, as no more came by, he was about to follow when an enemy straggler, roused from his sleep, came out of the darkness and hit him a violent blow with his club. Though tottering and stunned, he warded off his foe until his senses cleared and then dispatched him. Meanwhile his followers at the water's edge were about to turn back to look for him when they heard his horn and rode to welcome him tumultuously. On his return to the main army, Randolph asked him how he had fared. 'We have drawn blood,' he replied laconically.[21]

Randolph sought always to emulate his companion-in-arms and was eager to attack the English with a larger force, but Douglas dissuaded him by telling him the fable of the fisherman and the fox.* Instead they contrived once again to dupe the English. They remained quiet for several days and then, by much movement and marshalling of troops in the late afternoon, they gave the impression that they were preparing for a night attack. The English stood to arms but the Scots, leaving their camp fires burning brightly and scattered trumpeters sounding their horns, thinned away onto the apparently impassable marsh behind them. They had laid down a series of hurdles over the boggy patches and as they moved forward lifted them up as they went so that none could follow. When morning came and the English saw before them only a bare hillside, the Scots were many miles distant on their way to their native soil.[22]

The news was brought to the royal tent and when Edward III, who was only sixteen, realized that after all the hardships and misery of his first campaign the Scots had escaped without his ever having been able to show his prowess by a feat of arms, he burst into tears of vexation.[23]

His army was now in a pitiable condition and towards the end had only been buoyed up by the hope of a decisive battle. The chivalry of

* cf note XI

Flanders, which had cost him so dear, reduced by the privation of a form of war which they had never yet experienced, limped back on foot beside their English hosts to the city of York, bereft of their famous horses which were either dead or unserviceable. Once arrived there, the whole army was disbanded.

This was the signal for the completion of Bruce's strategy. He had neutralized Ireland, he had exhausted the English and allied troops by the cat-and-mouse tactics of his raiders: now, on his return to Scotland to welcome his fellow countrymen back, he marshalled a fresh army and early in September crossed into Northumberland at its head. One part of the force surrounded Norham Castle and the ingenious John Crab began to erect his siege engines for its destruction;[24] another invested Alnwick and passed the time until it should be starved into submission by conducting formal tournaments outside its walls. Such had become the consciousness of complete superiority among the Scots. The King himself made a leisurely progress through the countryside, hawking and hunting as he went, receiving tribute and letting it be known everywhere that he proposed to annex the northern counties and parcel them out among his followers.[25]

His bluff succeeded. Edward III and his regents were impotent. Their previous campaign had cost them £70,000, and when they summoned a parliament at Lincoln at the end of September to ask for funds to finance a further war, they met with a blank refusal.[26] Faced with the possibility of losing part of the kingdom, they had no alternative but to sue for peace. Early in October two English envoys empowered to open talks for a lasting peace waited on King Robert at Norham, where thirty-five years before Edward I had thrown off his mask and claimed the overlordship of Scotland.

On 18 October the Scottish King replied from Berwick with a letter dictating his terms. He was to have the kingdom of Scotland 'free, quit and entire' for himself and his heirs for ever without any kind of homage. His son was to marry Edward III's sister. No one in Scotland or England should hold lands in the other country. A pact of mutual support was to be concluded in so far as it did not infringe the Franco-Scottish treaty. The Scottish King would pay twenty thousand pounds within three years of peace being signed. The English King would use his good offices to persuade the Pope to revoke his interdict. If the King of England was prepared to accept these six demands, Scottish envoys would meet his representatives at Newcastle-on-Tyne to hammer out the details of a final peace.[27]

Still unable to accept the degree of England's humiliation, Edward III assumed the lofty language of a conqueror. He could only agree, he wrote from Nottingham on 30 October, to the second and fifth of the terms received and must reserve judgement on the rest. But when the Scots made clear that without a watertight agreement on the first there would be no negotiations, the weakness of his position compelled him to climb down. After appointing a commission on 23 November headed by the Archbishop of York and issuing safe conducts to the Scottish envoys on 25 January 1328, he summoned his Parliament to York in February. There on 1 March, in the presence of the Scottish representatives, the following letters patent were endorsed 'by the King himself and Council in Parliament' and placed in their hands.

> To all Christ's faithful people who shall see these letters, Edward, by the grace of God, King of England, Lord of Ireland, Duke of Acquitaine, greeting and peace everlasting in the Lord. Whereas, we and some of our predecessors, Kings of England, have endeavoured to establish rights of rule or dominion or superiority over the realm of Scotland, whence dire conflicts of wars waged have afflicted for a long time the Kingdoms of England and Scotland: we, having regard to the slaughter, disasters, crimes, destruction of churches and evils innumerable which, in the course of such wars, have repeatedly befallen the subjects of both realms, and to the wealth with which each realm, if united by the assurance of perpetual peace, might abound to their mutual advantage, thereby rendering them more secure against the hurtful efforts of those conspiring to rebel or to attack, whether from within or without: We will and grant by these presents, for us, our heirs and successors whatsoever, with the common advice, assent and consent of the prelates, princes, earls, barons and the commons of our realm in our Parliament, that the Kingdom of Scotland, within its own proper marches as they were held and maintained in the time of King Alexander of Scotland, last deceased, of good memory, shall belong to our dearest ally and friend, the magnificent prince, Lord Robert, by God's grace illustrious King of Scotland, and to his heirs and successors, separate in all things from the Kingdom of England, whole, free and undisturbed in perpetuity, without any kind of subjection, service, claim or demand. And by these presents we denounce and demit to the King of Scotland, his heirs and successors, whatsoever right we or our predecessors have put forward in any way in bygone times to the aforesaid Kingdom of Scotland. And, for ourselves and our heirs and successors, we cancel wholly and utterly all obligations, conventions and compacts undertaken in whatsoever manner with our predeces-

sors, at whatsoever times, by whatsoever Kings or inhabitants, clergy or laity, of the same Kingdom of Scotland, concerning the subjection of the realm of Scotland and its inhabitants. And wheresoever any letters, charters, deeds or instruments may be discovered bearing upon obligations, conventions and compacts of this nature, we will that they be deemed cancelled, invalid, of no effect and void, and of no value or moment. And for the full, peaceful and faithful observance of the foregoing, all and singular, for all time we have given full power and special command by our other letters patent to our well-beloved and faithful Henry de Percy our kinsman, and William de la Zouche of Ashby and to either of them make oath upon our soul. In testimony whereof we have caused these letters patent to be executed.[28]

At long last and in full measure the King of Scots and his people had received what for thirty years of warfare they had striven to obtain. The language suggests the hand of Bernard Linton and it is possible that it was drafted in Scotland and then presented to the English Parliament for acceptance as the necessary preliminary to treaty discussions.

These now moved swiftly to a conclusion. English commissioners, consisting of the Bishops of Lincoln and Norwich, Sir Geoffrey Le Scrope (the English Chief Justice), Henry Percy and William de la Zouche, travelled north to Edinburgh and reached the Scottish capital on 10 March with full powers to conclude and proclaim a final peace.[29] Within a week the terms of the treaty had been agreed and on 17 March there took place a ceremony which must rank as momentous in the annals of Scottish history.

'In a chamber within the precincts of Holyrood where the Lord King [of Scotland] was lying' stricken by a benumbing illness after his campaigning the previous summer, there gathered about him a great company of 'bishops, abbots, earls, barons, freeholders and sufficient persons delegated by the burghs' to receive the English representatives and witness the sealing of the documents.[30] Close beside him were his two commanders, James Douglas and Thomas Randolph, whom long ago when they were young men he had chosen as his lieutenants and whose feats of arms since then had made the name of Scotland renowned among the chivalry of Christendom. William Lamberton, the aged Bishop of St Andrews, was there – to die later that year – and must have murmured a Nunc Dimittis as he watched the culmination of his thirty years of unending toil for the nationhood of his country. The chief officers of the household were present: faithful Gilbert de la Haye the Constable, Robert Keith the Marischal, and many others who had fought beside Bruce from his earliest days. Only the Queen was not there to share his triumph. She had died on 26 October 1327 but had lived just long enough to know the certainty of his success.[31]

And success it was. All six articles of the terms he had dictated in October 1327 were written into the treaty in entirety, with the exception of the third which related to landholding in the two countries. The fourth article on the part of mutual support was enlarged by a clause that the Scots would not help the Irish if they rebelled against the English, nor the English the Hebrideans and the Manxmen if they rose against the Scots. In the second article on the marriage between Joan, Edward III's sister, and David, son of Bruce, the Scottish King undertook to settle £2000 a year on his daughter-in-law. She was to be allowed to return to England if she became a widow and so wished: but if she was pregant she would have first to obtain the permission of the Scots King and his barons.[32]

So much store did the English set by the royal marriage as a guarantee of the treaty that they asked for an indemnity of £100,000 from the Scots if it did not take place by Michaelmas 1338. In actuality both sides were anxious to hasten the event, and as soon as the English Parliament had met at Northampton and ratified the treaty signed at Edinburgh and Edward III had affixed his seal on 4 May, arrangements were put in hand for the wedding. Early in July Isabella, the Queen Dowager, and her daughter set out for Scotland and on 12 July Joan, aged six, and David, aged four, in the presence of a great gathering of prelates and noblemen from both countries, were married in the church at Berwick. The King of England could not bring himself to attend. The King of Scotland absented himself on the plea that he had not recovered from his illness.

It would appear, however, that this was a diplomatic excuse to counter the discourtesy of the English King, for within a few weeks Bruce had sailed for Ulster. William de Burgh, grandson and heir of the Red Earl of Ulster, Bruce's father-in-law, was a guest at the wedding. His patrimony and the control of Carrickfergus were in dispute. The truce between Bruce and Sir Henry de Mandeville was about to end. Throughout his life Bruce had taken an intense interest in maintaining a friendly presence in Northern Ireland. Now, on the understanding, presumably, that his great-nephew would ensure the continuance of amicable relations with Scotland, he escorted him with sufficient force to make certain the occupation of his Ulster heritage.[33]

★　　★　　★

It was Bruce's last military expedition. From now on he retired to his manor at Cardross and diverted himself by sailing on the Clyde or improving his garden and his orchards. His infirmity was increasing. Later medieval writers refer to it as leprosy, but this is highly unlikely for throughout the Middle Ages the segregation of lepers was so strict that even kings were cut off from their fellow men.

It is pleasantly related by Barbour that after Douglas and Randolph had escorted Queen Isabella and her cortege to the border on their way south from the wedding festivities, Bruce had sent for his two old companions to bring to his house the little bride and bridegroom and had there entertained them all.[34] For Bruce with his humane nature to risk infecting with a fatal disease two children, one of whom was his heir, is beyond belief. His symptoms much rather suggest recurrent increasingly serious attacks of scurvy.

He spent the Christmas of 1328 at Cardross and in February 1329, feeling a little better, he set out on a pilgrimage to the shrine of St Ninian near the southern coast of Wigtownshire. In October 1328 the Pope had at last removed his interdict from Scotland and excommunication from its King. But Bruce, as death approached, felt a stronger urge to make his peace with God and sought the intercession of the saint. St Ninian was the first missionary to bring Christianity to Scotland in the fifth century, and his name was linked in Bruce's memory with the first victorious clash at Bannockburn hard by St Ninian's kirk. The King was carried slowly in a litter along the coastal road of Ayrshire and had reached a little short of Castle Kennedy by Stranraer when he had a relapse. After resting there a month, he recovered sufficiently to continue south, reaching St Ninian's shrine at Whithorn on 1 April. Here he spent four or five days fasting and praying to the saint. From there by slow stages he travelled northwards through Galloway and Carrick. His route may have taken him by Glen Trool, the scene of his first victory, and to Turnberry Castle, where he had set up a household for his little son whom he had created Earl of Carrick. By the end of April he was back at Cardross.[35]

He now felt his weakness increase daily and sent letters to all the leading men in his kingdom to come to his bedside. When they were there assembled, he pledged them all to give their strength and loyalty to his son and obey him when he came of age to be their King.

'Sirs,' he then said to them, 'my day is far gone and there remains but one thing, to meet Death without fear, as every man must do. I thank God he has given me the space to repent in this life, for through me and my wars there has been a great spilling of blood and many an innocent man has been slain. Therefore I take this sickness and this pain as a penance for my sins.'[36]

He went on to say that he had made a vow to God that if he should live to see the end of his wars and be able to leave the realm in peace and security, he would go in person to fight against the heathen. But when that time had come his body had been stricken by mortal sickness and since it could not go forward he asked them to choose one among their number to carry his heart against the enemies of Christ.

At this they could not refrain from tears, but he chided them that it was better they set about what he had asked. So they retired and came back saying that they had chosen Sir James Douglas. To which the King replied that, ever since he had thought of this enterprise, he had longed that Sir James would undertake it, and since they were all agreed he was the more pleased if Sir James would consent.[37]

Then James Douglas knelt beside the King, and when he could speak for weeping he thanked him for all the benefits he had received since he first came into his service, but above all that he had been given the honour of taking into his keeping his master's heart, which all the world knew was so full of nobleness and valour. Then the King thanked him tenderly and 'there was none in that company but wept for pity'.[38]

A few days later on 7 June 1329, a little short of his fifty-fifth birthday, Robert Bruce, King of Scots, died. When he had been embalmed his heart was taken out* and given to Sir James Douglas, and his body carried in a funeral procession of great splendour to Dunfermline Abbey and buried in the choir near to his Queen Elizabeth and among the former kings and queens of Scotland. 'And when his people knew that King Robert was dead, the sound of sorrow went from place to place.'[39]

* cf note XII

# EPILOGUE

Douglas had a casket made of silver and enamel and in it he placed the heart of Robert Bruce and carried it always on a chain about his neck.[1]

Early in the spring of 1330, he set sail from Berwick in a ship fitted out in royal state so that all might know he was the bearer of the heart of Robert, King of Scotland, and on his way to lay it in the Holy Sepulchre in Jerusalem. He had on board six knights, linked in friendship, neighbouring landowners from the Stewart domains: Sir William Sinclair of Roslyn, Sir Robert and Sir Walter Logan, Sir William Keith, Sir Alan Cathcart and Sir Seymour Loccard of Lee, and one other knight unnamed. Twenty-six squires and gentlemen were there to serve them.[2]

Their first port of call was Sluys in Flanders. Here Douglas remained twelve days, entertaining liberally on gold and silver plate and letting it be known that any who wished to fight in the Holy Land were welcome to join his company. He then sailed in rough seas around the coast of Spain and up the Guadalquiver River to drop anchor in the city of Seville.

When Alfonso XI, King of Castile and Leon, heard that he had arrived he came to greet him and offer him hospitality, and many foreign and especially English knights who had flocked to Spain to war against the Moors called at his lodgings to give him welcome, for his military prowess was acknowledged above all others throughout the camps of Europe.[3]

Douglas and his company rested for a while at Seville after the hardships of their stormy voyage, but in March the Moorish King of Granada advanced against the city and the King of Castile and Leon marshalled his forces to meet him. He asked Douglas to lead the vanguard and placed under his command all the foreign knights.[4] On 25 March, at Zebas de Ardales, the armies came face to face.

Douglas gave the order to charge and both sides became locked in battle. But the Saracens employed a ruse with which Douglas was not acquainted. Suddenly they turned their horses and fled, pursued by the Christians. Douglas and ten of his followers had drawn far ahead of the vanguard when the Saracens sharply checked and swung round to encircle them. Douglas turned too and might have escaped through the gap, but saw that Sir William Sinclair had been overtaken. With the two knights who were beside him – Sir Robert and Sir Walter Logan – Douglas turned yet again to rescue his comrade. In a moment they were surrounded by a multitude of Moors and, fighting desperately, were all cut down.[5]

The rest of the vanguard were now approaching, and the Saracens once more wheeled round their horses and galloped from the field, leaving the four knights dead upon the ground. The heart of Robert Bruce within its casket was found still chained about the neck of Douglas and, according to the tradition of the Cathcart family, was taken up by Sir Alan Cathcart.

The body of Douglas was brought to his cousin, Sir William Keith, who had been prevented from taking part in the battle by a broken arm.[6] After having the body boiled so that the flesh parted from the bones, the flesh was buried in holy ground and the bones placed on shipboard.[7] Then Sir William Keith, in command of the remaining Scotsmen, sailed for home, and when they had made landfall, the heart of Bruce was carried to the Abbey of Melrose and interred with great reverence, and the bones of Douglas were buried in the Kirk of Douglas.[8]

Thomas Randolph, Earl of Moray, the last of the great captains, had taken over the government of Scotland on the death of Bruce, as regent for the young King, David II. Three years later he, too, was dead.

Within two years of Randolph's death Edward III disavowed the Treaty of Edinburgh on the grounds that he had been under age when he signed it. Warfare between England and Scotland began again and continued intermittently for the next four hundred years. The Scots suffered many defeats since their bravery was seldom equalled by their generalship. But never again was there the possibility of their becoming a subject race. Robert Bruce had forged a nation and his victory at Bannockburn had given to his people a self-confidence which never deserted them however serious their reverses.

> Scots wha hae with Wallace bled
> Scots wham Bruce has aften led
> Welcome to your gory bed
> Or to victorie.[9]

# BIBLIOGRAPHY

## *Primary*

### RECORDS

| | |
|---|---|
| *A.P.S.* | *Acts of Parliament of Scotland*, ed. T. Thomson and C. Innes (1814–1875) |
| *Cal. Doc. Scots* | *Calendar of Documents relating to Scotland*, ed. J. Bain (1881–8) |
| Dickinson | *A Source Book of Scottish History*, Vol. I, ed. W.C. Dickinson, G. Donaldson, Isabella A. Milne |
| Foedera | *Foedera, Conventiones, Literae*, ed. T. Rymer, 3rd edn (The Hague, 1739–45) |
| Palgrave | *Documents and Records illustrating the History of Scotland*, ed. F. Palgrave (1837) |
| *Rotuli Scotiae* | *Rotuli Scotiae*, ed. D. Macpherson and others (1814–1819) |
| Stevenson | *Documents illustrative of the History of Scotland*, ed. J. Stevenson (1870) |
| Stones | *Anglo-Scottish Relations 1174–1328*, ed. E. L. G. Stones (Nelson, 1964) |

### CHRONICLES

| | |
|---|---|
| Barbour | *The Brus*, J. Barbour, ed. and tr. G. Eyre Todd (1907) |
| *Flores Historiarum* | *Flores Historiarum by Mathew of Westminster*, tr. C. D. Yonge (1853) |
| Fordun | *Scotichronicon*, John of Fordun, tr. F. S. H. Skene, ed. W. F. Skene (1872) |
| Froissart | *Chroniques de Froissart*, Vol I., ed. Simeon Luce (Paris, 1869) |

| | |
|---|---|
| *Guisborough* | *The Chronicle of Walter Guisborough*, ed. H. Roth-well (1957) |
| *Lanercost* | *The Chronicle of Lanercost*, tr. Sir Herbert Maxwell Bt (1913) |
| Langtoft | *English Historical Documents*, Vol. III, Pierre Langtoft, pp. 230–265 |
| *Le Bel* | *Les Vraies Chroniques de Messire Jehan Le Bel*, ed. L. Poulain (Brussels, 1863) |
| Mathew Paris | *Chronica Majora*, ed. Luard. Rolls Series |
| *Pluscarden* | *Liber Pluscardiensis*, ed. F. H. Skene (1880) |
| *Rishanger* | *Chronica Willelmi Rishanger*, ed. H. T. Riley (1865) |
| *Scalaronica* | *Scalaronica*, Sir Thomas Gray, tr. Sir Herbert Maxwell Bt (1907) |
| *Song of Lewes* | *Song of Lewes*, ed. and tr. C. A. Kingsford (1890) |
| *Vita Edwardii* | *Vita Edwardii Secundi Monachi by the Monk of Malmesbury*, tr. N. Denholm-Young |
| Walsingham | *Historia Anglicana*, Thomas Walsingham, Vol. I, ed. H. T. Riley (1863). |
| Wyntoun | *Orygynale Cronykil of Scotland*, Andrew Wyntoun, ed. D. Laing (1872–9) |

## Secondary

| | |
|---|---|
| Balfour Paul | *The Scots Peerage*, Sir J. Balfour Paul (1904–14) |
| Barron | *The Scottish War of Independence*, 2nd edn, E. M. Barron (1934) |
| Barrow | *Robert Bruce and the Community of the Realm of Scotland*, 2nd edn, Professor G. W. S. Barrow (Edinburgh University Press, 1976) |
| Bingham | *Edward II*, Caroline Bingham (Weidenfeld and Nicolson, 1973) |
| Burton | *History of Scotland*, Vol. II, J. H. Burton, 2nd edn (1873) |
| Christison | *Bannockburn. The Story of the Battle*, General Sir Philip Christison Bt G.B.E., C.B., D.S.O., M.C., D.L., B.A., F.S.A.Scot. and I. Cameron Taylor (Scottish National Trust, 1962) |
| Dunbar | *Scottish Kings: a revised Chronology of Scottish History*, A. H. Dunbar (1906) |

| | |
|---|---|
| Duncan | *The Nation of Scots and the Declaration of Arbroath*, Professor A. A. M. Duncan (Historical Association, 1970) |
| E.H.R. | *English Historical Review* |
| Frame | *Irish Historical Studies*, Vol. XIX, 4–36, Robin Frame |
| Hailes | *Annals of Scotland from Accession of Malcolm III to the Restoration of James I*, Lord Hailes (1819) |
| Hay | *Europe in the 14th and 15th Centuries*, Denys Hay (Longman, 1970) |
| Howard | *War in European History*, Michael Howard (Oxford University Press, 1976) |
| Jenkins | *The Mystery of King Arthur*, Elizabeth Jenkins (New York, 1977) |
| Lucas | *The Great European Famine 1315–1317*, H. S. Lucas (Speculum 30, 1930) |
| Lydon | *The Bruce Invasion of Ireland*, J. F. Lydon *Historical Studies*, Vol. IV, 115–119 |
| MacKay | *Robert Bruce, King of Scots*, James A. MacKay (Robert Hale, 1974) |
| MacKenzie | *Robert Bruce, King of Scots*, A.M. MacKenzie (1934) |
| Nicholson | *Scotland. The Later Middle Ages*, Ranald Nicholson (Edinburgh University Press, 1974) |
| Powicke | *The Thirteenth Century 1216–1307*, F. M. Powicke (1953) |
| Ramsay | *Dawn of the Constitution 1216–1307*, Sir James Ramsay (1908) |
| Scott | *Tales of a Grandfather*, Vol. I, Sir Walter Scott (1828) |
| S.H.R. | *Scottish Historical Review* |
| Tout | *Edward I*, T. F. Tout (1872) |
| Tytler | *The History of Scotland*, Vol. I, P. F. Tytler (1887) |

# REFERENCES

## Part One

### CHAPTER 1

1 Dunbar, 98
2 ibid., 99
3 *Lanercost*, 40
4 *Guisborough*, 275
5 Fordun, 295
6 *Lanercost*, 156
7 Mathew Paris, 93
8 Howard, 2–4
9 *Wyntoun*, 266

### CHAPTER 2

1 Barrow, 37
2 Balfour Paul, 433–4
3 ibid., 428–30
4 Palgrave, 29
5 Stones, 79
6 *Lanercost*, 111–12
7 ibid., 112–13
8 MacKay, 19
9 Barrow, 38
10 *Pluscarden*, 194
11 Jenkins, 105
12 ibid., 98

### CHAPTER 3

1 *Lanercost*, 40–42
2 *Cal. Doc. Scots*, ii, 292; Stevenson, i, 4
3 Palgrave, 42

4 Fordun, 305
5 *Cal. Doc. Scots*, ii, 305; Stevenson, i, 21
6 *Song of Lewes*, 42
7 *Cal. Doc. Scots*, ii, 293; Stevenson, i, 22
8 ibid., ii, 298; ibid., i, 35
9 Palgrave, 42
10 Stevenson, i, 22
11 *Lanercost*, 59
12 *Cal. Doc. Scots*, ii, 386, 388
13 Dickinson, 105–7
14 *Cal. Doc. Scots*, ii, 392; Stevenson, i, 111
15 ibid., ii, 416
16 ibid., ii, 464
17 Dickinson, 107–9
18 Stevenson, i, 162
19 ibid., i, 172
20 Dunbar, 416

### CHAPTER 4

1 *Cal. Doc. Scots*, ii, 459; Dickinson, 109–10
2 ibid., ii, 465; Stones, 89
3 *Lanercost*, 77
4 *Rishanger*, 121
5 *Pluscarden*, 88
6 *Cal. Doc Scots*, ii, 473, 474
7 ibid., ii, 480; Stevenson, i, 228
8 *Rishanger*, 241
9 ibid., 242

10 Stones, 107
11 *Rishanger*, 245
12 Stones, 113
13 *Cal. Doc Scots*, ii, 485
14 ibid., ii, 516
15 *Pluscarden*, 95
16 ibid., 97
17 Fordun, 308
18 *A.P.S.*, i, 449
19 *Rishanger*, 274–80
20 ibid., 309–16
21 Stones, 119–25
22 Fordun, 309
23 *Rishanger*, 363
24 *Cal. Doc. Scots*, ii, 650
25 *Rotuli Scotiae*, i, 12a
26 Stones, 127–9
27 *Rishanger*, 371
28 *Cal. Doc. Scots*, ii, 660
29 ibid., ii, 658
30 Stones, 131–3
31 *Rishanger*, 372
32 *Cal. Doc. Scots*, 720
33 *Lanercost*, 77
34 Stevenson, ii, 23
35 Barrow, 92
36 *Cal. Doc. Scots*, ii, 635
37 ibid., ii, 716
38 ibid., ii, 675
39 Dunbar, 127
40 Fordun, 317
41 *Guisborough*, 270
42 ibid., 271–2; *Lanercost*, 134
43 *Lanercost*, 115
44 Palgrave, 149
45 Stevenson, ii, 25
46 *Rishanger*, 375
47 Stevenson, ii, 37
48 Stones, 141
49 Fordun, 317
50 *Cal. Doc. Scots*, ii, 742;
   Stevenson, ii, 26
51 Stevenson, ii, 26–8
52 *Cal. Doc. Scots*, ii, 840
53 ibid., ii, 823
54 Fordun, 319
55 Stevenson, ii, 31

CHAPTER 5
1 *Scalaronica*, 17
2 *Guisborough*, 294
3 *Cal. Doc Scots*, ii, 742
4 ibid., ii, 922, 931
5 *Scalaronica*, 18
6 *Guisborough*, 295
7 *Cal. Doc. Scots*, ii, 357
8 *Lanercost*, 163
9 Stevenson, ii, 114, *Cal. Doc. Scots*, ii, 852
10 *Guisborough*, 297–8
11 *Cal. Doc. Scots*, ii, 887
12 ibid., ii, 909; Stevenson, ii 192
13 ibid., ii, 910
14 Stevenson, ii, 205
15 Barrow, 120
16 *Cal. Doc. Scots*, ii, 917
17 *Rishanger*, 379
18 *Guisborough*, 297
19 ibid., 299
20 Barron, 33–57
21 *Cal. Doc. Scots*, ii, 972
22 *Guisborough*, 300
23 ibid., 300
24 *Scalaronica*, 19
25 ibid., 19
26 *Rishanger*, 180
27 *Guisborough*, 303
28 ibid., 307–8
29 Dickinson, 118
30 *Cal. Doc. Scots*, ii, 1178
31 *Guisborough*, 299
32 *Rishanger*, 384
33 *Guisborough*, 303–7
34 Fordun, 323
35 *Cal. Doc. Scots*, ii, 984
36 *Flores Historiarum*, ii, 578
37 *Guisborough*, 324
38 ibid., 325
39 *Rishanger*, 386
40 *Guisborough*, 324
41 ibid., 326
42 ibid., 326–7
43 ibid., 327
44 *Rishanger*, 385
45 *Guisborough*, 327

46 ibid., 328, *Fordun*, 323
47 ibid., 328
48 *Rishanger*, 388
49 ibid., 388

CHAPTER 6

1 *Cal. Doc. Scots*, ii, 1184
2 Barrow 147
3 ibid., 150
4 *Cal. Doc. Scots*, ii, 1071
5 ibid., ii, 1978
6 ibid., ii, 1092, 1111
7 *Rishanger*, 402
8 *Cal. Doc. Scots*, ii, 1109
9 Barrow, 158
10 *Rishanger*, 395
11 ibid., 440
12 Langtoft, 247
13 *Rishanger*, 440
14 ibid., 442; *Cal. Doc. Scots*, ii, 1147
15 ibid., 445
16 *Cal. Doc. Scots*, ii, 1069
17 Stones, 163–75
18 *Rishanger*, 447
19 *Cal. Doc. Scots*, ii, 1163
20 ibid., ii, 1193
21 Barrow, 161
22 *Cal. Doc. Scots*, ii, 1191
23 ibid., ii, 1236, 1239
24 ibid., ii, 1235
25 ibid., ii, 1250
26 ibid., ii, 1269, 1282
27 *S.H.R.*, xxxiv, 130–31
28 Barrow, 169
29 Stones, 237–9
30 Dunbar, 128
31 *Pluscarden*, ii, 169
32 *Rishanger*, 211
33 ibid., 211
34 ibid., 211
35 ibid., 213
36 *Cal. Doc. Scots*, ii, 1375
37 *Flores Historiarum*, ii, 564
38 Palgrave, 279
39 ibid., 286–7
40 ibid., 287

41 *Flores Historiarum*, ii, 570
42 *Cal. Doc. Scots*, ii, 1599
43 Palgrave, 276
44 Barrow, 193
45 ibid., 193

CHAPTER 7

1 *Cal. Doc. Scots*, ii, 1691
2 ibid., ii, 1745
3 Barrow, 175
4 *Cal. Doc. Scots*, ii, 1510; Stevenson, ii, 482
5 ibid., ii, 1495
6 ibid., ii, 1465
7 Barrow, 203; Langtoft, 262
8 *Cal. Doc. Scots*, ii, 1708, 1736
9 ibid., ii, 1657
10 Barron, 176
11 *Cal. Doc. Scots*, ii, 1493
12 ibid., ii, 1546
13 *Flores Historiarum*, ii, 572, 573
14 *Cal. Doc. Scots*, ii, 1817
15 Fordun, 330; Barbour, 13
16 *Cal. Doc. Scots*, ii, 1691
17 ibid., ii, 1696
18 *Pluscarden*, 174; Fordun 331
19 ibid., 175
20 ibid., 175
21 *Lanercost*, 176
22 Barrow, 208
23 *Pluscarden*, 175 and oral tradition
24 *Guisborough*, 366
25 Stones, 267
26 Palgrave, 348
27 Stones, 267
28 ibid., 261, 263
29 ibid., 267
30 ibid., 273
31 Barbour, 21
32 *Cal. Doc. Scots*, ii, 1914
33 Walsingham, 108; *Flores Historiarum*, ii, 584

## Part Two

CHAPTER 8

1 *Flores Historiarum*, ii, 586, 587

2 *Cal. Doc. Scots*, ii, 1748
3 ibid., ii, 1754
4 ibid., ii, 1908
5 Palgrave, 348, 349
6 *Cal. Doc. Scots*, ii, 1813
7 Palgrave, 330
8 Barron, 224–35
9 Barbour, 23
10 ibid., 25
11 ibid., 25
12 Langtoft, 261
13 Barbour, 27, 28
14 *Flores Historiarum*, ii, 588
15 ibid., ii, 588; *Cal. Doc. Scots*, ii, 1811
16 *Cal. Doc. Scots*, ii, 1909; Walsingham, 237
17 Barbour, 30
18 Pluscarden, 177
19 Barbour, 32
20 ibid., 34
21 ibid., 34 footnote
22 ibid., 36, 37
23 Barbour, 42
24 Local tradition
25 Barbour, 43
26 ibid., 43
27 Local tradition
28 Barbour, 44
29 ibid., 44
30 ibid., 45, 46
31 ibid., 48
32 ibid., 48
33 *Cal. Doc Scots*, ii, 1810
34 Barbour, 54
35 ibid., 57
36 Sampson, *Official Guide, Kildrummy Castle*
37 *Flores Historiarum*, ii, 591
38 ibid., ii, 591; *Scalaronica*, 33
39 *Flores Historiarum*, ii, 584
40 *Cal. Doc. Scots*, ii, 1851
41 *Scalaronica*, 31
42 Palgrave, 358
43 *Cal. Doc. Scots*, ii, 1910
44 ibid., ii, 1910
45 Palgrave, 357

46 *Cal. Doc. Scots*, ii, 1963
47 *Cal. Doc. Scots*, ii, 1833, 1834
48 Barbour, 51
49 *Guisborough*, 370
50 Fordun, 335; *Pluscarden*, 178
51 Local tradition that Bruce stayed at MacKenzie's castle of Eilanadoon
52 *Cal. Doc. Scots*, ii, 1889
53 ibid., ii, 1829
54 Barbour, 63–5
55 ibid., 67
56 *Guisborough*, 370; *Lanercost*, 179, 180
57 Barbour, 75–7

CHAPTER 9

1 *Cal. Doc. Scots*, ii, 1913, 1923, 1957
2 Barbour, 79
3 Ibid., 86–90
4 ibid., 77–8
5 Oral tradition
6 Barbour, 92–9
7 ibid., 80–84
8 *Cal. Doc. Scots*, ii, 1896
9 Mackay, 105
10 Barbour, 104–16
11 ibid., 117–18
12 ibid., 119–22
13 *Cal. Doc. Scots*, ii, 1923, 1942
14 Barbour, 123
15 ibid., 123–5
16 ibid., 125
17 *Lanercost*, 182
18 Barbour, 126–9
19 ibid., 131
20 ibid., 129–35
21 *Flores Historiarum*, ii, 595

CHAPTER 10

1 *Cal. Doc. Scots*, ii, 1926
2 *Flores Historiarum*, ii, 595
3 Walsingham, 114
4 *Lanercost*, 183, 184
5 *Cal. Doc. Scots*, ii, 1926
6 ibid., iii, 14, 15

7 ibid., iii, 12
8 ibid., iii, 80
9 Barrow and Barnes, *S.H.R.*, xlix, 57–9
10 *Cal. Doc. Scots*, iv, 1837
11 Barbour, 141–4
12 ibid., 145–6
13 *Pluscarden*, 181
14 Barbour, 147
15 ibid., 148
16 Barbour, 10, 266
17 ibid., 101–2
18 ibid., 137–9
19 ibid., 137; *Cal. Doc. Scots*, iii, 28
20 ibid., 159–60
21 Barrow and Barnes, *S.H.R.* xlix, 57–9
22 Barbour, 148
23 ibid., 161–4
24 Barron, 348
25 Barbour, 154
26 *Cal. Doc. Scots*, iii, 83, 84
27 ibid., iii, 235, 281
28 Barbour, 155, 156

CHAPTER 11

1 *Scalaronica*, 45
2 *Lanercost*, 186
3 *Vita Edwardii*, 2, 8
4 *A.P.S.*, i, 459
5 Dickinson, 122–4
6 *A.P.S.*, i, 459, i, 289
7 ibid., i, 459
8 ibid., i, 289
9 *Cal. Doc. Scots*, iii, 100
10 *Lanercost*, 190
11 Barrow, 272 footnote
12 *Cal. Doc. Scots*, iii, 190
13 MacKenzie, 220
14 Dickinson, 125
15 *Vita Edwardii*, 11
16 *Lanercost*, 190
17 *Cal. Doc. Scots*, iii, 166
18 *Pluscarden*, 181
19 *Cal. Doc. Scots*, iii, 171
20 ibid., iii, 203, 206
21 ibid., iii, 171

22 *Vita Edwardii*, 12
23 *Lanercost*, 191
24 *Cal. Doc. Scots*, iii, 176
25 *Foedera*, ii, 118
26 *Cal. Doc. Scots*, iii, 197
27 *Lanercost*, 191
28 ibid., 191
29 ibid., 193
30 ibid., 194
31 ibid., 195
32 ibid., 195
33 ibid., 196
34 *Vita Edwardii*, 22
35 ibid., 23
36 *Lanercost*, 196
37 *Vita Edwardii*, 24–8

CHAPTER 12

1 *Cal. Doc. Scots*, iii, 50
2 ibid., iii, 279
3 *Lanercost*, 197, 199–200
4 ibid., 205
5 *Vita Edwardii*, 48
6 *Guisborough*, 397
7 Barrow, 287, 288
8 Barron, 398
9 *Scalaronica*, 52
10 *Lanercost*, 201, 202
11 Barbour, 149–151
12 ibid., 152
13 ibid., 151
14 *Cal. Doc. Scots.*, iii, 304
15 Barron, 410
16 *Cal. Doc. Scots*, iii, 420
17 ibid., iii, 562
18 *Rotuli Scotiae*, i, 108
19 Barbour, 182
20 *Cal. Doc. Scots*, iii, 202
21 Barbour, 184
22 ibid., 165–8
23 *Cal. Doc. Scots*, iii, 186, 337
24 *Lanercost*, 195
25 Scott, 164
26 Barbour, 170–74
27 ibid., 169
28 ibid., 175–9
29 ibid., 181

CHAPTER 13

1 *Vita Edwardii*, 43
2 *Cal. Doc. Scots*, iii, 337
3 *Rotuli Scotiae*, i, 119a
4 Barrow, 292, 293
5 Bingham, 97
6 *Vita Edwardii*, 49–50; *Lanercost*, 206
7 Barbour, 224
8 *Lanercost*, 206
9 Barbour, 187
10 *Vita Edwardii*, 50–51
11 Barbour, 191
12 ibid., 189
13 Christison lecture
14 Barbour, 194, 195
15 ibid., 194
16 ibid., 194
17 ibid., 192
18 *Scalaronica*, 53
19 *Cal. Doc. Scots*, ii, 1757
20 ibid., iii, 4
21 Barbour, 200, 201
22 ibid., 202
23 ibid., 197
24 *Scalaronica* 54
25 Barbour, 198–9, 202–4
26 ibid., 204–5
27 *Scalaronica*, 55
28 *Lanercost*, 207
29 Barbour, 209
30 Christison lecture
31 Barbour, 210
32 Christison lecture
33 Barbour, extracts, 205–8
34 Barbour, 210
35 ibid., 210–212
36 *Vita Edwardii*, 52–4
37 *Lanercost*, 208
38 Barbour, 213
39 ibid., 216
40 ibid., 216
41 ibid., 217
42 ibid., 216, 217
43 Christison, 25
44 Barbour, 221
45 ibid., 223, 224; *Scalaronica*, 56; Walsingham, 246
46 ibid., 225
47 ibid., 222
48 *Lanercost*, 209
49 Barbour, 225
50 *Lanercost*, 209
51 Barbour, 227
52 ibid., 227
53 ibid., 226
54 ibid., 231–2
55 ibid., 228–30
56 ibid., 229
57 ibid., 229
58 Walsingham, 142
59 Barbour, 229
60 Walsingham, 142
61 Barbour, 234
62 Walsingham, 142
63 Barbour, 230
64 Burton, 270
65 Barbour, 234
66 *Cal. Doc. Scots*, iii, 393
67 ibid., iii, 131
68 ibid., iii, 244
69 *Rotuli Scotiae*, i, 85b
70 *Cal. Doc. Scots*, iii, 313
71 *Vita Edwardii*, 56

## Part Three

CHAPTER 14

1 Dickinson, 126
2 *Vita Edwardii*, 57
3 *Lanercost*, 210–11
4 ibid., 212
5 ibid., 213
6 Walsingham, 143
7 *Cal. Doc. Scots*, ii, 1260, 1277, 1763; *Rishanger*, 414; Stevenson, ii, 281
8 Lydon, 118
9 ibid., 119–20
10 Barrow, 434
11 Frame, 4
12 Barbour, 237; *Pluscarden*, 187
13 Dickinson, 128

14 *Lanercost*, 212
15 Barbour, 240–42
16 ibid., 245–6
17 ibid., 254–8
18 Lydon, 121
19 Barbour, 259–60
20 *Cal. Doc. Scots*, iii, 451; *Vita Edwardii*, 61, 67
21 ibid., iii, 448
22 *Lanercost*, 213–15
23 ibid., 216
24 *Cal. Doc. Scots*, iii, 452, 470, 477, 480
25 ibid., iii, 470
26 Barbour, 260–62
27 ibid., 263–6
28 *Cal. Doc. Scots*, iii, 527
29 *Lanercost*, 216
30 Barbour, 268
31 Barbour, 269
32 Nicholson, 94
33 Barbour, 269
34 ibid., 270–73
35 Lydon, 118
36 Frame, 23
37 ibid., 34–5
38 Barbour, 275
39 Frame, 36 and footnote 26
40 *Lanercost*, 218
41 *Vita Edwardii*, 75
42 *Lanercost*, 217
43 Barbour, 277–80
44 ibid., 282–5
45 *Vita Edwardii*, 78
46 Foedera, ii, 340
47 *Cal. Doc. Scots*, iii, 553
48 ibid., iii, 555
49 Barbour, 287–92
50 Barbour, 293
51 *Lanercost*, 220–21
52 *Cal. Doc. Scots*, iii, 707
53 ibid., iii, 858
54 *Lanercost*, 221

CHAPTER 15

1 *Cal. Doc. Scots*, iii, 519
2 ibid., iii, 549

3 ibid., iii, 562
4 Lydon, 115
5 Nicholson, 95
6 *Lanercost*, 225
7 Barbour, 311–17
8 Dickinson, 130
9 *A.P.S.*, i, 113
10 Barbour, 294–9
11 ibid., 302–7
12 *Vita Edwardii*, 96
13 ibid., 96
14 *Lanercost*, 226
15 *Vita Edwardii*, 96
16 *Lanercost*, 227
17 Barbour, 308
18 *Vita Edwardii*, 76, 97
19 *Lanercost*, 227
20 Barrow, 434
21 *Lanercost*, 228
22 *Cal. Doc. Scots*, iii, 677, 681, 738, 739
23 *Lanercost*, 228
24 Barrow, 419
25 Burton, 284–6 footnote; Dickinson, 131–4
26 *Cal. Doc. Scots*, iii, 725
27 Dunbar, 142
28 Barbour, 328, 329; Dickinson, *S.H.R.*, xlii, 84–5

CHAPTER 16

1 *Lanercost*, 229, 230; *Vita Edwardii*, 108
2 *Cal. Doc. Scots*, iii, 746
3 *Lanercost*, 230, 231
4 ibid., 231–4; *Vita Edwardii*, 124
5 *Cal. Doc. Scots*, iii, 754
6 ibid., iii, 752
7 *Lanercost*, 239
8 Barbour, 318
9 ibid., 318
10 *Pluscarden*, 190
11 *Scalaronica*, 69
12 *Cal. Doc. Scots*, iii, 790
13 ibid., iii, 791
14 Barbour, 320–25
15 Nicholson, *S.H.R.*, xlii, 38–9

16 *Lanercost*, 240
17 ibid., 240
18 *Cal. Doc. Scots*, iii, 773
19 Stones, 309–15
20 *Lanercost*, 242
21 ibid., 243
22 ibid., 245
23 ibid., 244
24 *A.P.S.*, i, 479–81
25 *Cal. Doc. Scots*, iii, 778
26 Nicholson, 106
27 Burton, 294–6
28 *Foedera*, ii, 541
29 ibid., ii, 541
30 ibid., ii, 542
31 Dunbar, 145
32 *Cal. Doc. Scots*, iii, 841
33 ibid., iii, 169
34 ibid., iii, 239
35 ibid., iii, 305
36 ibid., iii, 323
37 ibid., iii, 354
38 Barrow, 439–40
39 ibid., 406–7
40 Nicholson, 113
41 ibid., 113
42 Barrow, 396–402
43 Nicholson, 107
44 ibid., 107–8
45 ibid., 113–14
46 Barrow, 438
47 *A.P.S.*, i, 475
48 Fordun, 343; *Pluscarden*, 190
49 Barbour, 337
50 Balfour Paul, ii, 435

CHAPTER 17

1 *Lanercost*, 248, 249
2 ibid., 250, 251
3 Dickinson, 135–6
4 Walsingham, 184, 185
5 *Lanercost*, 256
6 ibid., 257
7 Walsingham, 189

8 Barbour, 332
9 *Cal. Doc. Scots*, iii, 907
10 ibid., iii, 914
11 ibid., iii, 922
12 Barbour, 334
13 ibid., 339
14 *Le Bel*, 34–40
15 ibid., 47
16 ibid., 52–8
17 *Cal. Doc. Scots*, iii, 936
19 *Le Bel*, 59–63
19 *Froissart*, 65
20 Barbour, 341
21 ibid., 343, 344
22 ibid., 345–8
23 *Lanercost*, 258
24 Nicholson, 119
25 Barbour, 350
26 Nicholson, 119
27 Stones, 317–21
28 ibid., 323–5; *Lanercost*, 261, 262
29 ibid., *S.H.R.*, xxix, 48
30 ibid., *S.H.R.*, xxviii, 125
31 Dunbar, 139
32 Stones, 329–41
33 Nicholson, *S.H.R.*, xlii, 34–8
34 Barbour, 353
35 Barrow, 438, 439
36 Barbour, 355
37 ibid., 356
38 ibid., 357
39 ibid., 357, 358

EPILOGUE

1 Barbour, 359
2 Cathcart MSS
3 Barbour, 360
4 ibid., 361
5 ibid., 362, 363
6 ibid., 364
7 ibid., 366
8 ibid., 366, 367
9 Robert Burns

# NOTES

I   The claim by many previous historians that Robert Bruce 'the Competitor' served as a royal judge in England and became the first chief justice to be appointed there is due to a confusion between his name and that of Robert de Briwes, a leading English lawyer at that time, cf. Professor A. A. M. Duncan, *S.H.R.*, Vol. xlv, 186

II  After being taken to the Tower of London, John Balliol was moved to a manor house in Hertfordshire where he was allowed a huntsman, a page and ten hounds with permission to hunt in any of the King's forests south of the Trent. Here he remained until he was handed over to the Pope in July 1299, cf. Stevenson, 121 and 163

III This is based on circumstantial evidence. According to *Rishanger*, 384, Wallace was knighted by a prominent man of the Scottish race, 'de illa natione praecipuus', which implies one of the earls. At that time the Earl of Fife was a minor. The Earls of Angus and Dunbar supported the English, the northern Earls of Caithness, Sutherland, Ross and Mar were remote from the sphere of action, the Earls of Atholl and Menteith were in France. The remaining earls were Buchan, Strathearne, Lennox and Carrick. Of these only the Earl of Carrick was related to the Wallaces for the uncle of William Wallace, Sir Richard Wallace, was married to a Bruce and the link continued into the next generation by the marriage between William Wallace's cousin, Sir Duncan Wallace, to Eleanora, Countess of Carrick, the widow of Alexander Bruce, Earl of Carrick. It is significant also that, when Wallace relinquished the post of guardian after Falkirk, the only earl to be chosen as one of the two succeeding guardians was Robert Bruce, Earl of Carrick.

IV  In the papal bull *Scimus Fili*, which was delivered to Edward I at Sweetheart Abbey on his return from his Galloway campaign in 1300, Pope Boniface admonished him that the kingdom of Scotland 'was not feudally subject to your ancestors . . . nor is it so to you'. In reply

241

Edward had an elaborate legal brief prepared in justification of his claim to the suzerainty of Scotland. This was presented to the papal court in 1301. In the same year the Scots sent a delegation of three to the Vatican bearing with them a *Processus* (legal document) to combat the English claims. Master Baldred Bisset, main author of the *Processus* and chief spokesman for the delegation, was a graduate of Bologna University and president of the bishops' ordinary court at St Andrews. Andrew Wyntoun calls him a 'wys and cunnand clerk' (Wyntoun ii, 351) and anyone who reads his counterblast to the English submissions to the court must regard it as a little masterpiece.

V    Later in the century a popular verse epitomized the methods of Robert Bruce, which paraphrased runs as follows:

> On foot should be all Scottish war
> Let hill and marsh their foes debar
> And woods as walls prove such an arm
> That enemies do them no harm.
> In hidden spots keep every store
> And burn the plainlands them before
> So, when they find the land lie waste
> Needs must they pass away in haste
> Harried by cunning raids at night
> And threatening sounds from every height.
> Then, as they leave, with great array
> Smite with the sword and chase away.
> This is the counsel and intent
> Of Good King Robert's Testament.

VI   Those illegitimate children of Robert Bruce of whom records exist are:
1. Sir Robert Bruce, received 500 marks yearly from the King, died at the battle of Dupplin, 12 August 1332
2. Nigel Bruce of Carrick, received £30 yearly from the King, slain at the battle of Durham, 17 October 1346
3. Margaret Bruce, married Robert Glen, mentioned in records as alive on 29 February 1364
4. Elizabeth Bruce, married Sir Walter Oliphant of Gask
5. Christian Bruce of Carrick, recorded as in receipt of a pension from the King in 1328 and 1329. The names of their mothers are not known cf. Dunbar 142

VII  Edward II was constantly changing his viceroys, as can be seen from the list below. It is probable that such an office in a hostile country was not popular.
28 Aug 1307 Earl of Pembroke continues in office
13 Sep 1307 Earl of Richmond takes over
21 Jun 1308 Earl of Angus and William de Ros relieve the Earl of Richmond

16 Aug 1309 They are joined by Henry Beaumont
20 Aug 1309 They are superseded by Robert Clifford
14 Sep 1309 Earl of Gloucester replaces Clifford
15 Dec 1309 Clifford replaces Earl of Gloucester
10 Mar 1310 John Segrave replaces Clifford

VIII The following Highland clans claim to have taken part in the Battle of Bannockburn, the majority serving under their own chiefs: Cameron, Campbell, Chisholm, Fraser, Gordon, Grant, Gunn, MacKay, MacIntosh, Macpherson, Macquarrie, Maclean, MacDonald, MacFarlane, MacGregor, MacKenzie, Menzies, Munro, Robertson, Ross, Sinclair and Sutherland, cf. Christison, 10

IX The steady rise in the population of western Europe throughout the thirteenth century had been accompanied by an increase in the spread of agriculture. But early in the fourteenth century two ominous factors intervened. 'The boundary of productive land had been pushed to its limits'. 'A change for the worse in the climate occurred. Winters were longer and colder. Summers were colder and wetter'. The margin between adequacy of food supplies and dearth narrowed to a hairline, cf. Hay, 31, 32. In the summer of 1315 there were torrential rains which began on 11 May and continued almost unceasingly throughout the summer and autumn, causing a failure of crops from the Pyrenees to Russia. The ground became so sodden that few sowings could be made for the harvest of 1316, so that by the autumn of that year famine had stalked through the western world for two years running. Thousands died from hunger and thousands from pestilence which attacked the emaciated frames of the populace, cf. Lucas, 343

X The abbey of Coupar-Angus was the daughter church of Melrose, the daughter of Rievaulx, the daughter of Clairvaux where St Malachy had died, cf. Barrow, 438

XI A fisherman had built himself a little hut beside the river so that he could watch his nets. Within it was a bed, a small fire and a single door. One night he rose to see to his nets and was away a long while. When he returned he saw by the light of the fire a fox inside the hut devouring a salmon. Quickly he stepped into the doorway and, drawing his sword, cried, 'Traitor, thou must die.'

The fox, in great fear, glanced on every side but could see no way of escape except through the door which was blocked by the man. Beside him, lying on the bed, was a woollen cloak. Seizing it in his teeth, he drew it across the fire. When the man saw his cloak burning he rushed to save it and the fox sprang through the door and made his escape.

The Scots, said Douglas, are the fox and the English the man and we shall escape as cleverly as the fox, cf. *Barbour*, 345, 346

XII During the reformation in the sixteenth century, the tombs of the Scottish kings and queens in Dunfermline Abbey and part of the Abbey itself were destroyed. In 1819 workmen repairing the floor of the abbey uncovered the skeleton of a man on the site assigned by tradition to the tomb of Robert Bruce. The skeleton was exhumed and examined by Robert Liston, an Edinburgh surgeon. Part of the breast-bone had been sawn away so that the heart could be removed, cf. MacKay, 180

# INDEX

245